IN-Depth

UK SLOgAN PoSTMArk

Listings

DETAILS OF ALL TOWNS USING MULTI-TOWN SLOGAN POSTMARKS
IN THE UK OVER FOUR DECADES 1960-1999

BY COLIN G PEACHEY

SUB TITLED "COLIN PEACHEY'S LIFE WORK"!

VOLUME 1 : THE SIXTIES

FOREWORD

Well it wasn't really my life's work, it just seemed like it! How I time-shared collecting slogans and recording all the data with a normal working life and a family, let alone my other postmark interests and the production of various postmark books, I shall never know. The point is that all the data has been retained and it seems a shame not to publish it, albeit to a limited audience of dedicated collectors. I have to say "dedicated" as it takes a certain undefinable dedication to collect slogans "in depth". This term is used to describe those who collect specimens of every town using every slogan.

I have kept this data on various handwritten or typed documents (up to 1988 when I was "converted" to a word processor), thus the production of this book has allowed me to bring the data altogether on disc and print it in more orderly fashion. I am planning to produce four volumes covering 10 years each.

I dedicate this work to Valerie, my wife of 33 years, who deserves sincere thanks for her endless tolerance, support and assistance.

Colin Peachey January 1996

Printed in Great Britain by
Prontaprint, and Published by
Colin G Peachey at
19 Moorland Road, Hemel Hempstead
Herts HP1 1NH, 1996

© ISBN 0 904548 08 2

CONTENTS

BOOK LIST

An extensive range of postmark related books is now available from Colin Peachey at 19 Moorland Road, Hemel Hempstead, Herts HP1 1NH, as follows :

COLLECT BRITISH POSTMARKS by Dr J T Whitney - published by British Postmark Society
- Sixth edition published 1993, edited by Colin Peachey and V Brian Crookes
- the complete "Postmarks Simplified" for beginner and advanced collector alike
- larger "chunky" format, complete review of most chapters, all postmarks are priced
- thousands of changes to early chapters, pre & post 1840, squared circles etc
- improved emphasis on 20th century - machines, railways, FPOs, tourist cachets etc
- awarded Vermeil Medal at Cardinal Spellman Literature Fair 1994, large silver in NZ
PRICE £12.50 plus £1.50 postage & packing (overseas £2.30)

COLLECTING SLOGAN POSTMARKS - "flagship" of the slogan postmark series of 4 books
- All 4 books in the series are written/published by the "Parsons, Peachey & Pearson" team
- this book published in 1986, suitable for both beginners and advanced collectors
- includes story of how slogan postmarks came about, and how they developed since 1917
- gives details of "what to look for" - triangles, late uses, inverted slogans, meters etc
- includes the "classic stories" of "World Refugee Year", "Mole Wrench" etc
- includes details of all slogans from 1917 to 1969 in its 220 pages, fully illustrated
PRICE £9.95 plus £1.30 postage & packing (overseas £2)

SLOGAN POSTMARKS OF THE SEVENTIES
- gives all details of slogans used 1970-1979 (published 1980)
- tells postcoding story, plus 1971 postal strike, county reorganisation etc
- includes early slogans of newly independent Channel Isles and Isle of Man
- the largest book in the series, at 260 pages, fully illustrated
- includes complete index 1917-1979 to help the thematic collector
PRICE £8.50 plus £1.50 postage & packing (overseas £2.30)

SLOGAN POSTMARKS OF THE EIGHTIES
- gives all details of slogans used 1980-1989 (published 1990)
- gives details of postal mechanisation and generic postmarks
- describes effects of 1988 postal strike and use of coloured inks
- describes deteriorating quality of slogan impressions and "rolled on by hand" slogans
- neat handbook format, 136 pages, fully illustrated, with 1980s index
PRICE £5.95 plus £1 postage & packing (overseas £1.50)

SLOGAN POSTMARKS OF THE NINETIES : PART 1 1990-1994
- gives all details of slogans used 1990-1994, fully illustrated, published 1995
- details new developments, the ink jet machine and "handstamp slogans"
- full listing of the popular "meter correction" slogans
- neat handbook format, 124 pages, includes Channel Isles/Isle of Man, with index
PRICE £6.95 plus £1 postage & packing (overseas £1.50)

TWENTY YEARS OF FIRST DAY POSTMARKS - published by British Postmark Society
- compiled by Brian Pask and Colin Peachey over 20 years, published 1983
- gives full details of all towns using these postmarks, plus Philatelic Bureau etc.
- neat handbook with card covers, 104 pages.
PRICE £3.50 plus 75p postage & packing (overseas £1)

SPECIAL EVENT POSTMARKS OF THE UK VOLUME I - published by British Postmark Society
- Fourth edition of George Pearson's work, compiled by Colin Peachey & John Swanborough
- published 1991, neat hardback book, all postmarks valued, fully illustrated (in colour)
- covers all Special handstamps/machine marks etc from 1851 to 1962, fully illustrated
- includes the "classic" events - Franco-British, Wembley Exhibition, 1958 Games etc
- also includes many discoveries made during the 1980s
PRICE £6 plus £1 postage & packing (overseas £1.50)

SPECIAL EVENT POSTMARKS OF THE UK VOLUME II - published by British Postmark Society
- compiled by Alan Finch and Colin Peachey, covers another 21 years, 1963-83
- published 1996, neat comb bound handbook, completed the split into separate volumes
- approx 5500 items listed, many illustrated - includes Channel Isles/Isle of Man
PRICE £6 plus £1 postage & packing (overseas £1.50)

SPECIAL EVENT POSTMARKS OF THE UK VOLUME III - published by British Postmark Society
- Neat softback book produced in 1994 by Alan Finch and Colin Peachey
- covers another 10 years 1984-1993 in same format as volume II - includes CI/Isle of Man
- many illustrations, and full details of Philatelic & "Tourist" handstamps
- summary of "first day" handstamps continuing from "Twenty Years of First Day Postmarks"
- awarded bronze-silver medal at Autumn Stampex 1995
PRICE £9.50 plus £1 postage & packing (overseas £1.50)

INTRODUCTION

1. THE "SLOGAN POSTMARKS OF THE UK" BOOKS

As a dedicated collector of slogan postmarks since 1960, most of the data I have compiled and suitable for the needs of most collectors is contained in the series of books "Slogan Postmarks of the UK" details of which (there are four volumes, with a fifth due in 2000) are shown opposite. These have been compiled under the authorship of "Parsons, Peachey & Pearson", since my two good friends Cyril Parsons and George Pearson started the lists in 1958 or thereabouts, and produced their first slogan catalogue in 1962. I joined in in about 1968 and have done most of the compilation and production work since the mid 1970s. George sadly died in 1989 but the work continued under the joint authorship as a tribute to George's sterling work. The last of the slogan postmark books, "Slogan Postmarks of the Nineties : part 2 1995-1999" is due to be published in 2000.

Readers of this volume are expected to be familiar with these books and the reference numbers are included as a cross reference to the "PPP" books. "Collecting Slogan Postmarks", the flagship of the series, gives the background to what slogans are, how they developed, and shows details of the usages of slogans from 1917 up to 1969.

2. THE REASONING FOR THESE BOOKS

One element of the data was missing from the "PPP" books, and that is the details of WHICH TOWNS (or "offices" as we tend to call the Post Office sorting offices involved) used the multi town slogans. "PPP" details these towns only up to 7 or 8 towns but not above that. To complete the picture IN DEPTH LISTINGS gives all details of slogans used at two or more towns. The lists are bulky and have taken many hours to compile - known colloquially by me as my "LIFE WORK"! The second element of this work is the EARLY and LATE USES. Post offices at many towns seem unable to stick to the announced dates of slogan campaigns and many hours have been spent logging all of this data, with lists of observed late uses sent in by other collectors. For the first time they are all listed here!

3. COMPLETENESS

Naturally I cannot claim the lists to be complete. Forgive me, but I do not wish to receive long lists of additions at this stage, at a time when I am completing my work on the topic. My suggestion is that you make additions to MY lists to make them YOUR lists! Please write to me if I have made a serious error (and a correction can appear in the next volume) but not for individual additions.

In the period to 1958-61, George Pearson compiled similar lists, with the help of BPS members, and this data (published in the BPS Quarterly Bulletins) I have used to enlarge my own lists, and such entries I have marked with "<". George stopped this arduous work in 1962 and Capt Haworth took over for part of 1962 and published similar lists, which I have used in a similar manner. From 1962 George published "list A" from the Post Office including all the offices that SHOULD have used all the national slogans. Although I have continued to include "<" entries based on this list it means the meaning of < has subtlety changed. Earlier it had meant "recorded seen by someone, not be me" and later it means "should have been used but not reported". As the 1960s progressed and many towns had LP and similar slogans of their own, list A became less reliable and I have dropped the use of "<", noting "announced but not used" towns where known.

While I have completed the data compilation, I have not done this without lists from other collectors, and this is much appreciated. There are too many to mention, but those who have helped over prolonged periods include Patrick Awcock, Kate Burnell, P J Dawling, Martin Grier, Andrew Gulliver, Frank Harwood, Colin Langston, Michael Middlemiss, John Newcomb, and last but not least several members of our own families, notably Tony Bosworth. The help of numerous others is appreciated: please note it is not too late to help with the remaining years of the 1990s!

4. THE TOWNS USING SLOGANS

Listed are all MULTI TOWN slogans, but exceptions are (a) LP slogans (b) IOM slogans used at Douglas, Ramsey etc and (c) Newmarket slogans shared with Cambridge, all of which are omitted. The reference numbers are those of the PPP books and are not consecutive since the one-town entries are all missing.

The town die (which should not be separated from the slogan) shows the town of posting. Further complications set in, as explained in sections 5 and 6. Then there is the "die letter" which distinguishes one stamp cancelling machine from another: these are explained in sections 7 and 8.

5. JOINT OFFICES AND GENERIC DESCRIPTIONS

The first complication, and one which goes back many years, is that of "joint offices" eg Brighton & Hove, Rochester & Chatham and so on. There were changes affecting such offices eg Burnley & Nelson became Burnley alone, later Burnley & Pendle. A further example of the sort of complication which I will not describe here is that after "Blackburn & Accrington" was introduced at Blackburn, separate Blackburn and Accrington dies both also continued in use for some years! The second complication is that of generic identities. With the march of concentration, which got under way in the 1960s, smaller towns gradually ceased to stamp mail and generic inscriptions were invented to describe a concentration area, this of course being used at the new "centre" or Mechanised Letter Office (MLO, enhanced and changed to APC in the 1990s) where mail was stamped instead. The first "generic inscription" was "Fylde Coast" used at Blackpool from 1966 (with several variations) and many more were to follow.

In some cases the expanded area, denoted by either a joint or generic inscription, was then changed again when the area expanded further. Examples are Harrow, changed to "Harrow & Wembley" then later to Harrow again, and Swansea, changed to "West Glamorgan" then to Swansea again and later still to "Swansea & SW Wales"! It would take more space but it is tempting to tell the story of each such town! However I will take space to give a listing of joint towns/generic identities even though it covers a period beyond the Sixties: I am not certain of the earlier dates, if anyone can help then I can correct these in readiness for the next volume!

* denotes Sunday only usage. + denotes still in use (1996) but only on locals/ missorts so seldom seen. Slogan usage is not taken into account in this list.

Generic/joint description	Town where used	Dates of use
London IS MLO	London Mt Pleasant (see section 6)	1980-
London E1-E18	London E1	1982-
London North	London N1	1995-
London NWMLO/RM London NW	London NW1	1986-95
Royal Mail London South	London SW MLO at SW8	1995-
London SW	London SW MLO at SW8	1983-95
West London	Paddington	1994-
Bethnal Green & Homerton E2	E2	1977-87
Bethnal Green E2.E8.E9	E2	1987-93
Poplar & Isle of Dogs E14	E14	1991-93
London N13/N21	N21	1971-93
Kennington/Walworth SE17	SE17	1966-93
Blackburn & Accrington	Blackburn	1961-73
Blackburn & NE Lancs	Blackburn	1973-75
Bolton & Bury	Bolton, Bury	1974-81
Bournemouth-Poole	Bournemouth	1933?-94
*Bournemouth District	Bournemouth	1990-94
Brighton & Hove	Brighton	1920s-78
Bromley & Beckenham	Bromley	1930s?-70
Buckhaven Methil Leven	Leven	1964-76
+Burnley & Nelson	Burnley, +Nelson (still in use)	1938?-76
+Burnley & Pendle	Burnley, Colne	1976-
Bury Bolton Wigan	Bolton, Bury	1981-
Camborne Redruth	Redruth	1935?-92
Cardiff Newport	Cardiff	1993-

5

```
+Chesham & Amersham        Amersham                                    1933-
Cheshire                   Crewe                                       1983-
Chester Clwyd Gwynedd      Chester                                     1982-87
Chester/Clwyd 1            Chester (one still going!)                  1987-88
Chester & Clwyd/1          Chester                                     1988-
Cleveland        Middlesbrough,Hartlepool,Stockton-on-Tees            1974-
                    (only Middlesbrough still in use)
Clwyd, Clwyd 2             Rhyl (still used at Xmas!)                   1972-83
Clwyd 1                    Chester                                     1972-82
Clyde Valley               Motherwell,+Biggar(Krag),+Lanark            1987-
Coatbridge & Airdrie       Coatbridge                                  1968-86
*Cornwall 1,2,3,4  Penzance,Truro(still going),St Austell,Bodmin 1990-92
Cornwall 'lettered dies'   Truro,Bodmin,Falmouth,Hayle,Helston,
              Newquay,Penzance,Redruth,St Austell,St Ives 1992-
               (St Ives ended, Penzance now *, others + except Truro)
Coventry & Warwickshire    Coventry                                    1980-
Croydon/Sutton             Croydon, Morden, Sutton                     1989-
Cumbria Dumfries & Galloway Carlisle                                   1993-
+Dorchester S & W Dorset   Dorchester                                  1994-
Dorset & SW Hants          Bournemouth (new APC at Poole)              1994-
Edinburgh Lothian Fife Borders  Edinburgh                             1982-95
Exeter (and) District      Exeter, Dawlish, Exmouth etc                1970-
Fylde Coast (variations)   Blackpool                                   1966-75
+Fylde Blackpool Wyre      Blackpool, Lytham                           1975-
Gatwick MLO                Redhill's MLO at Crawley                    1988-
+Glastonbury & Street      Glastonbury                                 1964-
Gloucestershire            Gloucester etc                              1970-
+Grimsby & Cleethorpes     Grimsby                                     1964-
+Gwent                     Newport Gwent                               1973-
*Gwynedd N (North)         Bangor Gwynedd                              1990-
*Gwynedd S (South)         Caernarfon                                  1990-
Harrow & Wembley    Harrow,Wembley,Northwood,Pinner,Ruislip           1965-80
Head Post Office West Lothian  Livingston                             1983-94
Hereford & Worcestershire  Worcester                                   1993-
                    ("Worcester District E" still on Paid mail)
+Huddersfield Halifax      Huddersfield, Halifax                       1976-
Ilford & Barking           Ilford                                      1951-70
+Isle of Wight             Newport IOW                                 1977-
Lancashire (or Lancs)      Preston and +others (still in use) 1975-93
Lancashire (and) S Lakes   Preston and +others                        1993-
Lancaster & Morecambe      Lancaster                                  1930s?-93
Leicestershire             Leicester                                   1993-
Llandudno-Colwyn Bay       Colwyn Bay (and later Xmas only)           1960-64
Lynton & Lynmouth          Lynton                                      1965-
Mablethorpe & Sutton on Sea Mablethorpe                               1964-77
Medway                     Chatham                                     1970-
Medway & Maidstone         Maidstone                                   1983-
+Mid Northumberland        Morpeth                                     1969-
*Royal Mail Midlands       Derby                                       1993-
Motherwell & Wishaw        Motherwell                                  1952-87
Newport Mon NP3            Ebbw Vale                                   1971-72
Northamptonshire           Northampton                                 1985-
North Devon                Barnstaple                                  1970-
North Herts (error)        Stevenage                                  1985 only
Perth Dundee Angus         Perth                                       1983-95
Plymouth Cornwall & W Devon  Plymouth,St Austell                      1980-
              (only Plymouth still in use, but others at Xmas)
*Plymouth & District       Plymouth                                    1990-92
Portsmouth & Southsea      Portsmouth                                 1930s?-81
Portsmouth & IOW           Portsmouth                                  1981-
Reigate & Redhill          Redhill                                    1920s-76
Rhondda                    Pontypridd etc                             1966-c78
Richmond & Twickenham      Twickenham                                 1930s?-70
Rochdale Oldham Ashton-u-Lyne  Oldham                                 1981-
Rochester & Chatham        Chatham                                    1920?-70
Romford & Dagenham         Romford etc                                 1951-70
Scottish Borders           Galashiels,Hawick,Kelso                     1992-94
Sennen & Lands End         Penzance                                   1957?-92
Shropshire & Mid Wales     Shrewsbury                                  1982-
Slough/Windsor SLO-9       Slough                                      1991-
South Coast (error)        Brighton                                   1989 only
South Devon                Torquay,Paignton(& others at Xmas) 1969-
*SE Division 1             Tonbridge                                   1994-
*SE Division 2             Croydon                                     1995-
+S W County Durham         Bishop Auckland                             1970-
```

Sussex Coast	Brighton, Hove	1978-
Swansea & SW Wales	Swansea	1994-
Teesside	Middlesbrough,Hartlepool,Stockton-on-Tees	1969-74
+Thanet	Margate,Ramsgate(ended),Broadstairs(ended)	1971-
Torquay & Paignton	Torquay	1940s only
Tyneside/NE/SR	Newcastle upon Tyne	1995-
Warwick & Leamington Spa	Leamington Spa	1920s?-90
West Glamorgan	Swansea etc	1975-80
Worcester District	Worcester	1973-83

(also at Droitwich, now ended, but still going at +Evesham,+Malvern)

6. LONDON MOUNT PLEASANT

For many years up to about 1994 the arrangements in London EC were that postings destined for London, Overseas and Country were processed separately. Double aperture pillar boxes allowed for "London and Overseas" to be collected separately from "Country" mail, then London mail was processed at EC Section and overseas mail at Foreign Section, both of which were housed in King Edward Building. Country mail was taken to Mount Pleasant (in Farringdon Road) where the postmark read purely "London" plus die letter. This inscription was changed to "London IS MLO" (meaning London Inland Section) from 1980. In 1994 the London EC postmark ceased and from then onwards all London EC mail was handled at Mount Pleasant (with Foreign Section moved there too, the FS machine postmark also having by that time ceased).

7. TOWN DIE LETTERS

Basically the town dies show the town of posting, plus a letter or number to show the individual stamp cancelling machine. There the simplicity ends however, as there are more exceptions than standard cases. The first development is that a town die WITHOUT a letter is then followed by one WITH one. For example Harrow had one machine with no letter in its town die and a second with A. These, when both used, are shown in the listings as "Harrow, and A" in order to be brief.

I am not certain why the main stamp cancelling machines at Birmingham in use in the 1960s were lettered A,E and G, and at Manchester C,F,K,L and P, but they were! The next complication is that at Manchester further die letters are H (Head Office), E (East), S (South), N (North) and W (West), along with SE (South East) and so on: however, at Birmingham E is at the Head Office (ie it is NOT East) but Manchester E means East and is used at the Eastern District Office. Only experience (or chapter 10 of "Collect British Postmarks") can tell the collector which is which, but I have left a space, each time listed, after the Head Office dies and before the District Office dies, eg Glasgow A,B,C, followed by a space before S,SE,SW,W,W3. This applies to Birmingham, Edinburgh, Glasgow, Liverpool and Manchester. At Birmingham the district offices are further complicated: these are ADO (Aston), CH (Camp Hill), ED (Eastern District), H (Hockley), and WDO (Western District Office), but by the 1990s "H" has become a normal machine at the MLO. Erdington and Moseley DO are listed alphabetically, as are Leith DO and Portobello DO of Edinburgh.

Chapter 10 of "Collect British Postmarks" (Sixth Edition) contains a full listing of towns (including District Offices) that used machines from 1933 onwards.

8. DIFFERENT TYPES OF MACHINE

I do not intend to repeat the descriptions of ALFs, FCTs and CFCs already included in the "PPP" books. Suffice it to say that the ALF machines had four streams and FCTs and CFCs have two streams each. Usually the town dies indicate this but sometimes not so. The first ones, namely the S and T ALF machines at Southampton, did not do so, there being four S or T dies though later changed to S1-4 and T1-4.

9. NUMBERS OF SLOGAN DIES

Throughout the listing I have attempted to show the numbers of dies used, and counting the numbers of TOWN DIES can be misleading. On the other hand there is nothing else to go on. For example there were frequently from 10 to 13 town dies used at London (Mount Pleasant) but how many slogan dies does this represent? The answer is usually less than the 10-13 number eg six dies. At smaller offices the number of town dies is more reliable eg Leeds A,B,C usually means three slogan dies. The conclusions are that (a) I have used a certain amount of judgement in assessing the numbers and (b) all numbers are approximate.

10. TOWN DIES NOT USED AT THE TOWN STATED

The most well known example is Wadhurst. Wadhurst had a Krag machine in the 1960s and used no slogans. But on Sundays mail was taken to Tunbridge Wells where a Wadhurst town die was used in the Tunbridge Wells machine. Thus slogans were used, and whenever a slogan was used at Tunbridge Wells it was to be found with a Wadhurst town die for this reason. Similarly, though I am less certain about these, I suspect Mossley (at Ashton-under-Lyne), Ramsbottom (at Bury??) and Willenhall (at Walsall??) were all used as shown here in brackets, possibly only on one collection per day, though I assume not confined to Sundays. Specimens from these towns seem to be difficult to find!

11. TOWN DIE LAYOUTS

At one point I used the Kneil/Parsons classification which used roman numerals to show the layout of the die and whether there were arcs between the inscription at the top and the inscription at the bottom eg 1.I meant town/county at top & bottom with no arcs, 1.II the same but with arcs. I have simplified things in this volume, however, by ignoring the layout and just saying whether the die has arcs or not, and then only when both exist, otherwise I have not mentioned it at all. Hence the terms "arcs" and "no arcs" in my listings. Others that are obvious are those such as Reading which showed a + sign to either side (later X) to distinguish one die from the others. Why they did not all use letters A to Z I will never know!

12. TOWN DIE LETTERINGS

The lists unashamedly use the "Peachey classification" of town die letterings, particularly where there are no differences between town die inscriptions, it is only the shape and font of the lettering that differs. See section 18 for details.

13. SLOGANS USED IN STANDARD AND TRANSPOSED POSITIONS

Although transposed slogans (with slogan on the LEFT) started in 1963 it took some time before "transposed" uses of national slogans appeared, and even in 1965-67 there were few, with more in 1968-69. I have noted transposed uses in one of two ways, as inspection of the listings will show. Where the majority are standard (slogan on the RIGHT) I have highlighted transposed by underlining. Where a mixture of both, as in 1968-69, I have shown each as "std" and "trans". If the reference number is suffixed by "t" (for transposed) ALL the towns were transposed.

14. SEQUENCE

By convention I have always listed London first, and under London (a) Mount Pleasant usually comes first followed by the other Central London "1" offices (known as the "District Offices" to the mid 1980s) (b) then the sub-districts if used (including SW11 and W2 which were also District Offices); these are typically only involved for "Christmas" slogans and a few others (c) the alphabetic lists, (d) early and late uses. Triangles, where known, are shown at the end, but I have usually excluded these if the period of use is uncertain (as they are not dated) and I have ignored diamonds even if their town of usage is known. Other varieties, such as Inverted slogans, are not normally listed though may have been included in a few instances.

15. FIRST DAY SLOGANS

For full details see "Twenty Years of First Day Postmarks" by Brian Pask & Colin Peachey, published 1983.

16. POSTCODE SLOGANS

With these slogans I have taken a DIFFERENT line. Instead of a more complex description, with every town die used and when it was used, I have decided the PPP books show these slogans in sufficient detail. Thus what is need is a SIMPLIFIED listing. Thus I have attempted to show the towns involved, and whether standard and/or transposed but not the dates of every change, and little else. For more details refer to the main listings of "CSP" and "Seventies", and chapter 4 of "Slogan Postmarks of the Eighties" and "Nineties".

17. SLOGAN DESIGNS WITH SUB-TYPES

There are four designs which involved the production of dies in such numbers and at different times that different manufacturers were probably involved. This in turn resulted in slight differences which are apparent to the keen eyed collector. Details are shown in sections 17.1 to 17.4 that follow :

17.1   RADIO TV LICENCES

Initially there were four sub-types A to D. Most specimens can be allocated to these four sub-types but there are one or two "rogue dies" that do not fit precisely. From 1965 a type G occurs. Types E and F were earlier distinguished but the differences are so slight I have dispensed with these two sub-types.

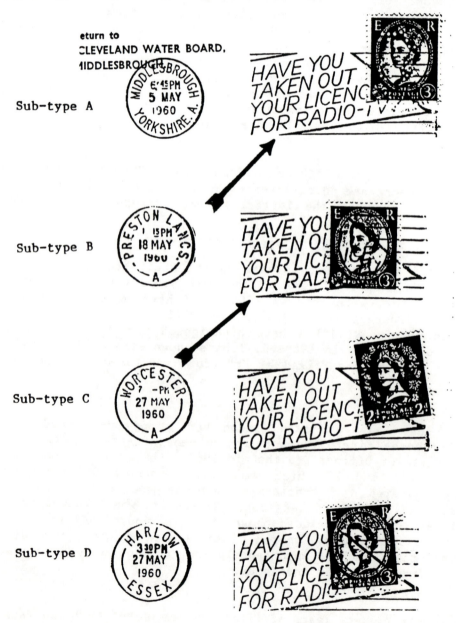

Sub-type G

Differences are difficult to describe, but (a) examine the point at the bottom of the design, which is under the R in type A and under the 0 in type B (b) examine the two Rs of FOR RADIO which are wide in types A and B, narrower in C and D, medium in G (c) the cross-bar of the A of RADIO which is low in type C, higher in type D and G (d) in type G both the shape of the Rs of FOR RADIO and the two Cs of LICENCE are distinctive.

17.2 VOTERS LISTS (also shown on page 34 of "Collecting Slogan Postmarks")

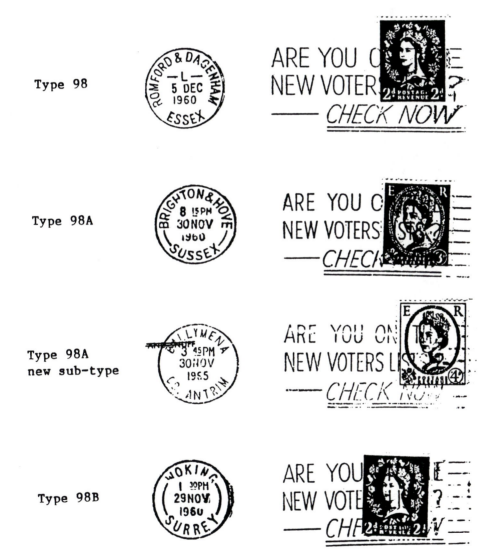

Type 98 has large letters and no lines at the right of the design. Type 98A has smaller lettering, lines at right of design, and the T of LISTS is to the left of the T of THE. Type 98B is similar but different shape to the C of CHECK and the T of LISTS is to the right of the T of THE. The fourth type was introduced in 1964 (1965 specimen shown here) and is listed as "type 98A new sub type" since like type 98A it has lines at right and the T of LISTS is to the left of the T of THE. But, more like type 98B, it has a distinctive shape to the C of CHECK and the R of VOTERS is also distinctive. There are two further sub types introduced in the 1970s.

17.3 POST EARLY FOR CHRISTMAS ("Candle" design)

The two sub types are shown here but are NOT distinguished in the lists since (a) I am not convinced their difference warrants it and (b) the data I have is not broken down by the two sub types. The lettering in the first sub type is thicker and the F of OF is to the left of the I of CHRISTMAS. In the second sub type the lettering is thinner and the F of OF is over the I of CHRISTMAS.

17.4 RECORDED DELIVERY

The two sub types are illustrated here, the "main type" being type 189. In the second sub type, type 189A, the lettering is thicker, the 6D is larger, and the shape of the letters R and C differs. Type 189A was only used in 1964.

Type 189

Type 189A

18. TOWN DIE LETTERINGS - THE PEACHEY CLASSIFICATION

The lettering of modern Universal machine town dies differs as different manufacturers are used. The "Peachey classification" of town dies used post war was first published in the British Postmark Society Quarterly Bulletin some years ago, and in 1991 was abbreviated and updated for publication in Royal Mail's British Postmark Bulletin - described here in totality even though it extends beyond the 1960s. It breaks the letterings into different styles or types. Readers should note the dies are not always easy to recognise, and the types are difficult to describe, but with some experience dies can be "dated" in that the types conform to respective periods of manufacture. Most offices with two or more machines seem to have town dies in use of more than one type since normally manufactured at different times, the exception being when a generic inscription is introduced then all the dies of one town are produced together, until replacements are later required and the cycle starts all over again!

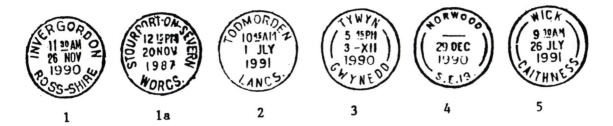

1   1a   2   3   4   5

Type 1 dies are termed "old large lettering" and had been in use from the 1920s; examples still in use in 1995 are Beckenham and Invergordon. Type 1a, old narrow lettering, has similar letters but narrower and not so rounded; rarely seen with arcs between town and county, and used for dies introduced from about 1945 into the early 1950s, and Stourport-on-Severn is a recent example.

Type 2, "old style", was used for many dies introduced between 1947 and 1958. Many such dies, presumably the lesser ones, have remained in use until quite recently - many of the London missort dies provide examples up to 1993 or so, also Emsworth a nice example with arcs and Todmorden without, both used to the early 1990s. Type 3, "narrow lettering", also applies to large numbers of dies since it was used for most of the dies produced between 1958 and 1967 and then from about 1970 to 1976, thus the first generics ("Rhondda" and "Fylde Coast" in 1966) and many of the "new county" dies introduced in 1975 were of this style; some of the small offices in East Sussex and in Wales are still using these dies.

A highly distinctive style of small squarish appearance was used for a short period of manufacture in 1963-64, and type 4 is known as "squat lettering" (as is style 12 in the 1990s). Only 54 dies are known and Glasgow B survives in 1995. Close on its heels was type 5, "narrow lettering new style", with new letters having flat sides and about 450 dies are recorded, introduced chiefly in 1964-65 and a few remained in use into the 1990s. Letters are not consistent, however, as comparing the two Cs in Wick will show.

Type 6 was similar to type 3, but in 1967 a few dies appeared with lettering closer together - only seen from Birmingham, Carlisle, Manchester and Newport Mon. Type 7, "new wider lettering", was more numerous again on new dies introduced from 1968 to 1971; like type 5 in terms of individual letters but letters wider.

6   7   8   9   10   11

Type 8 is very different, "very narrow lettering", used from about 1980, and dies lasted to the 1990s: the "&" is distinctive and is shown here. Type 9 is also distinctive in having a "bump" at top and bottom of the town die, and about 130 such dies were manufactured in about 1984. Very few of type 10 were made. Here the letters are further from the rim and close together, and most were short-lived - possibly a new material was used. Type 11 lasted for some years and most new dies in the period 1985-93 were of this style - narrow lettering and not unlike type 5. Type 12 (not shown here) is a clear squat type lettering and was introduced in late 1993, and new dies up to 1995 are of this style.

19. USE OF THE DATA IN THIS BOOK

Collectors, researchers and compilers of other works are encouraged to use the data from this book as they work on their own topics. However, they are asked to acknowledge the source.

20. SYMBOLS USED

< office listed by BPS or (later) from GPO list
E = earliest ("by" often used with similar meaning)
L = latest
(U) = unnanounced
(number in brackets) usually means number of SLOGAN dies used, sometimes my judgement!

21. THANKS

As well as those mentioned in section 3, particular thanks are due to Cary Knott and Phil Gains who have kindly helped check some of the lists and who have added some additional entries.

MAIN LISTINGS

294 World Refugee Year (with hand design) 1-8 Jan 1960

London <D,F,G,H,I,J,K,<M,O,<P,<T,   E1, and <A,   EC B,C,D,E,F,G,K,
       FS M,N,   N1 A,B,   NW1 <A,B,
       SE1 A,C,   SW1 A,B,C,G,   W1 D,E,F,
       WC B,C,D,

E <2,6,<8,11,15,<17,   N 4,<7,<16,17,22,   NW 2,3,6,9,10,10A,11,
SE 5,<6,9,13,<15,18,   SW 2,3,<4,6,7,9,11(types 2 & 3),15,16,<17,<18,19,
W 2 A, 3,4,<5,6,<8,12,14,

London missorts : 6A,<11,<27,<34B,35B,38,39,<39B,46B,55,57,<73,<88,<89.

Aberdeen A,<B,	Accrington,	Aldershot,
Altrincham,	Ashford Kent,	Ashton-under-Lyne,
<Aylesbury,	Ayr,	
Barnet,	Barnsley,	<Barrow,
Bath,	<Bedford,	
Belfast <A,C,	<Bexleyheath,	<Birkenhead,
Birmingham A,E,G, ADO,CH,ED,H,WDO,		Blackburn A,
<Blackpool A,B,	Bolton B,	<Bootle,
Bournemouth-Poole A,	Bradford Gt Brit B,	Brighton & Hove, and A,
Bristol <A,B,C,E,	Bromley & Beckenham,	<Burnley & Nelson,
Burton-on-Trent,	Bury St Edmunds,	
Cambridge,	<Canterbury,	Cardiff A,<B,
<Carlisle,	Chelmsford,	Cheltenham,
Chester A,	<Chesterfield,	Chichester,
Colchester,	Colwyn Bay,	Coventry A,B,
Crewe,	Croydon, and A,	
Darlington,	Dartford,	<Darwen A,
Derby A,	Dewsbury A,	<Doncaster,
<Dover,	Dudley A,	Dundee,
Durham,	Eastbourne,	<Edgware,
Edinburgh B,<C, NW,	<Enfield,	Epsom,
Exeter (two),	Falkirk,	<Farnborough,
Folkestone,	Glasgow A,B,C,<E, <E3,N,<S,<SW,<W,	
Gloucester A,<B,	Gravesend,	Grays,
Great Yarmouth,	<Greenock,	<Grimsby,
Guernsey,	Guildford,	
<Halifax,	<Harrogate,	Harrow, and A,
Hastings,	<Hayes,	<Hereford A,B,
High Wycombe,	Hounslow (short & long arcs),	
<Huddersfield,	Hull (types 2 & 3),	
Ilford & Barking,	Inverness,	Ipswich A,

Jersey,
King's Lynn,
Lancaster & Morecambe A,
Lincoln A,
<Llandudno,
<Lytham St Annes,
Maidstone,
Mansfield,
Moseley DO,
Newport Mon,
<Northwich,
<Oldham A,B,
Paignton,
Peterborough A,
Portsmouth & Southsea, and D,
Reading, and +,
Rochdale,
<Rotherham,
St Helens A,
<Scarborough A,
Sevenoaks,
Slough,
Southampton A,<B,
<South Shields,
<Stalybridge,
<Stockton-on-Tees,
Sutton,
Taunton,
Uxbridge A,
Wallasey,
Warrington <A,B,
Watford,
West Hartlepool,
Weymouth,
Winchester,
Woodford Green,

Keighley,
Kingston-on-Thames,
Leatherhead,
Liverpool A,B,<C,<D,
<Londonderry,
<Macclesfield,
Manchester C,<F,<K,<L,<P,
<Margate,
<Mossley,
Northampton No.1,<2,
Norwich,
<Oxford, and A,
Paisley,
Plymouth, and A,
Preston A,<C,
Reigate & Redhill,
Rochester & Chatham,
Rugby,
<Salford,

Sheffield <A,B,C,
Smethwick,
Southend-on-Sea,
<Stafford,
Stirling,
Stoke-on-Trent (2 dies),
<Swansea, and A,
Torquay,
<Wadhurst,
Walsall, and <B,
<Warwick & Leamington Spa,
Wembley A,
Weston-s-Mare A,
Wigan,
Woking,
Worcester A,

<Kendal,

Leicester A,B,
<ED,<ND,
Luton,
<Maidenhead,
  E,<N,SE,SW,
Middlesbrough A,
Newcastle upon Tyne A,B,
<North Shields,
Nottingham <A,B,C,

<Perth,
<Portobello DO,
<Ramsgate,
<Richmond & Twickenham,
Romford & Dagenham (2 dies),
St Albans,
Salisbury,

Shrewsbury A,<B,
<Southall, and Gt Brit,
Southport A,
<Staines,
Stockport A,
Sunderland,
Swindon,
Tunbridge Wells,
Wakefield,
Waltham Cross,

<West Bromwich,
Weybridge,
<Willenhall,
Wolverhampton <B,C,
Worthing.

Triangles : -CL-/MTP, EC, -L-/NW1, SE1, L/W2, SE15, KT, 445, 449, 733, 918, S7

Listed as 350 dies, about 332 dies listed above

Early use : 31 Dec 1959 Lancaster & Morecambe A

Late uses :
 9 Jan London NW1 B, NW9, SE13, SW3, Leicester B
10 Jan London NW1 A, NW2,10A,11, Brighton & Hove, Hastings, Uxbridge A
11 Jan NW3,6, Smethwick
12 Jan Inverness

ALSO Halifax "defaced version" **295** apparently used 9-11 Jan,

296 Correct Addressing 1 to 29 Feb 1960

Note : 296/297 were in use together, often at the same offices, as inspection of
the two lists will show. 175 dies of each design were in use, but the number
shown here exceeds that number: this difference is partly explained by Mount
Pleasant using both designs in all machines, probably 6 dies of each.

London D,F,G,H,I,J,K,<L,M,<O,P,<T,   E1,   EC D,<F,<K,
       N1 A,<B,   NW1 B,   SE1 <A,C,F,
       SW1 A,<B,C,   W1 D,E,<F,   WC D,

E <2,8,11,17,   N <7,<17,   NW 2,3,<9,10A,
SE 5,9,15,   SW 2,<4,<7,11(2 dies),18,<19,
W 2A,3,<5,8(old die),12,

London missorts : 4,23B,39B,87,91,

Aberdeen A,   Accrington,   <Aldershot,
Altrincham,   Ayr,   Barnet,
Barnsley,   Barrow,   Bath,
Bedford (2 dies),   Belfast <A,C,   Birmingham A,G, ADO,WDO,

Bolton B,   Bootle,   Bournemouth-Poole A,<B,
Bradford Gt Brit B, and <B,   Brighton & Hove, and A,
Bristol <A,B,   Burton-on-Trent,
Cambridge,   Cardiff A,<B,   <Carlisle A,
Chelmsford,   Chester B,   Colchester,
Colwyn Bay,   Coventry A,   Croydon,
Darlington (arcs & no arcs),   Dartford,   Derby A,
<Doncaster,   Dudley A,   <Dunfermline,
Eastbourne,   Edinburgh B, NW,   Epsom,
Exeter (2 dies),   Glasgow <A,E, <2, W,   Gloucester B,
Grays,   Great Yarmouth,   Grimsby,
<Harrogate,   Harrow,   Hastings,
Hayes,   Hereford B,   Huddersfield,
Hull (types 2 & 3),   <Inverness,   Ipswich A,
Jersey,   Kingston-on-Thames,
Lancaster & Morecambe A,   Leeds A,<B,   Leicester A,
Liverpool <B,<C,D, ND, Luton (2 dies),   Lytham St Annes,
Maidstone,   Manchester C,<K,<L,<P, <SE,   Mansfield,
Middlesbrough A,   Moseley DO,
Newcastle upon Tyne A,   Newport Mon (2 dies),   Northampton No.1,<2,
Northwich,   Norwich,   Nottingham C,
<Oxford, and A,   Perth,   Peterborough A,
Plymouth arcs & no arcs, <Preston C,   Reading,
Reigate & Redhill,   Rochdale,   Romford & Dagenham,
Rotherham,   <Salford,   <Sevenoaks,
<Sheffield A,B,   Southampton B,   Southend-on-Sea (2 dies),
Southport A,   Stafford,   Staines,
Stoke-on-Trent,   Sunderland,   Sutton (2 dies),
<Swansea, and A,   Swindon,   Torquay,
Warrington A,<B,   Watford,   Weston-s-Mare A,<B,
Weybridge,   <Woking,   <Woodford Green,
Worcester A,   York.

<Triangles : SE1,CIW(Clapham SW4),449,938,087

Listed as 175 dies, 190 shown above (see note).

Early uses :
29 Jan Altrincham
30 Jan Birmingham ADO

Late uses :
 1 March London N1 A, NW10A, SW2, missort 23B, Aldershot, Birmingham A,G,WDO,
Chelmsford, Epsom, Grays, Grimsby, Luton, Romford & Dagenham, Woking
 2 March SE9, Barnet, Oxford A, Rochdale, Salford
 4 March Leeds A,B
 6 March Lancaster & Morecambe A
 7 March SE15, W2A
 8 March Ayr
15 March Gloucester B, Hayes
23 March Maidstone, Reigate & Redhill
 6 April Northampton No.2

 - see also chapter 10 of "CSP" for FPO 774

297 <u>Please put your correct address</u> 1-29 Feb 1960

London D,F,G,H,I,J,K,L,M,O,<P,T,   E1 A,   EC B,C,E,G,
    <FS M,   <N1 A,B,   NW1 A,
    SE1 A,C,<F,   SW1 <B,C,D,G,   <W1 F,
    WC B,C,<D,

E <6,10,15,   N 4,16,<22,   NW 6,10,10A,11,
SE 6,13,18,   SW 3,6,9,15,16,   W 2A,4,6,8(new die)

London missorts : 6A,40,46,46B,57,60,71,73,87,88.

<Aberdeen B,   <Ashton-under-Lyne,   Aylesbury,
<Bexleyheath,   Birkenhead A,   Birmingham E, CH,ED,H,
Blackburn A,   Blackpool A,B,   Bournemouth-Poole A,B,
Bradford Gt Brit A,   Brighton & Hove, and A,   Bristol C,E,
Bromley & Beckenham,   <Burnley & Nelson,   Bury St Edmunds,

Canterbury,
<Chester A,
Crewe,
Dewsbury A,
Edinburgh C,
Farnborough,
Glasgow A,B,<C,   S,
<Greenock,
Halifax,
Hull (3 dies),
Keighley,
Kingston-on-Thames,
Leicester <A,B,C,
Liverpool A,C types 2 & 3, D,   <ED,
<Londonderry,
Mossley,
Northampton No.1,<2,
Nottingham A,B,
Paisley,
Portsmouth & Southsea,
Reading +,
Romford & Dagenham,
St Helens A,
Sheffield C,
Southall, and Gt Britain,
<Stalybridge,
Stockton-on-Tees,
Sutton,
Tunbridge Wells,
Wakefield,
Warwick & Leamington Spa,
Wigan,
Wolverhampton C.

Cardiff A,B,
Chesterfield,
Croydon A,
Dundee,
Enfield,
Folkestone,
Gloucester A,
<Guernsey,
Harrow A,
Ilford & Barking,
Kendal,
Leatherhead,
Lincoln A,
Manchester <F,K,   E,N,S,
Newcastle upon Tyne B,
North Shields,
Oldham A,B,
Plymouth A,
Preston A,
Richmond & Twickenham,
Rugby,
Salisbury,
Slough,
Southampton A,
Stirling,
Stoke-on-Trent, and <Gt Brit,
<Swansea, and A,
Uxbridge A,
Wallasey,
Wembley A,
Willenhall,

Cheltenham,
Coventry B,
Darwen A,
Durham,
Falkirk,
<Gillingham Kent,
Gravesend,
Guildford types 2 & 3,
High Wycombe,

<King's Lynn,
Leeds C,

<Llandudno,
<SW,   <Margate,
Newport Mon,
Norwich,
Paignton,
<Portobello DO,
Ramsgate,
Rochester & Chatham,
St Albans,
Scarborough A,
Smethwick,
South Shields,
Stockport A,
Taunton,
<Wadhurst,
Walsall,
West Hartlepool,
Winchester,

<Triangles : SE1,-L-/SE1,SW1,38,75,132,383,388,498,620,635,693,776,953,S81,SSS

Listed as 175 dies, 191 shown above (see note).

Early uses :
29 Jan Warwick & Leamington Spa
30 Jan Birmingham ED, Smethwick

Late uses :
 1 March SW6, Birmingham ED, Preston A, Romford & Dagenham, Sutton
 2 March NW6
 4 March Leeds C
 6 March Falkirk
 7 March W2A, Lincoln A
15 March Southall
16 March Enfield
20 March Gloucester A
 6 April Northampton No.1

298 World Refugee Year (revised design)   7 April to 4 May 1960

London D,F,G,H,I,J,K,<M,O,P,T,   <E1 and A,   EC <B,<C,<D,E,<F,<G,<K,
       FS <M,P,   N1 A,B,   NW1 <A,B,
       SE1 A,C,<F,   SW1 <A,B,C,D,<G,
       W1 D,F,<H,J,   WC <B,C,<D,

E 8,<11,15,<17,   <N 16,   <NW 2,3,6,10A,
SE 5,<9,<15,18,   SW <3,6,7,<9,11,<15,<16,17,<18,19,
W <2A,<3,<4,5,6,<8,12,

<London missorts : 4,6A,8B,27B,73,87,89,91.

Aberdeen A,<B,   <Abingdon,   Accrington,
Aldershot,   Altrincham,   <Ashford Kent,
Ashton-under-Lyne,   Aylesbury,   Ayr,
<Barnet,   <Barnsley,   Bath,
Bedford,   Belfast <A,C,   Bexhill-on-Sea,
Bexleyheath,   <Birkenhead A,

16

Birmingham A,E,<G,   ADO,CH,ED,H,WDO,   <Bishop Auckland,
Blackburn A,   Blackpool A,<B,   <Bletchley,
Bolton B,   Bootle,   Bournemouth-Poole A,<B,
Bradford <A,B,   <Bridgend,   Brighton & Hove, and A,
Bristol A,B,C,   Bromley & Beckenham,   <Burnley & Nelson,
<Burton-on-Trent,   Bury,   Bury St Edmunds,
Cambridge,   Canterbury,   Cardiff A,<B,
Carlisle A,   <Castleford,   Chelmsford,
Cheltenham,   Chester A,   <Chesterfield,
Chichester,   <Cleethorpes,   <Colchester,
<Colwyn Bay,   <Coventry A,B,   Crawley,
<Crewe,   Croydon, and <A,
Darlington,   Dartford,   <Darwen A,
Derby A,   <Dewsbury A,   <Doncaster,
Dover,   Dudley A,   <Dumfries,
Dundee,   <Dunfermline,   Durham,
Eastbourne,   Edgware,   Edinburgh B,C, NW,
Enfield,   Epsom,   <Erdington,
Exeter (2 dies),   <Falkirk,   <Farnborough,
Folkestone,   Glasgow A,<B,C,E, S,<SE,SW,<W,<W3,
Gloucester A,<B,   Gravesend,   <Grays,
Great Yarmouth,   Greenock,   Grimsby,
Guernsey,   Guildford,   Halifax,
Harlow,   Harrogate,   Harrow, and <A,
Hastings,   <Haywards Heath,   Hereford B,
High Wycombe,   Hitchin,   Hounslow short & long arcs,
Huddersfield,   Hull (2 dies),   Ilford & Barking,
Inverness,   Ipswich A,   <Jersey,
<Keighley,   <King's Lynn,   Kingston-on-Thames,
Lancaster & Morecambe A, Leeds A,B,<C,   Leicester A,B,C,
<Lewes,   Lincoln A,
Liverpool A,B,<C(2 dies),D,   <ED,<ND,   <Llandudno,
<Londonderry,   <Luton (2 dies),   <Lytham St Annes,
<Macclesfield,   Maidenhead,
Manchester <C,<F,K (types 2 & 3),L,P,   S,<SE,<SW, Mansfield,
Margate,   Middlesbrough A,   <Morpeth,
<Moseley DO,   <Mossley,   <Motherwell & Wishaw A,
Neath,   Newcastle upon Tyne A,B, Newport Mon,
Newton Abbot,   <Northampton No.1,2,   <North Shields,
Norwich,   Nottingham,   and <A,B,<C,
Oldham <A,B,   <Oxford,   and A,   Paignton,
Paisley,   Perth,   Peterborough A,
<Plymouth, and A,   <Pontefract,   Pontypridd,
<Portobello DO,   Portsmouth & Southsea, and D,
Preston A,<C,   <Ramsbottom,   <Ramsgate,
Reading, and <+   Reigate & Redhill,   <Rhyl,
<Richmond Yorks,   <Richmond & Twickenham,   Rochdale,
Rochester & Chatham,   Romford & Dagenham (2 dies),
Rotherham,   Rugby,   <St Albans,
St Helens A,   Salisbury,   Scarborough A,<B,
<Scunthorpe,   Sevenoaks,   <Sheffield,   and <A,<B,C,
<Shrewsbury A,   Slough,   <Smethwick,
Southall,   Southampton A,B,   Southend-on-Sea,
Southport A,   <South Shields,   Stafford,
Staines,   <Stalybridge,   Stockport A,
<Stockton-on-Tees,   Stoke-on-Trent (2 dies), Stroud,
Sunderland,   Sutton,   <Swansea,   and A,
Swindon,   <Taunton,   Torquay,
<Truro,   Tunbridge Wells,   Uxbridge A,
Wadhurst,   <Wakefield,   Wallasey,
<Walsall, and B,   Walton-on-Thames,   <Warrington A,B,
Warwick & Leamington Spa, Watford,   Wembley A,
<West Bromwich,   <West Hartlepool,   <Weston-s-Mare A,
<Weybridge,   Weymouth,   Wigan,
<Willenhall,   Winchester,   <Woking,
<Wolverhampton A,C,   Worcester A,   Worthing arcs & no arcs,
<Wrexham,   Yeovil,   York.

<Triangles : IS,SE1,SW1,SW/19,121,280,324,417,436,449,641,648,763,802,805,849,
923,I.14,S.36

Listed as 350 dies, about 356 listed above

Early uses :
 4 April Burton-on-Trent, Dumfries, Falkirk, Leeds ?, Swansea A
 5 April Dunfermline, Neath
 6 April Hounslow, Ilford & Barking, Keighley, Pontypridd, Rhyl

Late uses :
 5 May   NW2,6, Coventry B, Maidenhead, Southall
 8 May   Chichester
 9 May   Exeter (2 dies)
13 Sep   Sheffield ?

299 Radio-TV Licences 5-31 May 1960

There were four sub types of this slogan, shown below as A,B,C,D; at large
offices such as London Mount Pleasant town dies/slogan dies were not necessarily
used together for the whole period, thus the sub types used are shown once for
the office.

London D,F,G,H,I,J,K,M,O,<P,T(worn die and new one)(A and B),
       E1 (B), and <A,<B,
       EC <B,C,D,E,F,G,K (A and B),   N1 A, Gt Britain B (A),   NW1 A,B (A),
       SE1 A,C (A),   SW1 A,B,C,<G (A and B),
       W1 D,E,<F (C),   WC <A,<B,C,D (C),

E 8(B),11(A),15(A),17(B),   N 16(A),
NW 2(B),3(A),6(B),10(A),   SE 5(B),9(A),15(A),18(A),
SW 3(A),6(B),7(A),9(B),11(A),15(A),16(A),17(B),18(B),19(A),
W 2A(C),3(A),4(B),5(A),6(A),8(A),12(A),

London missorts : 4,6A,8B,35B,46B,57,60 (Kilburn 60 & London 60),61,73,87,88,91

Aberdeen A(C),<B,	Abingdon(D),	Accrington(C),
Altrincham(A),	Ashford Kent(B),	Ashton-under-Lyne(B),
Aylesbury(A),	Ayr(B),	Barnet(A),
Bath(A),	Bedford types 2 & 3(A),	Belfast A,C,<D(C),
Bexhill-on-Sea(D),	Bexleyheath(A), ADO(B),CH(B),ED(D),H(B),WDO(B),	Birkenhead A(C),
Birmingham A,E,G(A and B),		
Bishop Auckland(D),		
Blackburn A(C),	Blackpool A,B(C),	Bletchley(D),
Bolton B(C),	Bootle(B),	Bournemouth-Poole A(A),
Bradford A,B(B),	Bridgend(D),	Brighton & Hove, and A (B),
Bristol A,B,C,E(B),	Bromley & Beckenham(B),	Burnley & Nelson(C),
Burton-on-Trent(A),	Bury(B),	Bury St Edmunds(B),
Cambridge(A),	Canterbury(A),	Cardiff A,B(B),
Carlisle A(C),<B,	<Castleford,	Chelmsford(B),
Cheltenham(A),	Chester A(A),<B,	Chesterfield(A),
Chichester(A),	Colchester(B),	<Colwyn Bay,
Coventry A,B(A and B),	Crawley(C),	Crewe(A),
Croydon, and A(A and B),	Darlington(A),	Dartford(B),
Darwen A(C),	Derby A(A),	Dewsbury A(A),
Doncaster (arcs)(B),	Dover(A),	Dudley A(C),
Dumfries(A),	Dundee(B),	Dunfermline(B),
Durham(A),	Eastbourne(C),	Edgware(A),
Edinburgh A,B(A and D),	NW(A),	Enfield(A),
Epsom(B),	Erdington(A),	Exeter (2 dies)(B),
Falkirk(A),	Farnborough(A),	Folkestone(A),
Glasgow A,B,C,E(A and D),	S(B),<SE,SW(C),W(C),<W3,	Gloucester A,<B(A),
Gravesend(A),	Grays(B),	Great Yarmouth, and A(A),
Greenock(D),	Grimsby(A),	Guernsey(A),
Guildford(D),	Halifax(B),	Harlow(D),
Harrogate(B),	Harrow, and A(B),	Hastings(A),

Haywards Heath(D),   Hereford B(A),   High Wycombe(B),
Hitchin(D),   Hounslow long & short arcs(B),
Huddersfield(A),   Hull (2 dies)(A),   Ilford & Barking(A),
<Inverness,   Ipswich A(A),   Jersey(B),
<Keighley, and Gt Brit,   King's Lynn(B),   Kingston-on-Thames(A),
Lancaster & Morecambe A(C),   Leeds A,B,<C(A and B),
Leicester A,B,C(A and D),   Lewes(D),   Lincoln A(A),
Liverpool A,B,C,<D(A and C),   <ED,<ND,   Llandudno(A),
Londonderry(C),   Luton types 2 & 3(A),
Lytham St Annes (type 2, replaced by type 3 E 28 May)(C),
Macclesfield(B),   Maidstone(A),
Manchester C,F,K,L,P(A and D),   E(A),<S,SE(D),SW(D),   Mansfield(A),
Margate(B),   Middlesbrough A(A),   <Morpeth,
Moseley DO(A),   <Mossley,   Motherwell & Wishaw A(D),
Neath(D),   Newcastle upon Tyne -A-,   then A E 25 May, B(A and B),
Newport Mon(B),   Newry(D),   Newton Abbot(A),
Northampton No.1,2(C),   North Shields(B),   Norwich(A),
Nottingham A,B,C(B),   Oxford A(A),
Paignton(D),   Paisley(A),   Perth(D),
<Plymouth, and A(A),   <Pontefract,   Pontypridd(D),
Portobello DO(A),   Portsmouth & Southsea, and D(A),
Preston A,<C(B),   <Ramsbottom,   Ramsgate(B),
Reading, and +(A),   Reigate & Redhill(A),   Rhyl(D),
Richmond Yorks(D),   Richmond & Twickenham(A),   Rochdale(C),
Rochester & Chatham(C),   Romford & Dagenham (2 dies)(A and B),
Rotherham(?),   Rugby(B),   St Albans(A),
St Helens A(C),   Salisbury(A),   Scarborough A(B),
<Scunthorpe,   <Sevenoaks,   Sheffield <A,B,C(B)
Shrewsbury A(A),   Slough(B),   Smethwick(B),
Southall, and Gt Britain(A),   Southampton A,B(A), Southend-on-Sea (2 dies)(C),
Southport A(C),   South Shields(B),   <Stafford,
Staines(A),   Stockport A(A),   Stockton-on-Tees(A),
Stoke-on-Trent types 2 & 3(A),   <Stroud,   Sunderland(B),
Sutton(B),   Swansea, and A(D),   Swindon(A),
Taunton(B),   Torquay(B),   <Truro,
Tunbridge Wells(A),   Uxbridge A(B),   <Wadhurst,
Wakefield(A),   Wallasey(C),   Walsall, and B(C and D),
Warrington <A,B(A),   Warwick & Leamington Spa(A),   Watford(A),
Wembley A(D),   West Bromwich(A),   <West Hartlepool,
Weston-s-Mare A(A),   Weybridge(A),   Weymouth(B),
<Wigan,   Willenhall(D),   Winchester(B),
Woking(B),   Wolverhampton C(D),   Worcester A(C),
<Worthing,   Yeovil(A),   <York.

<Triangles : EC,SE1,-L-/SE1,SW1,W5,W6,5,32,132,235,383,405,470,498D,575,625,635,
648,675,888,938,S.31,S.33,S.42,S.174,SSS(N16)

Listed as 350 dies used, approx 344 shown above.

Early uses :
 4 May Keighley, Lancaster & Morecambe A

Late uses :
 1 June London EC C,E, NW3,6,10, SW6,9,19, W3, Hounslow, Ilford & Barking,
Kingston-on-Thames, Rhyl, Truro
 4 June Lewes
11 June Enfield
14 June Weybridge

301 Ceramic Congress 23 to 28 May 1960

London FS M (and ?second die),   SW1 A,B,C,   W1 D,

Triangle : FS

?6 dies used

302 King George's Jubilee Trust (1st use) 1 to 30 June 1960

London D,F,G,H,<I,<J,K,<L,M,O,P,T,   <E1, and A,B,   EC <C,E,F,G,
  N1 A,   NW1 <A,B,   SE1 A,C,F,
  SW1 A,B,C,<D,<G,   W1 <C,D,E,F,   WC B,C,D,

E <8,<11,15,17,   <N 4,   NW 2,3,6,10A,
SE 5,9,<15,18,   SW 3,<6,7,<9,15,<16,17,<18,19,
W 2A (two, one more spaced),<3,<4,6,8,<12,14,

<London missorts : 4,6A,27B,46B,57,60,73,79,87,88,91

Aberdeen A,<B,   <Abingdon,   <Accrington,
<Aldershot,   <Altrincham,   <Ashford Kent,
<Ashton-under-Lyne,   <Aylesbury,   <Ayr,
<Barnet,   Belfast <A,C,   <Bexleyheath,
Birmingham A,E, ADO,CH,<ED,<H,WDO,   <Bishop Auckland,
Blackpool B,   <Bletchley,   Bolton B,
<Bootle,   <Bournemouth-Poole B,   Bradford <A,B,
<Bridgend,   <Brighton & Hove, and A, Bristol <A,C,
Bromley & Beckenham,   Bury,   <Bury St Edmunds,
Cardiff A,B,   <Castleford,   Chichester,
Colwyn Bay,   <Coventry A,   Crawley,
<Crewe,   Darlington,   Dartford,
<Derby A,   <Dewsbury A,   Doncaster (two),
<Dumfries,   Dundee,   <Dunfermline,
Durham,   Eastbourne,   <Edgware,
Edinburgh A,B, <NW,   <Epsom,   <Falkirk,
Glasgow <A,B,<C,E,   <N,<S,<SE,<W,W3,   Gloucester A,B,
<Grays,   <Greenock,   Guernsey,
Guildford,   <Halifax,   <Harrogate,
<Harrow, and <A,   Haywards Heath,   <Hitchin,
Hounslow long & short arcs, and <Gt Brit,   <Ilford & Barking,
<Inverness,   Jersey,   <Keighley,
King's Lynn,   Kingston-on-Thames (two), Leatherhead,
Leeds B,   Leicester B,C,   <Lewes,
Lincoln A,   <Liverpool A,B,C,   Llandudno,
<Londonderry,   Luton (two),   <Lytham St Annes,
<Macclesfield,   Maidenhead,   Maidstone,
<Manchester C, <E,<S,<SE,<SW,   <Morpeth,   <Mossley,
<Motherwell & Wishaw A,   Newcastle upon Tyne A, Newry,
Newton Abbot,   Northampton No.1,   North Shields,
Norwich,   Nottingham B,   <Oldham A,B,
<Paisley,   Perth,   <Plymouth (two), and A,
<Pontefract,   <Portobello DO,   Portsmouth & Southsea,
Preston A,   <Ramsbottom,   Reading, and +,
Reigate & Redhill,   Richmond Yorks,   Richmond & Twickenham,
Rochester & Chatham,   Romford & Dagenham (two),
<St Helens A,   <Salford,   <Salisbury,
Scunthorpe,   <Sheffield C,   <Slough,
<Southall,   Southampton B,   Staines,
<Stalybridge,   <Stoke-on-Trent,   Stroud,
Sutton,   <Swansea,
Taunton,   Torquay,   Truro,
<Wakefield,   <Walsall B,   <Warwick & Leamington Spa,
<Watford,   <Wembley,   West Bromwich,
<Weybridge,   Willenhall,   Winchester,
<Windsor,   <Woking,   Wolverhampton C,
Worthing arcs & no arcs,   <Yeovil,   York.

<Triangles : IS,SW15,132,547C,805,890,S.33,PA

Listed as 225 dies, but about 244 shown above.

Early use : 31 May Luton

Late uses :
  1 July E 11,15,17, NW 6, SE 9, SW 6,9,17, W 4, Birmingham ED, Edgware, Jersey,
Staines, Sutton
  2 July SE 15, SW 7
  4 July Motherwell & Wishaw A
 12 July Newry

303 June Dairy Festival 1 to 30 June 1960

London <E1,   EC B,D,<K,   SW1 B, <Gt Britain F,

<N 7,9,16,   <SE 11,13,   SW 11,
W 5,

<Barnsley,   <Barrow,   <Basingstoke,
Bath,   <Bedford (two),   <Bexhill-on-Sea,
<Birkenhead A,   <Birmingham G,   Blackburn A,
Blackpool A,   Bognor Regis,   <Boreham Wood,
Bournemouth-Poole A,<B,   <Bracknell,   <Bradford A,
Brighton & Hove, and <A,   Bristol B,<C,<D,E,   <Burnley & Nelson,
Burton-on-Trent,   <Caernarvon,   Cambridge,
<Canterbury,   Cardiff A,B,   <Carlisle A,
Chelmsford,   Cheltenham,   <Chester A,
<Chesterfield,   <Cleethorpes,   Colchester,
Coventry B,   <Derby A,   Dover,
Dudley A,   <Enfield,   <Erdington,
Exeter (two),   Exmouth,   <Fareham,
<Farnborough,   Feltham,   Folkestone,
Gloucester A,B,   <Gravesend,   <Great Yarmouth,
<Grimsby,   <Halifax,   <Harlow,
<Harrow, and <A,   Hastings,   Hereford <A,B,
High Wycombe,   <Hucknall,   Huddersfield,
<Hull (two),   <Ilfracombe,   Ipswich A,
<Kidderminster,   Lancaster & Morecambe A, Leeds A,<C,
Leicester A,   Liverpool <A,B,   <Llanelly,
<Lowestoft,   Manchester F,K,<L,<P,   <Mansfield,
Margate,   <Merthyr Tydfil,   Middlesbrough A,
<Mitcham,   <Monmouth,   Moseley DO,
<Neath,   <Newbury,   Newcastle upon Tyne B,
Newport Mon,   Northampton No.<1,2,   <Norwich,
<Nottingham A,C,   <Nuneaton,   <Oswestry,
<Oxford, and A,   Paignton,   <Penzance,
Peterborough A,   <Pinner,   Plymouth A,
<Pontypridd,   <Porthcawl,   <Portsmouth & Southsea, and D,
<Port Talbot,   <Preston C,   <Pwllheli,
<Ramsgate,   <Reading, and +,   Rhyl,
<Rochdale,   Romford & Dagenham,   <Rotherham,
<Rugby,   Ryde,   <St Albans,
<Scarborough A,   <Sevenoaks,   Sheffield <A,B,
<Shrewsbury A,   <Skegness,   <Smethwick,
Southampton A,   Southend-on-Sea,   Southport A,
<South Shields,   <Stafford,   Stockport A,
Stockton-on-Tees,   Stoke-on-Trent,   Sunderland,
<Swansea A,   Swindon,   <Tenby,
Tunbridge Wells,   <Uxbridge A,   <Wadhurst,
Walsall,   <Warrington A,B,   Wembley A,
West Hartlepool,   Weston-s-Mare A,   Weymouth,
Wigan,   <Wolverhampton A,   Worcester A,
<Wrexham.

<Triangles : SE11,13,61,176,383,391,632

Listed as 175 dies, about 170 shown above

Early use : 31 May Burnley & Nelson

Late uses :
 1 July Feltham, High Wycombe
 4 July Hastings

307 Cadet Forces Centenary 1 to 30 July 1960

Not used 7 July (with exceptions) since not relevant to stamp issue that day;
used concurrently with no.308

London <D,F,G,H,<I,J,<K,<O,P,T,   EC G,   SW1 <A,B,C,<D,
     W1 F,   WC C,D,

London missorts : 6A,73

Aylesbury,   Bedford (two),   Belfast C,
<Birkenhead A,   Birmingham A,E,G,   <Blackburn A,
<Bolton B,   Bournemouth-Poole B,

Bristol B,C (worn die, replaced by new die E 21 July), E,
Cambridge,   Cardiff A,B,   <Colchester,
Coventry B with arcs L 21 July, new die no arcs E 31 July,
<Darwen A,   Derby A,   Dundee,
Edinburgh A,B,   Glasgow A,B,<C,   Huddersfield,
Hull (two),   Ipswich A,   King's Lynn,
Leeds A,C,   Leicester A,<B,   Lincoln A,
<Liverpool B,C,D,   Manchester C,K,<P,   <Middlesbrough A,
<Newcastle upon Tyne A,B,   <Northampton No.2,   Norwich (two),
Nottingham A,<C,   <St Albans,   Sheffield A,<B,<C,
Stockport A,   Stoke-on-Trent,   Willenhall,
Wolverhampton <A,C.

Triangles : 107,158,466H,675

Listed as 75 dies, approx 73 shown above.

Late uses :
 2 Aug Bedford
 4 Aug Aylesbury

308 World Mental Health Year 1 July to 31 Aug 1960

Not used 7 July (with exceptions) since not relevant to stamp issue that day;
used concurrently with no.307

London D,F,G,H,I,<J,<K,L,O,P,<T,BB,   E1, and <B,
       EC B,C,D,E,F,K,   N1 A,   NW1 B,
       SE1 A,   SW1 B,<C,<D,G, and <Gt Britain D
       W1 <C,D,E,H,   WC A,<B,C,D,

W 2A (old with dot after Paddington and new without),

Aberdeen A,   Aldershot,   Barnsley,
Bath,   Birmingham CH,H,WDO,   Blackpool A,
<Bootle,   Bournemouth-Poole A,   Bradford B,
Brighton & Hove, and A,   Bristol <A,<B,E,   Burnley & Nelson,
Bury St Edmunds,   Cardiff A,B,   Carlisle A,
Chelmsford,   Colwyn Bay,   Coventry A,
Croydon, and A,   Darlington,   Derby A,
Doncaster,   <Dundee,   Edinburgh B, <NW,
Enfield,   Exeter (two),   Glasgow <A,B,C,
Gloucester A,   Great Yarmouth,   Grimsby,
Halifax,   Harlow,   Harrow, and A,
Hounslow short & long arcs, Hull (two),   Kingston-on-Thames,
Leeds B,<C,   Leicester A,B,C,   Liverpool A,B, <ED,
Llandudno, but Llandudno-Colwyn Bay by 23 Aug,
Luton (two),   Manchester C,F,K,L,   <Merthyr Tydfil,
Newcastle upon Tyne A,B,   Newport Mon,   <Northampton No.1,
Nottingham A,B,   Oldham A,<B,   Oxford A,
Plymouth arcs & no arcs, and A,   <Pontypridd,
<Portobello DO,   Portsmouth & Southsea, and D,
Preston A,<C,   Reading, and +,   Rhyl,
Rochdale,   Rochester & Chatham,
Romford & Dagenham (two), and <Gt Brit,   Rotherham,
St Helens A,   Salford,   Sheffield C,
Slough,   Southampton A,B,
Southend-on-Sea type 2, type 3 E 24 July,   Southport A,
South Shields,   Stoke-on-Trent types 2 & 3,
Sunderland,   <Swansea, and A,   Swindon,
Wallasey,   Warrington <A,B,   Watford,
West Bromwich,   <Wigan,   Woking,
Wolverhampton A,C,   Worthing arcs & no arcs,
Wrexham,   York (two).

Listed as 150 dies, approx 145 shown above.

<Triangles : EC,-L-/EC,-L-/NW1,SE1,SW1,78,132,394,449,466,,466Q,498,498D,523,
625,628,096

Late uses :
 1 Sep Blackpool A, Northampton No.1
 2 Sep Slough
20 Sep Hounslow

313 Greetings Telegrams 1 to 18 Sep 1960

London D,F,G,I,J,K,<M,O,P,T,BB,   E1, and A,<B,
    EC B,<C,D,E,F,G,K,   N1 A,<B,   NW1 <A,B,
    SE1 A,C,F, <Gt Britain F   SW1 A,B,C,D, <Gt Britain,
    W1 <C,D,E,F,   WC <B,C,D,

E 8,11,15,17,   N 16,   NW 2,3,6,10A,
SE 5,9,15,18,   SW 3,6,7,9,11(two),15,16,17,18,19,
W 2A,3,4,5,6,8,12,

London missorts : 6A,10,11,34B,35B,39,39B,46B,57,73,87,88

Aberdeen A,	Accrington,	Aldershot,
Altrincham,	Ashford Kent,	Ashton-under-Lyne,
Aylesbury,	Ayr,	Barnet,
Barnsley,	Bath,	Bedford types 2 & 3,
Belfast <A,C,	<Bexhill-on-Sea,	Bexleyheath,
Birkenhead A,	Bishop Auckland,	Blackburn A,
Blackpool A,<B,	Bletchley,	Bolton B,
Bootle,	Bournemouth-Poole A,<B,	Bradford A,B,
Bridgend,	Brighton & Hove, and A,	Bristol A,B,C,E,
Bromley & Beckenham,	Burnley & Nelson,	Burton-on-Trent,
Bury,	Bury St Edmunds,	Cambridge,
Canterbury,	Cardiff A,B,	Carlisle A,
Castleford, and <GB,	Cheltenham,	Chester A,
Chesterfield,	Colchester,	Coventry A,B,
Crawley,	Crewe,	Croydon, and A,
Darlington,	Dartford,	<Darwen A,
Derby A,	Dewsbury,	Doncaster,
Dudley A,	Dumfries,	Dundee,
Dunfermline,	Durham,	Eastbourne,
Edgware,	Edinburgh A,B, NW,	Epsom,
Exeter (two),	Falkirk,	Farnborough,
Folkestone,	Glasgow A,B,C,E, N,S,W3,	
Gloucester A,<B,	Gravesend,	Grays,
Great Yarmouth,	<Greenock,	Grimsby,
Guernsey,	Guildford,	Halifax,
Harlow,	Harrogate,	Harrow, and <A,
Hastings,	Haywards Heath,	Hereford B,
High Wycombe,	Huddersfield,	Hull types 2 & 3,
Ilford & Barking,	Inverness,	Ipswich A,
Keighley,	King's Lynn,	Kingston-on-Thames arcs & no arcs,
Lancaster & Morecambe A,	Leeds A,B,<C,	Leicester A,B,C,
Lewes,	Lincoln A,	Liverpool A,B,C,D, ED,<ND,
Llandudno-Colwyn Bay,	Londonderry,	Luton types 2 & 3,
Lytham St Annes,	Macclesfield,	Maidstone,
Manchester C,F,K,L,<P, E,S,SE,SW,		Mansfield,
Margate,	Middlesbrough A,	Morpeth,
<Mossley,	Motherwell & Wishaw A,	Neath,
Newcastle upon Tyne A,B,	Newport Mon,	<Newry,
Northampton No.1,2,		
<North Shields,	Norwich,	Nottingham A,B,C,
Oldham <A,B,	Oxford A,	Paignton,
Paisley,	Perth,	Peterborough A,<B,
Pontefract,	Pontypridd,	Portobello DO,
Portsmouth & Southsea, and D,		<Ramsbottom,
Ramsgate,	Reading, and +,	Reigate & Redhill,
Rhyl,	Richmond Yorks,	Richmond & Twickenham,
Rochdale,	Romford & Dagenham (two),	
Rotherham,	Rugby,	
St Albans,	<St Helens A,	Salford,
Salisbury,	<Scarborough A,B,	Scunthorpe,
Sevenoaks,	Sheffield A,B,C,	Shrewsbury A,
Southall, and GB,	Southampton A,B,	Southend-on-Sea,
Southport A,	South Shields,	Stafford,
Staines,	<Stalybridge,	Stockport A,
Stockton-on-Tees,		
Stoke-on-Trent (two),	Stroud,	Sunderland,
Sutton,	Swansea, and A,	Swindon,
Taunton,	Torquay,	Truro,
Tunbridge Wells,	Uxbridge A,	Wadhurst,
Wakefield,	Wallasey,	Walsall, and B,
Warrington A,B,	Warwick & Leamington Spa,	Watford,
<Wembley A,	West Hartlepool,	Weston-s-Mare A,
Weybridge,	Weymouth,	Willenhall,

23

Winchester,   Windsor,   Woking,
Wolverhampton <A,C, Worcester A,   Wrexham,
Yeovil,   York.

<Triangles : IS,-CL-/MTP,EC,-L-/EC,N1,SE1,SW1,E17,SE15,12,163,228,388,405,406,
923,938

Listed as 350 dies, about 320 dies shown above.

Early uses : 31 Aug London G,BB, Bolton B, Gloucester A,B, Reading

Late uses :
19 Sep NW10A, missort 46B, Accrington, Hastings, Kingston-on-Thames
20 Sep Belfast C, Crawley
21 Sep Ashton-under-Lyne, Mossley, Southampton A
26 Sep London SW1 C, Willenhall, Wolverhampton C
27 Sep London SW1 B
29 Sep Edgware, Weybridge
13 Oct Burnley & Nelson, Southall)
15 Oct Truro   ) probably joined up with 318 on 19 Oct
17 Oct Southall GB, Staines   )

315 Civil Defence - Join Now (one line) 20 Sep to 18 Oct 1960

Used in conjunction with 316-7.

Accrington,   Barnet,   Birkenhead A,
Blackpool A,<B,   Bletchley,   Bolton B,
Bootle,   Brighton & Hove,   Burnley & Nelson,
Burton-on-Trent,   <Carlisle A,   Crawley,
<Crewe,   Croydon, and A,   Dartford,
Derby A,   Enfield,   Epsom,
Farnborough,   Harrow, and A,   Hounslow long arcs,
Lancaster & Morecambe A,   Leeds A,   Leicester A,C,
Liverpool A,B,C(two),D,   <ED,<ND,   <Lytham St Annes,
Macclesfield,   Manchester C,F,K,L,P,<Gt Britain C,   S,SE,SW,
Newcastle upon Tyne A,B,   Nottingham A,   Oldham A,<B,
Oxford A,   Portsmouth & Southsea,   Reigate & Redhill,
Richmond & Twickenham,   Rochdale,
Romford & Dagenham, and <Gt Britain,   Rugby,
St Albans,   St Helens A,   <Sandbach,
Sevenoaks,   Sheffield A,   Southport A,
Stockport A,   Stoke-on-Trent,   Sutton arcs & no arcs,
Tunbridge Wells,   <Wadhurst,   Wallasey,
Walsall, and B,   Watford,   Wembley A,
Weybridge,   <Wigan,   Woking,
Wolverhampton A,   Worcester A.

<Triangles : 491, 697, 849

Listed as "about 90 dies", about 81 shown above

Late uses :
19 Oct Carlisle A, Derby A, Hounslow
20 Oct Farnborough
31 Oct Reigate & Redhill

316 Civil Defence - Join Now (two lines) 20 Sep to 18 Oct 1960

Used in conjunction with 315, 317

<Abingdon,   Aldershot,   Altrincham,
Ashford Kent,   <Ashton-under-Lyne,   Aylesbury,
Bedford types 2 & 3,   Bexleyheath,   Blackburn A,
Blackburn & Accrington,   Bradford A,B,   Brighton & Hove, and A,
Bromley & Beckenham,   Bury St Edmunds,   Cambridge,
Canterbury,   Chelmsford,   Colchester,
Coventry A,B,   Darwen A,   Doncaster,
Dudley A,   Eastbourne,   Edgware,
Folkestone,   Gravesend,   Great Yarmouth,
Guildford,   Hastings,   High Wycombe,
Hounslow short arcs,   Hull (two),   Ilford & Barking,
Ipswich A,   King's Lynn,   Leeds B,C,
Leicester B,   Luton types 2 & 3,   Maidstone,

<Manchester E,   Mansfield,   <Margate,
Middlesbrough A,   Northampton No.1,<2,   Norwich,
Nottingham B,C,   Peterborough A,   Portsmouth & Southsea D,
Preston A,   Ramsgate,   Reading, and +,
Rochester & Chatham,   Sheffield, and B,C,   Slough,
Southend-on-Sea,   Stafford,   <Stalybridge,
Stoke-on-Trent,   Uxbridge A,   Walsall,
Warrington <A,B,   Warwick & Leamington Spa,
Willenhall,   Wolverhampton C,   Worthing arcs & no arcs

<Triangles : 31,132,405,625

Listed as "about 90 dies", about 77 shown above

Early use : 1 Sep Margate

Late uses :
19 Oct Canterbury, Hastings, Northampton No.1, Norwich
20 Oct Folkestone, Luton, Uxbridge A
21 Oct Aldershot

317 Civil Defence is common sense 20 Sep to 18 Oct 1960

Used in conjunction with 315-6.

London D,F,G,<I,J,K,<L,M,O,P,R,T,BB,   E1, and A,
       EC B,C,D,E,F,G,K,   N1 A,
       NW1 A,B,   SE1 A,C,<F,
       SW1 A,B,D,G,   W1 D,E,F,   WC B,C,D,

E 8,11,15,17,   N 16,   NW 2,3,6,10A,
SE 5,9,15,18 (two),   SW 3,6,7,9,11(two),15,16,17,18,19,
W 2A,3,4,5,6,8,12,

London missorts : 4,6A,34B,35B,39B,46B,57,73,79,88,89

Aberdeen A,<B,   Ayr,   <Barnsley,
Bath,   Belfast C,D,   Bishop Auckland,
Bournemouth-Poole A,B,   Bridgend,   Bristol, and <A,B,C,E,
Bury,   Cardiff A,B,   <Castleford,
Cheltenham,   Chester A,   <Chesterfield,
Darlington,   Dewsbury, and Gt Britain,   Dumfries,
Dundee,   Dunfermline,   Durham,
Edinburgh A,B, NW,   Exeter (two),   <Falkirk,
Glasgow A,B,<C,<E,<F, <N,S,<SE,<W,<W3,   Gloucester A,B,
Grays,   Greenock,   Grimsby,
Guernsey,   Halifax,   Harlow,
Harrogate,   Haywards Heath,   Hereford B,
Huddersfield,   <Inverness,   Keighley,
Kingston-on-Thames arcs & (two) no arcs,   Lewes,
Lincoln A,   Llandudno-Colwyn Bay,   <Londonderry,
<Morpeth,   <Motherwell & Wishaw A,   <Neath,
Newport Mon,   North Shields,   Paignton,
Paisley,   Perth,   Pontefract,
Pontypridd,   Portobello DO,   <Ramsbottom,
Rhyl,   <Richmond Yorks,
Romford & Dagenham types 2 & 3 (3 in all),   Rotherham,
Salford,   Salisbury,   Scarborough A,
Scunthorpe,   Shrewsbury A,   Southampton A,B,
<South Shields,   <Stockton-on-Tees,   Stroud,
Sunderland,   <Swansea, and A,   Swindon,
Taunton,   Torquay,   Wakefield,
<West Hartlepool,   Weston-s-Mare A,   Weymouth,
Winchester,   Wrexham,   Yeovil arcs and no arcs,
York.

<Triangles : -L-/NW1,SE1,E15,SE/18,W8,392,668,874,S.174

Listed as 175 dies, about 183 shown above.

Late uses :
19 Oct London SW1 B, SW7, W8, Missort 11, Haywards Heath,
20 Oct Gloucester A
21 Oct Londonderry
25 Oct Rhyl
28 Oct Lewes
 3 Nov Weymouth

318 Greetings Telegrams 19 to 31 Oct 1960

London D,<I,J,<K,M,O,P,T,BB,   E1, and <A
       EC B,C,D,E,F,G,<H,K,   N1 A,   NW1 A,B,
       SE1 A,C,   SW1 A,B,G,
       W1 D,<E,<F,   WC <B,<C,D,

E 8,11,15,17,   <N 16,   NW 3,6,10A,
SE 5,9,15,18,   SW 3,6,7,9,<11(two),15,<16,17,18,19,
W 2A,3,4,5,6,8,12,

London missorts : 6A,46B,57,60,73,79,88

Aberdeen A,   Aldershot,
Altrincham,   Ashford Kent,   Ashton-under-Lyne,
Ayr,   Barnet,   <Barnsley,
Bath,   Belfast C,   Bexleyheath,
<Birkenhead A,   Blackburn & Accrington,
<Blackpool A,B,   <Bletchley,   Bolton B,
Bootle,   Bournemouth-Poole A,   Bradford A,B,
<Bridgend,   Brighton & Hove, and <A,   Bristol A,B,C,E,
Bromley & Beckenham,   Burnley & Nelson,   Burton-on-Trent,
Bury,   <Bury St Edmunds,   Cambridge,
Canterbury,   Cardiff A,<B,   <Carlisle A,
Chelmsford,   Cheltenham,   Chester A,<B,
Chesterfield,   Colchester,   Coventry A,B,
Crawley,   Croydon, and A,
Darlington,   Dartford,
Derby A,   Dewsbury,   <Doncaster,
Dudley A,   <Dumfries,   Dundee,
<Dunfermline,   Durham,   Edgware,
Edinburgh A,B, NW,   Enfield,   <Epsom,
Exeter,   Falkirk,   <Farnborough,
Glasgow A,B,C,<E, <N,S,<SE,<W,<W3,   Gloucester A,<B,
Gravesend,   Grays,   Great Yarmouth,
<Guernsey,   Guildford,   Halifax,
<Harlow,   <Harrogate,   Harrow, and <A,
<Haywards Heath,   Hereford B,
High Wycombe,   <Huddersfield,   Hull (two, type 3 seen),
Ilford & Barking,   <Inverness,   Jersey,
<Keighley,   Kingston-on-Thames arcs & no arcs,
Lancaster & Morecambe A,   Leeds A,B,<C,   Leicester A,B,C,
<Lincoln A,   Liverpool A,B,<C,   <ED,<ND,
<Llandudno-Colwyn Bay,   Luton type 3,
<Lytham St Annes,   Macclesfield,   Maidstone,
Manchester <C,K,L,P, <S,SE,<SW,   Mansfield,
<Middlesbrough A,   <Morpeth,   Motherwell & Wishaw A,
<Neath,   Newcastle upon Tyne A,B, Newport Mon,
Northampton No.1,<2,   North Shields,   Nottingham A,B,C,
Oldham <A,B,   Oxford A,   Paignton,
<Paisley,   Perth,   Peterborough A,<B,
Pontefract,   Portsmouth & Southsea, and D,   Preston A,
<Ramsbottom,   <Ramsgate,   Reading, and +,
<Richmond Yorks,   Richmond & Twickenham,   Rochdale,
Rochester & Chatham,
Romford & Dagenham (two),   Rotherham,   Rugby,
<St Albans,   <St Helens A,   <Salford,
Salisbury,   <Scarborough A,   Scunthorpe,
<Sevenoaks,   Sheffield <B,C,   <Shrewsbury A,
Slough,   Southall, and GB,   Southampton A,B,
Southend-on-Sea,   Southport A,   <Staines,
Stockport A,   Stockton-on-Tees,
Stoke-on-Trent (two),   Stroud,   <Sunderland,
Sutton,   <Swansea, and A,   Swindon,
Taunton,   Torquay,   <Truro,
Tunbridge Wells,   Uxbridge A,   <Wadhurst,
Wakefield,   <Wallasey,   Walsall, and B,
Warrington <A,B,   Warwick & Leamington Spa,   Watford,
<Wembley A,   West Bromwich,
<West Hartlepool,   Weston-s-Mare A,
Weybridge,   Wigan,   Willenhall,
Winchester,   <Windsor,   Woking,
Wolverhampton A,C,   Worcester A,   Worthing,
Yeovil,   York.

<Triangles : EC,W1,E8,NW3,49,132,364,466B,868,ABO,WAY

Listed as 350 dies, about 295 shown above

Early uses : see late uses of 313
18 Oct   about 13 offices

Late uses :
 1 Nov E11, NW6, Aldershot, Stockport A
16 Nov Manchester SE
21 Nov King's Lynn

319 Cheap rate trunk calls 1-27 Nov 1960

London D,G,H,<I,J,K,M,O,P,T,BB,   E1, and <A,
       EC B,C,D,E,F,G,K,   N1 A,<B,
       NW1 <A,B,   SE1 A,C,<F,
       SW1 A,B,C,<D,G,   W1 D,<E,F,
       WC <A,C,D (new D die, letters closer, E 15 Nov),

E <8,<11,15,<16,   <N 16,   NW 2,3,6,<10A,
SE <5,9,<15,18(two),   SW <3,6,7,<9,11(two),<15,16,<17,<18,19,
W 2A,3,4,<5,6,8,12,

<London missorts : 4,6A,73,WC/73,88

Aberdeen A,<B,	<Abingdon,	<Accrington,
Aldershot,	<Altrincham,	<Ashford Kent,
Ashton-under-Lyne,	Aylesbury,	<Ayr,
<Barnet,	<Barnsley,	Bath,
<Bedford,	Belfast C,	Bexhill-on-Sea,
Bexleyheath,	Birkenhead A,	
Birmingham A,<E,<G, <ADO,<CH,<ED,H,WDO,		<Bishop Auckland,
Blackburn & Accrington,	Blackpool A,<B,	<Bletchley,
Bolton <A,B,	Bootle,	Bournemouth-Poole A,<B,
Bradford <A,B,	Brighton & Hove, and A,	Bristol <A,B,C,E,
Bromley & Beckenham,	Burnley & Nelson,	Burton-on-Trent,
Bury,	<Bury St Edmunds,	Cambridge,
Canterbury,	Cardiff A,<B,	<Chelmsford,
Cheltenham,	<Chester A,	<Chesterfield,
<Chichester,	Colchester,	Coventry A,<B,
<Crawley,	<Crewe,	Croydon, and A,
Darlington,	<Darwen A,	Derby A,
<Dewsbury,	<Doncaster,	Dudley A,
<Dumfries,	Dundee,	Dunfermline,
<Durham,	Eastbourne,	Edgware,
Edinburgh A,B,<C, NW,	Enfield,	Epsom,
<Erdington,	Exeter (two),	<Falkirk,
Farnborough,	Folkestone,	
Glasgow A,B,C,E, <N,<S,<SE,		Gloucester A,B,
Guernsey,	Guildford,	<Harlow,
Harrogate,	Harrow, and <A,	Hastings,
Haywards Heath,	Hereford B,	High Wycombe,
<Hitchin,	Hounslow (long arcs),	Huddersfield,
Hull types 2 & 3,	Ilford & Barking,	<Inverness,
Ipswich A,	Jersey,	Keighley,
Kingston-on-Thames,	Lancaster & Morecambe A,	Leeds A,B,<C,
Leicester A,B,<C,<D,	<Lewes,	Lincoln A,
Liverpool A,B,<C,D,	Llandudno-Colwyn Bay,	<Londonderry,
Luton type 3,	Lytham St Annes,	<Macclesfield,
<Maidenhead,	Maidstone,	
Manchester <C,<F,<K,<L,P, E,<S,SW,		<Mansfield,
<Margate,	Middlesbrough A,	<Morpeth,
Moseley DO,	<Motherwell & Wishaw A,	<Neath,
Newcastle upon Tyne A,<B,	Newport Mon,	Newton Abbot,
Northampton No.1,<2,	North Shields,	Nottingham <A,B,C,
<Oldham A,B,	Oxford A,	Paignton,
Paisley,	Perth,	Peterborough A,
Plymouth, and <A,	<Pontypridd,	Portsmouth & Southsea, and D,
Preston A,<C,	<Ramsbottom,	<Ramsgate,
Reading, and <+,	Reigate & Redhill,	<Rhyl,
Richmond & Twickenham,	Rochdale,	Rochester & Chatham,
Romford & Dagenham types 2 & 3,	<Rotherham,	Rugby,
St Albans,	<St Helens A,	Salisbury,
<Scarborough A,	<Scunthorpe,	<Sevenoaks,
Sheffield <A,<B,C,	<Shrewsbury A,	<Slough,
Smethwick,	<Southall, and Gt Brit,	Southampton A,B,

598t National Savings Golden Jubilee Year (first use) 1 Jan to 24 March 1966

Dumfries,   Dunfermline,   Falkirk,
Kirkcaldy,   Motherwell & Wishaw A,   Paisley,
Perth (type 2, but type 5 by 31 Jan),   St Andrews.

Triangle : S62

8 dies used

Late use : 25 March Paisley

National Eisteddfod 66

600/t (first use) 3-9 Jan 1966 and **602/t** (second use) 7-13 Feb 1966

This slogan was not announced until mid January, and permission was given for
collectors' covers to be stamped, hence the "exceptional" entries shown below.

	First use	Exceptional use	Second use
Cardiff A (wide C,R)	std		
Cardiff A (narrow C,R)		28 Jan std	std
Cardiff B	std	13 Jan std	std
Carmarthen	std		trans
Llanelly	trans	3 Feb trans	trans
Neath	std	4 Feb trans	7 Feb 10.15am std, trans by 7 Feb 2pm
		(and late use 14 Feb trans)	
Pontypridd	std (& late use 10 Jan)		trans
Port Talbot	std	1 & 3 Feb std	trans
Swansea, and A	std		trans

Triangle : 162 std

9 dies used

601/t Help save your doctor's time 10 Jan to 6 Feb 1966

London D,F,G,H,I,J,K,P,T,   El A, and Gt Britain B,   EC D,E,F,G,
       N1 A,B,   NW1 A,C,   SE1 F,4V,
       SW1 A,B,C,D,E,G,   W1 D,E,F,   WC C,D,

E 8,11,15,17,   N 16,   NW 2,3,6,10A,
SE 5,9,15,18(types 2 & 3),   SW 3,6,9,11,15,16,17,18,19,
W 2A,B(types 2 & 3), 3,4,5,6,8,12,

London missorts : 6A,11,67,75(two diff)

Aberdeen A,B,   Abingdon,   Aldershot,
Altrincham A,   Ashford Kent,   Ashton-under-Lyne,
Aylesbury,   Barnet,   Barnsley,
Bedford,   Bexleyheath,   Birkenhead B,
Birmingham A,E,G,J, ADO,ED,H,WDO,   Blackburn & Accrington,
Bletchley,   Bolton B,   Bootle,
Bradford A,B,   Bromley & Beckenham,   Burnley & Nelson,
Burton.on.Trent,   Bury,   Canterbury,
Cardiff (wide & narrow C,R),B,   Castleford,
Chelmsford,   Chesterfield,   Chichester,
Colchester,   Coventry A,B,   Crewe,
Croydon, and A,   Darlington,   Dartford,
Derby A,   Dewsbury,   Doncaster A,
Durham A,   Edgware,
Edinburgh C transposed,   Enfield,
Erdington,   Exeter,   Farnborough,
Glasgow B (type 3 & squat), C,F,   S,W,   Gloucester A,B,
Gravesend,   Grays,   Greenock,
Guernsey,   Guildford,   Halifax,
Harlow,   Harrogate,   Harrow & Wembley, and A, and *,
Haverfordwest,   Haywards Heath,   Hereford A,
High Wycombe,   Hitchin,   Hounslow,
Huddersfield,   Hull A,B,   Ilford & Barking,
Ipswich,   Keighley types 2 & 3,   King's Lynn,
Kingston-upon-Thames 1,3,   Leatherhead,   Leeds A,B,C,
Leicester A,B,C,   Lewes,   Lincoln A,
Londonderry,   Luton types 2 & 3,   Macclesfield,
Maidenhead,   Maidstone types 2 & 3,   Manchester S,SE,SW,
Middlesbrough A,   Morpeth,   Moseley DO,

Mossley,
Newport Mon types 3 & 5,
Norwich A2,
Oxford A,
Preston A,B,
Richmond Yorks,
Rochester & Chatham,
Rugby,
Scunthorpe,
Slough,
Southampton A,B,
Staines,
Stoke-on-Trent arcs,
Swansea, and A,
Uxbridge,
Warrington A,
Watford types 2 & 3,
Wigan,
Wolverhampton A,B,
Wrexham,

Neath,
Newry,
Nottingham A,B,C,
Pontefract,
Ramsgate,
Richmond & Twickenham A,
Romford & Dagenham B,C,L,
St Helens A,
Sevenoaks,
Smethwick,
South Shields,
Stockport A,
Stroud,
Swindon A,
Wakefield A,

West Bromwich,
Winchester,
Worcester A,
Yeovil.

Newcastle upon Tyne A,B,
Newton Abbot,
Oldham A,B,
Pontypridd,
Reigate & Redhill,
Rochdale,
Rotherham,
Salford,
Sheffield A,B,C,
Southall,
Stafford A,
Stockton-on-Tees,
Sutton,
Truro,
Walsall, and B,

Weybridge,
Woking,
Worthing,

Triangles : SE15,929, S33 trans

Listed as "about 256 dies std", 1 transposed, as shown above

Late uses :
 7 Feb W6, Aylesbury, Birmingham H, Keighley, Newport Mon, Warrington A
 8 Feb E 8,17, Bolton B, Sutton
 9 Feb Romford & Dagenham B
10 Feb Bedford
14 Feb SW11,16, Cardiff A (exceptional after "Eisteddfod", listed as E.44)
15 Feb SW15
17 Feb Richmond & Twickenham A
24 Feb Chesterfield
 1 March Canterbury, High Wycombe
 4 March Stockport A
25 March Weybridge - see also Exceptional Use at Bury in April - E.45

609-610/t   Bath & West Show 1 March to 31 May 1966

Bristol E std type 378A in error L 15 March, std type 378   E 21 March
Devizes std type 378 in error L 21 March, 10.45am,
        std type 378A 21 March, 4.45pm & 6.45pm
        trans type 378A E 22 March,   Dorchester trans type 378A

Triangles : 134 std types 378A/378

1 die of type 378, 3 dies of type 378A used

611/t   Dr Barnardo's Homes (first use) 7 March to 3 April 1966

London G,
      SE1 E,4V,

E 2,
W 2A,B,C,   3,11,

E1 A, Great Britain B,
SW1 B,

N 4,7,8,17,

N1 A,
W1 A,D,E,

SW 2,3,5,6,11,

London missorts : 34B,75

Aldershot,
Bradford B,
Bromley & Beckenham,
Colchester,
Dartford,
Godalming,
Guernsey,
Harrogate,
Hitchin,
Ilfracombe,
Kendal,
Loughborough,
Neath,
Nottingham A,B,C,
Rochester & Chatham,
Southampton A,
Swansea,
Wigan,

Birmingham H,
Brentwood,
Burton.on.Trent,
Croydon transposed L 10 March, std by 13 March,
Dundee B,
Goole,
Halifax,
Hemel Hempstead,
Huddersfield,
Ipswich,
Leeds A,B,
Lowestoft,
North Shields,
Oxford A,
Rugby,
Stockport A,
Tonbridge,
Wolverhampton B,

Bournemouth-Poole C,
Bristol NDO,
Chesterfield,

Glasgow B,
Grantham,
Hamilton,
High Wycombe,
Hull A,
Keighley,
Leicester A,B,
Manchester S,SE,SW,
Norwich,
Rochdale,
Southall,
Stourbridge,
Walsall, and B,
Yeovil.

Triangle : 210

75 dies used

Early use : 6 March London W1 ?

Late uses : 4 April Birmingham H, Manchester F,
  but also see others which continued and joined up with second use, see 622/t

616/t Radio-TV Licences 4 April to 3 May 1966

There were five sub types of this slogan, shown below as A,B,C,D,G where sub-type is known; at large offices town dies/slogan dies were not necessarily used together for the whole period, thus the slogan types used are shown once for the office.

For this issue I have a PO list of die allocations so the < entries are ones on this list that have not been seen. Others announced but not used at Guernsey, High Wycombe (both still using "Dr Barnardo's", London EC (7), Dundee (LP slogan), Manchester (5) and Taunton. The numbers of dies are from that list and are here shown in brackets, one die if not indicated.

London G,H,I,J,K,O,P,T (A and B)(8),   E1 A, Great Britain B(A and G)(2),
    N1 A,B,C (A and G)(2),   NW1 A,C (A and B)(2),
    SE1 E (A)(3),   SW1 C,D,G (A and B)(5),
    W1 D,E (B and C)(3),   WC D (B)(1),

E 8(A)(PO list has E11 not E8),15(A),17(B),
N 4(A),16(A),
NW 2(B),3(A),10 seen 4 May,   SE 5(A),9(B),18(A),
SW 3(A),6(B),
W 2A,B,C(A and C)(2), 3(A),4(D),5(A),<6,8(A),<12,

London missorts :

<Abingdon,   Aldershot(A)(2),   Altrincham A(A),
Ashford Kent(G),   Aylesbury(A),   Barnet(A),
Barnsley(C),   Bexleyheath(A),   Birkenhead B(A),
Birmingham A,E,G(A and B)(3), ADO(A),CH(B),WDO(B),
Bletchley(A),   Bolton B(C),   Bournemouth-Poole A(A),
Bradford A,B(A and B)(2),   Bristol E,Z(A and B), NDO(A)(2),
Burnley & Nelson(C),   Burton.on.Trent(A),   Bury(B),
Carlisle A(C),   Castleford(D),   Chesterfield(A),
Chichester(D),   Coventry A,B (A and B)(2), Crewe(A),
Croydon, and A(A and B)(2), Darlington(A),   Derby A(A)(2),
Doncaster A(A),   Dumfries(B),   Dunfermline(A),
Edgware(A),   Edinburgh C transposed(C)(3),
Enfield(A),   Epsom(B),   <Falkirk,
Farnborough(A),   Folkestone(A),   <Glasgow 2(Waterloo St)
Gloucester A,B(A and B)(2), Grays(B),   Greenock(A),
Guildford(D),   Halifax(A),   Harlow(B),
Harrogate(B),   <Harrow(1),   Hitchin(D),
Hounslow(B),   Huddersfield(A),   Hull A(A)(2),
<Ilford & Barking(1),   Keighley(B),   Kingston upon Thames 1(A)(2),
Leeds A,B,C(B)(3),   Leicester A,B(B and C)(3), Lewes(D),
Lincoln A(A),   <Londonderry,   Lowestoft(A),
Maidenhead(B),   Manchester S(D),SE(A),<SW,
Morpeth(A),   Moseley DO(B),   Motherwell & Wishaw A(D),
Neath(D),   Newcastle upon Tyne A,B(G)(2),
Newport Mon types 3 & 5(A and B), <Newry,   <Newton Abbot,
North Shields(A),   Nottingham A,B,C(A,B and G)(4), Oxford A(A),
Paisley(C),   Peterborough A(A),   Plymouth arcs, and A(A and B),
Pontefract(D),   Pontypridd(D),   Preston A,B(B),
Ramsgate(B),   <Reading(2),   Richmond Yorks(D),
Richmond & Twickenham A(A),   Rochdale types 2 & 3(C),
Rochester & Chatham(B),   Romford & Dagenham B,C(A and B)(2),
Rugby(B),   St Albans(A),   St Helens A(A),
Salford(A),   Scunthorpe(B),   Sheffield A,B,C(A and B)(3),
Slough types 2 & 3(B),   Smethwick(A),   Southall(A),
Stafford A(A),   <Stalybridge,   Stoke-on-Trent types 3 & 5(A),
Swansea, and A(D)(2),   Swindon A(A),   Truro(B),
Uxbridge(B),   Walsall, and B(C and D)(2), <Watford,
Weybridge(A),   Wigan(C),   Winchester(B),
Woking(B),   Wolverhampton A,B(C and D)(2),
Worthing arcs & no arcs(B), Wrexham(G),   York(B).

Listed as "about 220 dies used", about 190 listed above, not including <
entries.

Late uses :
 4 May   too many to list
 6 May   Pontypridd
 7 May   Weybridge
 8 May   Pontypridd Glam Gt Britain, Weybridge
12 May   Grays
23 May   Manchester S
24 May   Bury
12 Aug   Manchester SE
20 Sep   Rugby
11 Dec   Hitchin

618/t <u>National Savings Golden Jubilee (second use) 7 April to 24 June 1966</u>

Aberdeen A (new die with shorter arcs E 22 June), B std (2),
Glasgow B (squat, type 5 E 29 May), C,F std (3)
Glasgow S,SEDO,W all trans

Triangle : AB std

8 dies used

620/t <u>Kent County Show 12 April to 12 July 1966</u>

Dartford std L 18 April, trans E 19 April,
Maidstone arcs types 2 & 3, and no arcs (20-22 June only seen), trans.

Triangles : 236 std and trans

2 dies used

622/t <u>Dr Barnardo's Homes (second use) 18 April to 15 May 1966</u>

+ denotes used in "first use" also and may have been used continuously (there
was only a two week gap), see later uses for ++ and +++ entries.

London F,+G,H,I,J,   SW1 A,   W1 B,C,D,   WC C,

E 3,4,8,   N +4,22,   NW 6,   SE 3,13,15,
SW 9,   London missort : 66

Andover,   Beeston,   Bishop's Stortford,
Blackburn & Accrington,   Boston,   +Brentwood,
+Bromley & Beckenham,   Canterbury types 2 & 3,   Chelmsford,
Chippenham,   +Colchester,   Dewsbury,
Durham A,   Edinburgh NW,W,   Ellesmere Port,
Enfield,   Erdington,   +Guernsey,
Harrow & Wembley, and *,   Haywards Heath,   +Hemel Hempstead,
Hereford A,   +High Wycombe,   Horsham,
Hounslow,   Ilford & Barking types 3 & 5,   Kettering,
Kidderminster,   Lancaster & Morecambe A,   Leatherhead,
+Loughborough,   Manchester F,   Newcastle upon Tyne A,B,
Oldham A,B,   Oxford A,   Penzance,
Perth,   Redditch,   Reigate & Redhill,
Rotherham,   +Rugby,   Sevenaoks,
South Shields,   Staines,   Stalybridge,
+Stockport A,   Stoke-on-Trent,   Stroud,
Sutton,   Wakefield A,   Warrington A,
Wellingborough <u>transposed</u>,   Wellington Shropshire,
West Bromwich,   Worcester A,   +Yeovil.

74 dies used standard and 1 transposed.

Late uses :
16 May Warrington A
17 May Guernsey
but see also ++ entries in "third use" denoting possibly continuous use

624 <u>Remploy 21st Anniversary (first use) 20 April to 4 May 1966</u>

Although only used at one office, included here to show all uses of this slogan.

Cardiff A,B.   Triangle : 162   1 die used

625t <u>Devon County Show 22 April to 19 May 1966</u>

Barnstaple,   Exeter,   Plymouth, and A.

Triangles : 50,285,620

3 dies used

627/t <u>Epilepsy Week 1-7 May 1966</u>

London G,H (2 dies),   W1 F,J (two dies),

Blackheath Birmingham,   Bristol A,D (two dies),   Cardiff A,
Gosport <u>transposed</u>,   Halesowen,   Hull A,
King's L<u>ynn</u>,   Leeds A,   Leicester B,
Manchester C,   E,   Newcastle upon Tyne A,   Nottingham B,
Oldbury,   Sheffield B.

Triangles : 320 trans, 449 std

20 dies used

Late uses : 8 May Cardiff A, Leeds A

629/t <u>United Counties Show 1 May to 12 Aug 1966</u>

Cardigan trans,   Carmarthen trans (1 May to 17 July and 1-12 Aug),
Haverfordwest std, trans by 4 May,
Swansea, and A,L trans (same dates as Carmarthen)

Triangle : 167 trans

4 dies used

633 <u>Remploy 21st Anniversary (second use) 3-17 May 1966</u>

Although only used at one office, included here to show all uses of this slogan.

Manchester A,H.   2 dies used

634/t <u>Imperial Cancer Research 'Cancer Week' 4-17 May 1966</u>

London G,H,I,J,T std,   E1 A std,   EC F std,   N1 A std,
    NW1 A std,   W1 D std,

N 16 trans,   SE 5 trans,
SW 3 std, 11 std L 7 May, trans E 12 May, 16 std, trans by 13 May,
    19 std, trans by 17 May,
W 2A,B,C std,   5,6,12 all trans,

London missorts : 11 std,75 std

Asford Kent std,   Barnsley trans,   Birmingham ED std,
Bolton B trans,   Bradford B std,   Bristol NDO std,
Chesterfield std,   Chichester trans,   Coventry A trans,
Crewe std,   Croydon std,   Derby trans,
Gloucester A std,   Grantham trans,   Hull A std,
Leeds B std,   Leicester A trans,   Manchester P std,
Nottingham A std,   Nuneaton trans,   Oxford A,B std,
Peterborough A trans,   Preston A trans,   Romford & Dagenham B std,
Sheffield B std,   Slough type 3 std,   Solihull std, trans by 6 May
Stourbridge trans,   Sutton Coldfield trans,
Watford types 2 & 3 std L 9 May, trans by 12 May,
Winchester trans,   York trans.

Triangle : 668 std

50 dies used: about 27 std, 18 trans, 5 "both"

Early use : 3 May Derby trans
Late uses :
18 May Slough type 2 std
19 May London EC F std
20 May Manchester P std

635/t CBSO International Wind Competition 4-25 May 1966

Birmingham A,E,G std (3),   ADO trans, CH std, WDO trans,
Moseley DO trans,   Smethwick trans type 3 L 6 May, type 5 by 23 May.

Triangles : 75CH std, 75M trans

8 dies used

636/t Suffolk Show 4-31 May 1966

Bury St Edmunds trans,
Ipswich trans, and A std L 9 May, trans by 13 May (two dies),
Lowestoft std L 9 May, trans by 13 May.

Triangles : 97 trans, 405 trans, 478 trans

4 dies used

637 County Show Stafford 9-22 May 1966

Burton.on.Trent,   Leek,   Lichfield,
Stafford A,   Stoke-on-Trent arcs type 3, type 5 by 15 May,
Walsall,   Wolverhampton B.

7 dies used

641/t Dr Barnardo's Homes (third use) 30 May to 26 June 1966

+ denotes used in previous "second use", ++ denotes used in previous two uses
also and may have been used continuously from first/second uses (there was only
a two week gap from the previous use), see later use for +++ entries.

++London G,   N1 A,   +W1 C,H,
        WC D (worn type 5 then type 3 with dot after London),

E 11,14,17,   NW 3,11,   SW 3,16,19,
W 6,8,9,12,

London missort : 4

Ashford Kent,   Barry,   Birmingham E,G, ADO,WDO,
Bodmin,   Burnley & Nelson,   Bury,
+Chelmsford,   Chesham & Amersham,   Crewe,
Darlington,   Doncaster, and A,
Dorchester transposed, std by 6 June,   Dundee A,
Dunstable,   Farnham,   Feltham,
Glasgow B,   Goole seen late,   Grays,
Halifax,   Hamilton,   +Hereford A,
++High Wycombe,   Huddersfield,   King's Lynn,
Kingston-upon-Thames 1, Macclesfield,   Malvern,
+Manchester F,   Moseley DO,   Newton Abbot,
North Shields,   Northwich,   Norwich,
Oxford A type 3, type 5 by 9 June, C,   Port Talbot,
Preston A,   Richmond & Twickenham, and A,
Rickmansworth,   Romford & Dagenham C,   Ruislip,
Sale,   Smethwick,   ++Stockport A,
+Stoke-on-Trent,   Truro,   Watford types 2 & 3,
Wellington Shropshire, Welwyn Gdn City A,   Wigan,
Winchester,   Woking.

Triangle : 960

75 dies used

Late uses :
27 June Hamilton, Richmond & Twickenham A
 3 July Northwich
 6 July Goole

643/t Learn to Swim Week 30 May to 4 June 1966

Dumfries trans,   Dunfermline trans,   Edinburgh C, NW both trans,
Falkirk trans,

Glasgow B trans L 31 May, std by 2 June,
           C std 30 May but backdated philatelic item,
Kirkcaldy trans,   Motherwell & Wishaw A trans,
Paisley std 30 May (6am seen), trans by 4pm 30 May,   Perth trans.

Triangles : S42 std, S64 trans.

10 dies used

Late use : 5 June Paisley trans

644/t Dairy Festival Time for sport 31 May to 31 July 1966

London F,G,H std,

Birmingham A,E std,   Bootle trans,   Bradford A,B std,
Bristol D std,   Cardiff A (wide C,R and narrow),B std,
Eastleigh trans,   Leeds A std,   Manchester P std,
Nottingham B std,   Plymouth A std,   Scunthorpe std,
Stoke-on-Trent std,   Sunderland E 15 June std (announced as trans),
Swindon A std, trans by 26 July.

Triangles : 881 std and trans

15 dies used

Late uses :
 4 Aug Birmingham E
 8 Aug Bristol D

652 Remploy 21st Anniversary (third use) 13-27 June 1966

Although only used at one office, included here to show all uses of this slogan.

Sheffield A,B,C,D   3 dies used

656t Royal Counties Show 1967 26 June to 6 Sep 1966

Basingstoke (to 5 Sep),   Newbury.

2 dies used

660 Remploy 21st Anniversary (fourth use) 29 June to 13 July 1966

Although only used at one office, included here to show all uses of this slogan.

Bristol A,E,Z, NDO   3 dies used

672/t The Country Code - keep your dog under control 7 July to 31 Aug 1966

London F,G std,

Birkenhead B trans,   Birmingham A std,   Bradford A,B std,
Bristol E std,   Cardiff A std, new die with narrow C by 14 July std,B,
Darlington std,   Exeter trans,   Leeds B std,
Manchester A,F std.

Triangles : 134 std, 233 std, 466H trans.

10 dies used

Late uses :
 6 Sep London G
18 Sep Cardiff A
20 Sep Manchester F

673/t National Savings Golden Jubilee (third use) 8 July to 24 Sep 1966

Arbroath trans,   Ardrossan trans,
Coatbridge trans, new town die by 12 Aug with Coatbridge more spaced, trans,
Dumbarton trans,   Galashiels trans,   Kilmarnock trans,
Oban trans,   Stirling std, trans by 21 July.

Triangles : S5,S6,S23,S63,S98(handstamp triangle added), all trans

8 dies used

675/t Dr Barnardo's Homes (fourth use) 11 July to 7 Aug 1966

+ denotes used in previous "third use" also and may have been used continuously (there was only a two week gap), ++ denotes used for previous two uses, and +++ denotes used for all three previous uses, probably continuously

London +++G,H,   El A,   NW 1A (dot & no dot after 1),
   SW1 B,C,   ++W1 H,   +WC C,D,

SE 5,6,
SW 12,15,17 <u>all 3 transposed</u> for short period (11 July, but SW15 to 13 July), then std,   W 3,5,

Barnet,	Barnsley,	Bexleyheath,
Birmingham CH,	Bolton B,	+Bradford B,
Bridgwater,	Bristol D, NDO,	Canterbury,
Colchester,	Croydon,	Derby,
Dewsbury,	+Doncaster, and +A,	Dumfries,
Edgware,	Falkirk,	Fareham,
Gloucester A,	Grantham,	Gravesend,
+Halifax,	Hereford A squat, type 3 by 4 Aug,	
+++High Wycombe,	Horsham,	Hull A,B,
+Kingston-upon-Thames 1,	Leeds A,	Leicester B,
Maidtsone types 2 & 3,	Motherwell & Wishaw A,	Orpington, and Gt Britain,
Pontypool,	+Preston A,	Pwllheli,
Romford & Dagenham B,	Rotherham,	St Helens A,
Slough,	Solihull,	Stafford A,
Stevenage,	+++Stockport A,	++Stoke-on-Trent types 3 & 5,
Sutton Coldfield,	Uxbridge,	Wakefield A,
Walsall,	Waltham Cross,	Warrington A,
+Welwyn Gdn City A,	+Wigan,	+Woking,
Wolverhampton A,B,	Woodford Green,	Worcester A,
Wrexham.		

72 dies used standard, and 3 both standard & transposed.

Late uses :
18 Sep High Wycombe
19 Sep Woking

676/t National Eisteddfod (third use) 18-31 July 1966

Bridgend trans,   Cardiff A,B std (2 dies),   Carmarthen trans,
Llanelly trans,   Neath trans,   Port Talbot trans,
Swansea, and A,L all trans (2 dies).   9 dies used

684 Remploy 21st Anniversary (fifth use) 16 Aug to 22 Nov 1966

London F,G,H,   SW1 B,C (new die with shorter arcs by 20 Oct),
   W1 A,D.   3 dies used,

and a further 3 dies used 8-22 Nov : El, and A,   N1 A,   W1 B.

Late use : 23 Nov London (die letter unreadable)

688 Remploy 21st Anniversary (sixth use) 30 Aug to 13 Sep 1966

Newcastle upon Tyne A,B (2),   Wallsend.   3 dies used

697/t Stop Accidents 16 Sep to 14 Oct 1966

Armagh trans,   Ballymena trans,   Bangor Co Down trans,
Belfast C trans (reported std but not confirmed), Coleraine trans,
Cookstown trans,   Downpatrick trans,   Dungannon std,
Enniskillen trans,   Lisburn trans,
Londonderry std, trans by 20 Sep,   Lurgan trans,
Omagh trans,   Portadown trans,   Strabane std, trans by 27 Sep.

15 dies used

Triangles : -I-/9 std, I14 trans, I20 trans

698 St Andrew's Home & Club for Boys Westminster 16-29 Sep 1966

London SW1 B,C,G,   W1 B,   Triangle : W1.   2 dies used

699-700/t Muscular Dystrophy Week 19 Sep to 16 Oct 1966

699 Last year's design used in error :

London SE1 F (19-28 Sep), V4 (28 Sep),
Kingston upon Thames 1 (19 Sep, presumably am)(not seen).

700/t New design.

London F,H std,   EC F std,   SE1 F from 29 Sep std, V4 E 10 Oct std,
    WC D std,

Birmingham WDO (new town die by 7 Oct) std,   Blackburn & Accrington std,
Bolton B trans,   Bristol E std,   Cardiff A std,
Croydon trans,   Darlington std L 27 Sep, trans by 29 Sep,
Derby trans, A trans by 20 Sep,   Durham A std,
High Wycombe std L 13 Oct, trans by 17 Oct,
Kingston upon Thames 1 std E 19 Sep 2.45pm, new town die (no dots) by 7 Oct, 3,
Leicester B std, type 5, type 3 by 25 Sep,
Luton Beds dot & no dot both type 3, trans,
Maidstone types 2 & 3 both trans,   Manchester F std,
Nottingham B std,   Reading arcs, no arcs, and + all std,
Stoke-on-Trent arcs types 3 & 5.

Triangles : 134 std, 482 trans

22 dies used

Late uses :
17 Oct Blackburn & Accrington std, Bolton B trans
23 Oct Maidstone trans
28 Oct Reading + std

701 National Savings Group (first use) 19 Sep to 13 Nov 1966

Although only used at one office, included here to show all uses of this slogan.

Birmingham A,E,G (3 dies).   Triangle : 75   3 dies used

702 National Savings Group (second use) 24-30 Sep 1966

Although only used at one office, included here to show all uses of this slogan.

Wrexham.   1 die used.

704 Premium Bonds Prize Investment (first use) 26 Sep to 16 Oct 1966

Although only used at one office, included here to show all uses of this slogan.

Nottingham A,C,D.   Triangle : 583   3 dies used

705/t Wage war on warble grubs 1-31 Oct 1966

Aberdeen A std,   Dumfries trans,   Glasgow B std 19-31 Oct only,
Hawick trans,   Perth trans.

Triangles : S29 trans, AB std

5 dies used

707/t NABC Club Week 3 Oct to 6 Nov 1966

Used for varying periods within the dates shown above.

London SE1 A,F,V1 std 17-30 Oct,   W1 B std 17-30 Oct,
    WC C,D std (announced as 2 dies) 3 Oct - 6 Nov,

Corby std (announced as trans and a "rolled on" trans obtained when trans
requested), 17-23 Oct,
Coventry A trans (reported but not seen)(not certain of dates)
Edgware trans, 17-30 Oct,
Enfield (announced as trans) trans (17 Oct), std by 25 Oct, 17-30 Oct,
Hounslow trans, 17-30 Oct,
Kettering trans, 17-23 Oct,
Kingston upon Thames 3 std (announced as trans), 1 by 18 Oct, 10-30 Oct,
Manchester F,P (types 3 & 5) std (2 dies), SE,SW both std, all 24 Oct - 6 Nov,
Northampton 1 trans, 17-23 Oct,

Nottingham A,B std (2 dies), 24 Oct - 6 Nov,
Peterborough A trans, 17-23 Oct,
Richmond & Twickenham A trans, 17-30 Oct,
Southampton C trans, 24-30 Oct,
Stockport A trans, 24 Oct - 6 Nov,
Swindon A std in error from 4 Oct (not 3 Oct as announced), trans from 7 Oct
  (seen std and trans both 12.15pm 7 Oct),
Winchester trans, 3-16 Oct.

Triangles : 498 std, 888 trans

23 dies used

710 Remploy 21st Anniversary (seventh use) 4-18 Oct 1966

Although only used at one office, included here to show all uses of this slogan.

Glasgow B,C,F.   Triangle : S42   3 dies used

711t National Savings Golden Jubilee (fourth use) 8 Oct to 31 Dec 1966

Edinburgh C,D, Gt Britain D, then B by 15 Dec(swopped with "Musselburgh Racing")
(announced as 2 dies at HO but one used at EC),   EC,NW,SW,W,
Glasgow E3 (only seen 20 Dec, which die was borrowed?), N,NW,
Hamilton.

8 dies used

Late use : 1 Jan 1967 Edinburgh B

713 Public Works Congress 17 Oct to 15 Nov 1966

London G,H,I,M,T (2 dies),   EC F,   WC D,

W 6 (types 2 & 5).   London missort : 39,   Triangle : W6

5 dies used

Late use : 16 Nov W6

714 National Savings Group (third use) 22 Oct to 5 Nov 1966

Although only used at one office, included here to show all uses of this slogan.

Leicester A (see 715 below). Triangle : 449.   1 die used.

715 Premium Bonds Prize Investment (second use) 22 Oct - 5 Nov 1966

Although only used at one office, included here to show all uses of this slogan.

Leicester B,C (see 714 above). Triangle : 449.   2 dies used.

716/t John Groom's 31 Oct to 31 Dec 1966

Ended generally 10 Dec but extended to 31 Dec at six offices as noted below

N 14 trans (to 31 Dec),
NW 3 std (trans reported but not confirmed), 4 trans, 7 trans (both to 31 Dec),
SE 21 std, trans by 10 Nov (to 31 Dec),
SW 3 std L 14 Nov, trans by 21 Nov, 15 std, trans by 19 Nov,
W 2A,B,C std, 8 trans,

London missorts : 5 trans, 11 std, 75 std.

Barnet trans,   Bromley & Beckenham trans, Edgware trans,
Enfield trans,   Harrow & Wembley trans, Orpington trans (to 31 Dec),
Richmond & Twickenham, and A, both trans,
Romford & Dagenham B trans,
Sevenoaks std L 23 Nov, trans by 27 Nov,
Watford types 2 & 3 (2 dies) trans L 9 Nov, std by 1 Dec,
Woodford Green std, trans by 30 Nov (to 31 Dec).

Triangles : NW3 std, NW4 trans, 586 trans

22 dies at 20 offices (not sure of the second office that had 2 dies, Watford
being one)

Late uses :
11 Dec Romford & Dagenham B trans (due to end 10 Dec)
10 Jan 1967 NW4 trans
14 Jan 1967 NW7 trans
17 Jan 1967 N14 trans, Woodford Green trans

717/t Reedham School 7 Nov - 4 Dec 1966

London F,H,I,J,K,O,P,T std,   EC B,E std,
       SW1 A,D std,   WC C std,

Dorking std, trans by 14 Nov,   Dumfries trans,
Dunfermline trans,   Epsom trans,   Farnham trans,
Godalming trans,   Guildford trans,   Kilmarnock trans,
Kirkcaldy trans,   Leatherhead trans, Motherwell & Wishaw A trans,
Weybridge trans,   Woking std in error, also with red square Paid.

Triangles : EC std, S29 trans

17 offices, not certain if one die each

Late use : 8 Dec London EC B std

718/t Sue Ryder Homes 7-20 Nov 1966

London F,H,J std,   W1 C std,

Birkenhead B std,   Birmingham WDO std,
Chelmsford std (announced as trans),   Colchester std (announced as trans),
Glasgow B trans,   Harrogate trans, Hereford A std (announced as trans),
Huddersfield, and GB, both trans,
Manchester F (types 3 & 5),L,P std (2 dies),
Newport Mon (types 3 & 5) trans (one slogan die),
Northampton 1 trans,   Preston A trans,   Rugby std, trans by 11 Nov,
Sheffield A,C std (2 dies).

Triangles : 210 std, 387 trans, 466H std

18 dies used at 16 offices (std 11 dies at 9 offices, trans 6 at 6, "both" 1)

Late uses :
21 Nov Birkenhead B std, Colchester std
22 Nov London F,H std, Hereford A std

720/t Britain leads - helping spastics 14 Nov - 11 Dec 1966

London D,F,G,H,I,K,L,O,P,T,   EC E,F,   NW1 A,B,C,
       SE1 F,V1,   SW1 C,F,I,   WC D,

E 8,   SW 6,9,11,16,   W 5,9,12,

Birmingham A,E,G,   Blackburn & Accrington,   Bolton A,B transposed,
Bradford A,B,   Bristol B,D,E,   Cardiff A (wide & narrow C),B,
Clacton-on-Sea,   Coventry A,B,   Derby A,
Hertford,   Hull A,B,   Ipswich, and A,
Leeds A,B,C,   Leicester A,B,   Manchester A,F(types 3 & 5),P,
Nottingham A,B,C,   Oxford A(types 3 & 5),B,
Plymouth, and A,   Sheffield A,B,C,   Southampton A,C transposed,
Sutton std L 4 Dec, transposed by 5 Dec,   Swansea, and A,L,
Tonbridge,   Wolverhampton A,B, both transposed.

Triangles : 86 std, 905 trans

About 70 dies used, 63 std, 6 trans, and 1 "both"

Late uses :
12 Dec Birmingham A
14 Dec Manchester F type 3
17 Dec Manchester P
29 Dec Hertford

723-725 Voters Lists 28 Nov to 11 Dec 1966

A new sub type was used for the first time in 1964, and used again in 1965-6 is
here shown at the end of 724 - type 98A. Note there are two transposed uses
here, of 724t. < entries are shown by comparison wit the Post Office listing
which I have for this slogan. Thus they are more substantive data than the
previous years and they are shown in a separate list at the end.

723 Type 98

London N1 A,B,

E 2,3,4,10,17,	N 4,7,8,9,19,	NW 2,10A,
SE 3,5,6,	SW 19,	W 4,11,

Londonmissort : 67

Barnsley,	Bedford (GPO list says 2 dies),	Bishop Auckland,
Canterbury,	Chelmsford,	Chichester,
Crewe,	Darlington,	Doncaster,
Durham A,	Hereford A,	Hexham,
Kidderminster,	Luton types 2 & 3 dot & no dot,	
Maidenhead,	Neath types 2 & 3,	North Shields,
South Shields,	Stoke-on-Trent arcs types 3 & 5,	
Wallsend.		

Listed as "about 50 dies", as shown above.

Late uses :
12 Dec NW2, Darlington
14 Dec E10, Kidderminster, Maidenhead
17 Dec W11
20 Dec NW10

724/t Type 98A

London NW1 C,

E 6,11,15,	N 16,17,22,	NW 6(types 3 & 5),8,10,11,
SW 2,4,5 (philatelic cover unfortunately rolled on by hand),		W 3,

Aberdeen A,	Aldershot,	Andover,
Aylesbury,	Barrow-in-Furness,	Basingstoke,
Birkenhead B,	Bridgwater,	Burnley & Nelson,
Burton.on.Trent,	Bury,	Chippenham,
Cirencester,	Coatbridge,	Coleraine,
Dumbarton,	Exeter,	Falkirk,
Fareham,	Farnborough,	Galashiels,
Glasgow B,	Gloucester A,	Halifax,
Harrogate,	Huddersfield,	Keighley,
Kettering,	Lanark,	Lancaster & Morecambe A,
Leigh,	Lincoln A,	Londonderry,
Lymington,	Maidstone arcs types 2 & 3, and no arcs,	
Malvern,		
Newbury,	Newport Mon,	Newton Abbot,
Northampton 2 <u>transposed</u>, later 1 (E 2 Dec)(see below for 2nd die),		
Northwich,	Oldham A,B,	
Paisley,	Penzance,	Perth,
Peterborough A,	Preston A,	Retford,
Rochdale,	Rossendale arcs & no arcs,	
Rotherham,	St Helens A,	Stockport A,
Stroud,	Truro,	Wakefield A,
Warrington A,	Wigan,	Winchester,
Workington,	York.	

New sub-type :   Ballymena std 28 Nov, then <u>transposed</u> E 29 Nov 9.15am,
L 3 Dec, then std again by 6 Dec,   Bangor Co Down,
Barry,   Beeston,   Boston,
Bridgend,   Grantham,   Loughborough,
Northampton 1 <u>transposed</u>, later 2,
Nuneaton,   Stamford.

Listed as "about 90 dies" as shown above

Early uses :
10 Nov Rossendale arcs
24 Nov Huddersfield

Late uses :
12 Dec N22, W3, Andover, Bridgwater, Bury, Huddersfield, Newbury
14 Dec Lanark, Rochdale
15 Dec Cirencester
16 Dec NW10
17 Dec Rossendale arcs
24 Dec Rossendale no arcs (E 15 Dec)(the 2 must have been used together)
 4 Jan 1967 Rossendale arcs again (E 27 Dec)

725 Type 98B

E 7,   SE 13,

Ashford Kent,   Camberley,
Rochester & Chatham,   Slough,   Windsor.

Listed as "about 7 dies", as shown above.

Late uses :
12 Dec Windsor
18 Dec Ashford Kent

Additional offices listed by GPO but not seen - clearly I do not know which type
these are : SE15, Greenock, Portadown, St Andrews, Yeadon.

Others announced but not thought to have used the slogan : SW 9,13,17,
Brentwood, Derby, Leicester, Macclesfield, Reigate & Redhill

731t-732/t Post early for Christmas   12-19 Dec 1966

These two designs were not announced at all, thus the dates shown above are
merely those of 733/t below. **731t** is the old holly design, used transposed only
at Taunton.

732/t is the Candle design. Two sub-types exist, thin lettering with F over I,
thick with F left of I, but these are not distinguished in this list.

Barry,   Brentwood,   Bridgend,
Bury Lancs Gt Britain,   Canterbury,   Carlisle A,
Chesham & Amersham,   Chester B,   Chesterfield Gt Britain,
Chippenham,   Croydon, and A,   Edgware, and Gt Britain,
Enfield,   Fylde Coast 3,4,5,6,   Godalming,
Guernsey,   Harrow & Wembley A,   Keighley,
Llandudno-Colwyn Bay (two), Lowestoft,   Luton,
Newport Mon seen early,   Norwich std and transposed, and A-1-4 std,
Oxford B,   Penzance,   Peterborough A,
Slough,   Southport A,
Sunderland squat & type 3, and Gt Britain,   Swindon B,
Taunton type 3,   Walsall, and B,   Warwick & Leamington Spa 1,
Watford (seen 19 Dec),   Worthing arcs (two) & no arcs.

Listed as "about 48 dies standard", and one transposed, as shown above.

Earliest uses :
 1 Dec Fylde Coast 1,4, Harrow & Wembley * (up to 11 Dec), Newport Mon
 5 Dec Carlisle A, Fylde Coast 3, Harrow & Wembley A

Late uses :
20 Dec about 14!
21 Dec Barry, Penzance, Sunderland, Worthing no arcs
24 Dec Bury Lancs Gt Britain

733/t Post your Christmas cards   12-19 Dec 1966

London F,G,H,I,J,K,O,P,T,   E1, and A,
       EC B,D,E,F,G,H,   N1 A,B,   NW1 A,C,   SE1 A,B,F,
       SW1 A,C,D, and Gt Britain C,D,   W1 A,B,C,E,G,   WC A,C,D,

E 8,11,15,17,   N 16,   NW 2,3,6,10A,
SE 5,9,15(types 2 & 3),18,
SW 3,6(types 3 & 5),7,9,11(two sim),15(types 3 & 5),16(dot & no dot),
   17(two similar),18,19,
W 2A,B,C, 3,4,5,6,8,12,

London missorts : 6A,10 (SW7) <u>transposed</u>, 75,91

Aberdeen A,B,	Abingdon,	Aldershot arcs & no arcs,
Altrincham A,	Ashford Kent,	Ashton-under-Lyne,
Aylesbury (types 2 & 3)		
Barnet,	Barnsley, and A,	Batley,
Bedford,	Belfast A,C,D,	Bexleyheath,
Birkenhead B,	Birmingham A,E,G, ADO,CH,ED,WDO,	
Bishop Auckland,	Blackburn & Accrington (two), and B,	
Bletchley,	Bolton B,	Bradford A,B,
Bromley & Beckenham,	Burnley & Nelson, and B,	Burton.on.Trent,
Bury, and Gt Britain,	Canterbury,	Cardiff A,B,
Castleford,	Chelmsford,	Chichester,
Colchester,	Coventry A,B,	Crewe,
Darlington arcs & no arcs,	Dartford types 2 & 3,	Derby A,B,
Doncaster A,	Dudley B std and <u>transposed</u>,	
Dumfries,	Dunfermline,	Durham A,
Edgware <u>transposed</u>,	Enfield,	Epsom, and Gt Britain,
Erdington,	Exeter,	Falkirk,
Farnborough,	Folkestone,	Gloucester A,B,
Gosport <u>transposed</u>,	Gravesend,	Grays,
Grimsby & Cleethorpes (broken & unbroken town dies), and A,		
Guildford,	Halifax,	Harrogate, and A,
Harrow & Wembley, and A, and *,		Haywards Heath,
Hereford A,	High Wycombe A,	Hitchin,
Hounslow,	Huddersfield, and A,	Hull A,B,
Ilford & Barking,	Ipswich,	King's Lynn,
Kingston-upon-Thames 1,3,	Lancaster & Morecambe A,	
Leatherhead,	Leeds A,B,C,	Leicester A,B,C,
Lewes,	Lincoln A,	
Londonderry,	Luton dot & no dot,	Macclesfield,
Maidenhead,	Maidstone no arcs,	Manchester S,SE,
Morpeth,	Moseley DO,	Motherwell & Wishaw A,
Neath <u>transposed</u>,	Newport Mon,	
Newton Abbot,	Northampton 1,2 both <u>transposed</u>,	
North Shields,	Nottingham A,B,C,	
Oldham A,	Oxford A,	Paisley,
Perth,	Plymouth arcs, and A types 3 & 5,	
Pontefract,	Pontypridd,	Portadown,
Preston A,B,	Reading, and +,	Reigate & Redhill,
Richmond Yorks,	Richmond & Twickenham A,	Rochester & Chatham,
Rockferry,	Romford & Dagenham B,C,L,	Rotherham,
Rugby,	St Albans,	St Helens A,
Scunthorpe, and A,	Sevenoaks,	Slough,
Smethwick,	Southall,	Southampton B,C,D all <u>transposed</u>,
South Shields,	Stafford A,	Staines,
Stockport A,	Stoke-on-Trent arcs types 3 & 5,	
Stroud,	Sutton,	Swansea, and A,
Swindon A,B,	Tonbridge,	Truro,
Uxbridge,	Wakefield A,	Warrington A,
Watford (two),	West Bromwich,	
Weybridge,	Wigan,	Winchester,
Woking, and red square Paid,	Wolverhampton, and A,B,	
Worcester A,	Wrexham,	
Yeovil,	York.	

Triangles; 190 std, 570 trans

Listed as "about 260 dies" standard, and about 7 transposed, as shown above

Early uses :
  2 Dec Maidenhead
  6 Dec Stafford A
  9 Dec Epsom
 11 Dec E17, Halifax

Late uses :
 20 Dec too many to list (all standard)
 21 Dec NW6, Bishop Auckland, Sutton
 22 Dec Bury, Gravesend, Hitchin
 28 Dec SW15

734/t <u>Christie's Bicentenary Exhibition   26 Dec 1966 to 14 Jan 1967</u>

London SW1 A,B,C (philatelic items dated 26 Dec)(originally planned to have 3
dies at SW1 but in practice only one used), later I, all trans,
      W1 A,B,C,E std (3 dies)

SW 6,7 both trans 10-14 Jan - these dies were due to be used at SE1 4-14 Jan,
but there were problems fitting the dies to the machines, hence used elsewhere.

London missorts : 10,46B both trans

6 dies used

Late uses :
16 Jan 1967 London W1 B std, SW6 trans, Missort 10 trans
17 Jan 1967 SW7 trans

736/t	<u>Are you under insured (first use) 23 Jan - 19 Feb 1967</u>		
773/t	<u> ditto (second use) 17 April - 14 May 1967</u>		
856/t	<u> ditto (third use) 24 July - 20 Aug 1967</u>		
904/t	<u> ditto (fourth use) 23 Oct - 19 Nov 1967</u>		

Four uses shown in 4 columns, "same" means "same as previous use"; not every
change of town die is included in the listing. In brackets are supposed numbers
of slogan dies where different from number of town dies in first use.
< shows repeat uses not seen but probably used
+ denotes continuous use from previous use, ++ two prev uses, +++ three

First use	Second use	Third use	Fourth use
London H,I,J,T (6),	D,H,I,K,T,	D,H,I,T,	T,AA,BB
E1, and A,	same	same	same
EC B,D,E,F,G,	same	F only,	same
N1 A,B,	same	same	same
NW1 A,B,	<A,B,	C only,	B only,
SE1 F (3)	same	same	same
SW1 A,C,D (4)	+A,C,D,I	++A,C,I,K,	A,B,C,F,
W1 A,B,	same	+same	A,C,
WC B,C,D,	same	same	C,D,
E 8,11,15,17,	5,7,10,11,14,+17,	15,++17,	8,<11,<15,<17
N 16,	same	same	xxx
NW 2,3,6,10,	2,3(two),+6,10A,	3,6,10A,	2,3,6(two),10
SE 5,9,15,18,	5,9,15,18,	same (18 t 2 & 3)	5,9,15,18,
SW 3,6,7,9,	same (+7,+9) same	(++SW7)(9 types 3 & 5) SW 3,6,7	
11 std & transposed	trans	trans	trans
15,16,17,18 & SDO,19,	15,16,17,18 SDO,19,	same	same 18 not SDO
W 2A,B(types 2 & 3),C,	same	W2 A,B,	W2 <A,B,
3,4,5,6,8,12	same (+4, 5 two)	3,4,5,<6,8,<12,	3,4(two),5(two),
			<6,8,12,

London missorts : 6A,10,27B	6A,+10,75	75	75,87

Aberdeen A,B,	+B,	A,<B,	A,B,
Abingdon,	same	same	same
Aldershot,	same	same	same
Altrincham A,	same	same	used again
Ashford Kent,	same	<	same
Ashton-under-Lyne,	same	same	same
Aylesbury,	same	same	same
Ballymena,	same	same	same
Bangor Co Down,	same	<	<
Barnet,	same		A,
Barnsley,	same	same	type 3,
Bedford type 3,	+types 2 & 3	type 2,	same
Bexleyheath,	same	same	B,
Birkenhead A,	same	same	+same
Birmingham A,E,G,	after "Antiques"	same	same
ADO,CH,ED,WDO,	same (+ADO)	same	same
Bishop Auckland,	same	used again	same
Blackburn & Acc (2),	xxx	xxx	xxx
Blackheath Birmingham,	xxx	++same	+++same
Bletchley,	+same		
Blyth seen 20 Feb,	Blyth	same	same
Bolton B,	same	same	same

Bootle,	xxx	xxx	xxx
Bradford A,B,	same	same	A(two),B,
	Bristol NDO	<	used again
Bromley & Beckenham t5,	types 3 & 5,	type 5,	same
Burnley & Nelson,	Burnley,	same	same
Burton.on.Trent,	same	same	Burton-on-Trent
Bury,	+same	++same	same
Canterbury,	Deal,	Canterbury & Deal,	Canterbury
Cardiff A (type 3),B,	A types 3 & 5,B,	as 1st use	same
Castleford,	same	same	same
Chelmsford,	same	same	same
Chichester,	same	xxx	used again, squat & t3
Colchester,	same	same	same
Coleraine,	same	same	same
Coventry A,B,	same	same	Nuneaton
Crewe,	same	+same	same
Darlington,	Stanley,	xxx	Stanley,
Dartford,	same	same	same
Derby A (2),	same. also Belper	xxx	xxx
Doncaster,	Doncaster A,	same	same
Driffield,	same	same	same
Dumfries,	same	<	used again
Dunfermline,	same	same	same
Durham A,	same	same	same
Edgware,	same	same	<
Enfield,	same	same	same
Epsom,	same	same	same
Erdington,	same	xxx	used again
Exeter,	same	Crediton and Ilfracombe	Exeter,
	Falkirk transposed,	same	same
Farnborough,	same	same	same
Folkestone,	same	same	<
Gainsborough,	same	same	same
Gloucester A,B,	same	same	same
Gosport transposed	same	same	same
Gravesend,	same	same	dot & no dot
Grays,	same	same	same
Guildford type 5,	types 3 & 5,	type 3,	type 5,
Halesowen,	+same	xxx	xxx
Halifax,	same	same	same
Harrogate A,	same	xxx	same, and GB
Harrow & Wembley, A & *,	same	same	same
Haywards Heath,	same	same	same
Hereford A,	same	same	same
High Wycombe A,	same	same	same
Hitchin,	same	same	+types 2 & 3
Hounslow (2),	long & short arcs	short arcs,	long & short arcs
	Hoylake (from 6 March),	xxx	used again
Huddersfield,	same	same	same
Hull A,B,	same	xxx	xxx
Ilford & Barking,	same	same	<
Ipswich, and A,	Woodbridge,	Ipswich,	same
King's Lynn,	same	same	same
Kingston-upon-Thames 1,3,	same	same	same
Lancaster & Morecambe A,	same	A types 3 & 5,	A type 3,
Leatherhead,	same	same	same
Leicester A,B,C (3),	same	same	Hinckley,
		also Loughborough	Loughborough, Melton Mowbray,
Lewes,	same	same	same
Lincoln A,	seen late	used again	E 22 Oct
Littlehampton,	same	same	same
Louth,	same	same	same
Macclesfield, arcs	same	xxx	used again, no arcs
Maidenhead,	types 2 & 5,	type 5,	same
Maidstone types 2 & 3 (2)	Faversham std & Sittingbourne transposed	Maidstone trans L 10am, 2 Aug, std E 6.45pm 2 Aug, arcs, later no arcs,	std, arcs & no arcs,
Manchester S (2)	same	same	same
Morpeth,	same	<	used again
Moseley DO,	same	same	same
Motherwell & Wishaw A,	same	Carluke E 21 Aug to L 15 Sep,	Bathgate trans,
Neath type 2,	same	same	types 2 & 3,

Newport Mon t 3 & 5 (2),	type 6,	type 5 & 6,	same
Newton Abbot,	xxx	used again	same
Northampton 1,2,	same	same, also Corby,	same, also Corby,
		Kettering,	Wellingborough,
North Shields,	Wallsend,	same	same
Nottingham A,B,C,	same	same	Grantham,Sleaford
Oldbury,	xxx	xxx	xxx
Oldham A,B,	same	same	+same
Omagh,	same	same	<
Oxford A,	Oxford, and A,	A,	A(from 22 Oct),C
		Paisley,	same
Perth,	same	same	seen 20 Nov
			Peterborough A,
Plymouth, and A,	same	same	same, not
		also St Austell trans	St Austell
		std by 14 Aug	
Pontefract,	same	same	same
Pontypridd,	+same	same	same
Portadown,	<	used again	Armagh
Preston A,B,(2)	A,	A, and Chorley	A no Chorley
Reading, and + (2),	also arcs, +Reading+	arcs & +	arcs t2/5, no arcs & +
Reigate & Redhill t 2 & 5,	same	type 2,	same
Richmond Yorks,	same	same	same
Richmond & Twickenham A,	same	same	same
Rochdale,	same	same	same
Romford & Dag B,C,L (3)	+B,C,	++B,	+++B,
Rotherham,	same	same	same
Rugby A,	same	same	same
St Albans,	same	same	same
St Helens A,	same	+same	<
Scunthorpe,	same	same	same
Sevenoaks,	xxx	used again	same
Slough,	same	same	same
Smethwick	same	same	Warley B,
Southall,	same	same	same
Southampton C,D (2),	same	xxx	xxx
South Shields,	Hebburn,	xxx	Hebburn,
Stafford,	same	same	same
Staines,	same	same	same
Stockport A,	same	same	same
Stoke-on-Trent arcs,	arcs & no arcs, also	types 3 & 5, and	no arcs t2/3,
	Kidsgrove, Uttoxeter 10 May,	no arcs,	arcs type 5,
	when Stoke replaced by "Show"		also Leek,
Stroud,	+same	same	same
Sudbury,	same	same	same
Sutton types 3 & 5,	type 3,	type 5,	same
Swansea, and A(2)	and A,L,	same	and A,
Swindon A trans,	std only	same	trans,
std by 3 Feb,			std by 16 Nov,
Tonbridge,	same	same	same
Truro,	same	Camborne Redruth,	same
Uxbridge,	same	same	same
Wakefield A,	same	same	same
Warrington A,	same	D	same
Watford types 2 & 3 (1)	xxx	xxx	xxx
West Bromwich,	same	same	same
	Weston s Mare B,	xxx	xxx
Weybridge,	same	same	+same
			Weymouth trans,
			std by 2 Nov,
Wigan,	types 2 & 3,	A,C,	A,
Winchester,	same	xxx	used again
Windsor,	same	same	same
Woking,	same	same	same
Wolverhampton A,B,	A, B types 2 & 3	as first use	same
Worcester A,	same	same	same
	Worksop,	same	same
Wrexham,	same	same	same
Yeovil,	same	same	same
York,	xxx	xxx	xxx
Triangles :			
EC,320,881 trans	547	75S	SW/19

About 240 dies used

FIRST USE late uses (not including + entries which joined up with second use) :
20 Feb EC B, W5, Ashton-under-Lyne, Blyth, Darlington, Lincoln A, Rotherham, Weybridge
21 Feb London EC D, SW11 <u>transposed</u> again, Bolton B, Bradford A, Huddersfield, Hull A, Warrington A
22 Feb W12, Manchester S
23 Feb Reigate & Redhill
27 Feb NW2
 2 March Bootle
10 March St Helens A
12 March Birkenhead A
13 March London W1 B, NW10
14 March Blackheath Birmingham
20 March Aberdeen A (prob to 25 March before "Opera" slogan)
21 March Motherwell & Wishaw A
31 March London W1 A, Dartford
13 April Oldbury, then see + entries

SECOND USE early use :
16 April Cardiff A

SECOND USE late uses (not incl +/++ entries which joined up with third use) :
15 May Aylesbury, Bexleyheath
16 May SW3, Barnet, Burnley, Faversham, Warrington A
18 May E14
22 May Ilford & Barking (from 21 May after "Redbridge")
23 May SW6
28 May Birmingham E
 5 June SW15, Aberdeen A (from 28 May after "Opera"), B (both up to P Code 6 J)
 6 June Birmingham G
 7 June Ashford Kent, Birmingham WDO
 8 June Birmingham A
15 June Romford & Dagenham C
26 June Derby A
 3 July Doncaster A
 7 July Hull A,B (prob up to "Gateway" 10 July)
13 July London SW1 C (prob to 17 July "Litter")
14 July Hoylake
16 July Lincoln A (E 19 June up to 17 July "Litter"),   then see +/++ entries

THIRD USE late uses (not incl +/++/+++ entries which joined up with fourth use):
21 Aug W2 A, Dartford, Wakefield A
22 Aug Edgware
27 Aug W8
29 Aug SW15
30 Aug E15
 2 Sep Bury
 3 Sep London SW1 C
 6 Sep SW7, Hoylake
 8 Sep London SW1 A, SW9 (two)
11 Sep Oxford A (type 5)
 9 Oct Ashton-under-Lyne, then see +/++/+++ entries

FOURTH USE late uses :
20 Nov London I, Aylesbury, Hinckley, Perth
21 Nov E8, Bolton B
22 Nov Worksop
23 Nov London NW1 B
26 Nov Sudbury
27 Nov Hereford A, Paisley, Peterborough A, Rugby A
30 Nov Warley B
 3 Dec Hitchin
 6 Dec Weymouth std
10 Dec Bletchley, Romford & Dagenham B
11 Dec Birmingham CH type 5
12 Dec SW7
18 Dec Hounslow long arcs
20 Dec Birmingham CH type 3
30 Jan 1968 Birmingham CH squat (E 29 Dec)(wavy lines 31 Jan)

740 <u>National Savings Group (fourth use) 18-25 Feb 1967</u>

Wolverhampton A,   1 die used

742t <u>Scottish stamps & FDCs 20-28 Feb 1967</u>

Edinburgh C,   Glasgow S,   Paisley,
Perth.

Triangles : S70,PA

4 dies used

743t <u>New stamp issue Wales & Monmouthshire 21 Feb - 1 March 1967</u>

Aberystwyth,   Cardiff A,B (B rolled on by hand),
Colwyn Bay,   Llandudno,   Llanelli,
Newport Mon,   Swansea, and A,L,

Triangles : 2,162,470,561,763,096

7 dies used

744t <u>New Stamp Issue Northern Ireland 21 Feb - 1 March 1967</u>

Belfast A,C,   Londonderry.   Triangle : I5

2 dies used

746/t <u>Medway Dutch Week 1 March - 17 June 1967</u>

Gillingham std in error 1 March 9.45am, then trans,
Rochester & Chatham types 2 & 3 trans (2 dies),
Sheerness trans.

Triangles : 650,650A,699

4 dies used

751 <u>BOAC South Pacific Air Route 15 March - 12 April 1967</u>

London F,G,H,T (3),   FS M,N,   SW1 C,   W1 A,B (2),

E 15,   NW 5,   SE 8,17,   W 8,

Beverley,   Birkenhead A,   Blaydon-on-Tyne,
Bootle,   Glasgow S,W,   Goole,
Keighley,   Kettering,   Kirkcaldy,
Manchester F,P (1),   Newport Mon types 5 & 6,   Northallerton,
Nuneaton,   Peterborough A,   Stirling,
Sutton Coldfield.

30 dies used at 26 offices

Early use : 13 March Keighley

752 <u>Antiques Fair Solihull 19 March - 29 April 1967</u>

Birmingham A,E,G,   Solihull, and A (one die). Triangles : 75,753

4 dies used

756t <u>Blood Donors save lives Newcastle/Tyne 1 April 1967 - 30 March 1968</u>

North Shields,   South Shields.   2 dies used

Other similar designs used at relevant towns, all one-town slogans

757 <u>National Savings simply grow (first use) 1 April - 23 June 1967</u>

Glasgow E3,N,NW,-S- L 24 May (then Glasgow S/- by 3 May), SEDO,SW,W,W3.

Triangle : S42F

8 dies used

766/t Kent County Show 12 April - 11 July 1967

Canterbury std in error, trans by 18 April,
Maidstone arcs types 2 & 3, and no arcs, all trans,
Sevenoaks trans.

Triangles : 493,697

3 dies used

774/t Devon County Show 20 April - 17 May 1967

Barnstaple trans,   Exeter trans,
Newton Abbot std L 27 April 8.15pm, trans by 28 April 10.15am,
Plymouth A std 20 April 7.30am, trans by 20 April 8pm,
   also Plymouth by 25 April.

Triangles : 50 trans, 567 std, 620 trans, and diamond ex Exeter (trans)

4 dies used

777 Redbridge Arts Festival 24 April - 20 May 1967

E 4,11,15,

Ilford & Barking,   Romford & Dagenham B,   Woodford Green.

Triangles : E4,E11,E15,920,IAD

6 dies used

778 Cystic Fibrosis Week 29 April - 13 May 1967

London EC F,

N 14,   SE 3,17,   SW 12,   W 11,

London missort : 45 used for stamping collectors' covers at SE17.

Belfast C,   Bridgwater,   Chippenham,
Clacton-on-Sea,   East Kilbride,   Edinburgh NW,
Ellesmere Port,   Evesham,   Fylde Coast 5,
Haslemere,   Hemel Hempstead,   Hexham,
Horsham,   Loughborough,   Newport IOW,
Northwich,   Retford,   Romford & Dagenham D,
Saffron Walden,   Salford,   Selby,
Spalding,   Stourbridge,   Tamworth,
Taunton,   Trowbridge,   Walsall, and B,
Welwyn Gdn City A,   Wisbech.

Triangle : 953

Listed as 40 dies, about 36 dies shown above

Late uses :
14 May Horsham, Northwich, Tamworth
15 May Bridgwater, Ellesmere Port, Evesham, Retford, Spalding, Stourbridge
22 May Fylde Coast 5

781t United Counties Show 1 May - 11 Aug 1967

Cardigan,   Carmarthen,   Haverfordwest.

Triangle : 164

3 dies used

785/t Suffolk County Show 3-30 May 1967

Bury St Edmunds trans,
Ipswich A std first day only seen, otherwise trans, B std (2 dies),
Lowestoft trans.

Triangles : 97 trans, 478 trans

4 dies used

Late use : 31 May Bury St Edmunds trans

789/t <u>County Show Stafford   10-23 May 1967</u>

Burton.on.Trent trans,
Leek std 17 May, trans by 19 May,
Lichfield std L 15 May, trans by 16 May,
Stafford std L 14 May, trans by 16 May,
Stoke-on-Trent std, arcs and no arcs, L 13 May,
               trans, arcs types 3 & 5 and no arcs, by 17 May,
Walsall, and B std L 17 May, trans (not seen B) by 23 May,
Wolverhampton A type 3 std L 13 May
            A type 2 trans by 16 May

Triangle : 152 trans

7 dies used

791/t <u>Alcan Golf Championships St Andrews   12 May - 1 Aug 1967</u>

Arbroath std L 6 June, trans by 8 June,
Carnoustie std L 17 May, trans by 24 May,
Cupar trans to 11 July, transferred to Dundee B trans from 12 July,
St Andrews std, new town die with shorter arcs by 26 May.

Triangles : S5 std, -S-/19 std, S76 std

4 dies used

805/t-806t <u>Learn to swim week   29 May - 3 June 1967</u>

805/t short design with lines at right :

Glasgow B std 29 May 9.30am (probably B die, I have not seen this),
       B squat, C trans 29 May 8.30am, presumably continued trans

Triangle : S42 trans

Late use : 5 June 9.30am Glasgow B

806t long design with no lines at right :

Dumfries,	Dunfermline,	Edinburgh C, NW,
Falkirk,	Greenock,	Kirkcaldy,
Paisley,	Perth.	

Triangle : S70

1 die of short design, 9 dies of long design

807 <u>Five Million Arthritis Victims   1-30 June 1967</u>

London E1, and A (one die),   EC F,   NW1 B,   SW1 D.

4 dies used.

815t-828 <u>All Britain Crusade</u>

815t <u>Mecca Car Park Blackpool   6-30 June 1967</u>

Fylde Coast 6,   Triangle : 953   1 die used

817t <u>Regal Cinema Oxford   9-30 June 1967</u>

Oxford A,B,   Triangle : 603   1 die used

819 <u>1967 TV Relays Bingley Hall   11 June - 1 July 1967</u>

Birmingham A,E,G,   ADO,CH,WDO,   Triangle : 75   6 dies used

820t <u>Eastville Bus Depot   11 June - 1 July 1967</u>

Bristol A,C,D,E,   NDO,   Triangle : 134   5 dies used

822t <u>ABC Cinema Plymouth   12-30 June 1967</u>

Plymouth A,   Triangle : 620   1 die used

823 Nottingham Ice Stadium 12-27 June 1967

Nottingham A,B,C,   Triangle : 583   3 dies used

828 ABC Cinema Northampton 16-30 June 1967

Corby,   Kettering,   Northampton 1,2,
Wellingborough.

Triangle : 570

4 dies used

827/t The Dairy Festival 15 June - 31 July 1967

London NW1 A std (announced as N1 trans),

Ashford Kent std,   Banbury std,
Blaydon-on-Tyne std (instead of Hexham),   Bolton B std (from 19 June),
Cardiff A trans 15 June - 23 July, B std seen 23 July only, then transferred to
Cwmbran trans 24-29 July,
Dudley B trans (announced as std),   Fylde Coast 5 std,
Keighley std,   Kidderminster std,   Nottingham C std,
Swindon A std,   Walsall, and B both std,
Winchester std (to 23 July),   Yeovil std (instead of Weymouth).

Triangles : 162 trans, 263 trans, 578 trans, 881 std

15 dies used at 16 offices

Early use : 14 June Dudley A trans

844/t Country Code avoid damaging hedges etc 2 July - 26 Aug 1967

London NW1 B std,
Chesterfield Derbyshire std (instead of Sheffield), trans DYS by 26 Aug,
Hexham trans at first, then std, both seen 2 July 5.30pm, L 11 July, then trans
again by 13 July,
Leeds A std (2-23 July and 21-16 Aug),
Manchester P types 3 & 5 trans,
Market Harborough trans (type 2, type 5 by 15 July),
Nottingham B,C std, trans in C by 7 July, later trans B,D also,
Preston A trans,   Taunton std (announced as trans),   Trowbridge std

Triangle : 511 trans, 813 std but applied by hand

10 dies used

846/t National Savings simply grow (second use) 8 July - 23 Sep 1967

Bathgate std, trans by 2 Aug,
Callander std, trans by 9 Aug,
Edinburgh NW std, trans by 21 Aug,
Edinburgh W std, trans by 1 Aug,
Hawick std, trans by 9 Aug,
Kirkcaldy std, trans by 26 July,
Oban std, trans by 31 July,
Stirling std, trans by 2 Aug, to 6 Aug (assumed) then transferred to Falkirk
    trans from 7 Aug

Triangles : S68 std and trans

8 dies used

850/t National Anti-Litter Week 17-23 July 1967

London EC F,H std,   N1 A std,   SE1 F std,   SW1 C std,

Belfast C std,   Birmingham E std (announced as trans),
Bradford B std,   Bristol C trans,   Coventry A trans,
Doncaster std,   Dunfermline trans,   Durham A std,
Glasgow S std,   Guildford trans,   Ipswich, and A, both std,
Lincoln A std,
Manchester F,K,P std (K prob exceptional since "Gateway" only seen in K),
Nottingham B trans,   Plymouth A trans,   Stoke-on-Trent trans,
Wakefield A std,   Warrington A,D std,   York std.

Triangles : 107 std, 547 trans

23 dies used

864t Alcan Golf Championship one putt for £21,430 2 Aug - 30 Sep 1967

Arbroath,   Carnoustie,   Dundee B,
St Andrews,

Triangle : S76

4 dies used

878 Save at work (first use) 11 Sep - 11 Nov 1967

Cheltenham short arc town die, 14-21 Oct only,
Chester-le-Street,   Doncaster, and A,
Gloucester A,B, 11 Sep - 22 Oct only,   Huddersfield,
Stoke-on-Trent, arcs types 3 & 5, and no arcs, 11 Sep - 22 Oct,
Wrexham, 11 Sep - 22 Oct.

Triangle : 255

7 dies used

Late uses :
23 Oct Gloucester A (due to end 22 Oct)
13 Nov Huddersfield

889/t Oxfam 25th year 1 Oct - 31 Dec 1967

E 12 std in error, then trans, both seen 5.15pm 1 Oct,
N 6 std in error L 5 Oct, trans by 13 Nov (seen dated 30 Dec 1968)
SW 18 trans,

Bristol C std in error 2 Oct, trans by 5 Oct,
Chesterfield trans,
Corby std (not seen by me), then supposedly transferred to -
   Kettering trans but seen 12.15pm and 5.30pm 1 Oct (types 2 & 3 town dies),
Glasgow.S. trans, Glasgow -S- town die by 9 Dec,
Manchester F,P trans,
Oxford B trans.

9 dies used at 10 offices.

Late uses :
 4 Jan 1968 Glasgow -S- trans
15 Jan 1968 Manchester F trans

893/t NABC Club Week 2 Oct - 5 Nov 1967

Used for varying periods within the above dates.

London EC F std, 16-22 Oct,
       SE1 F std, 16-22 Oct,
       WC D std, 2-15 Oct,

NW 4 std, 10A std, both 16-22 Oct,   W 5 std, 16-22 Oct,

Bristol D, NDO, both trans 16-22 Oct, Enfield std, 16-22 Oct,
Harrow & Wembley std, 16-22 Oct,   Kingston upon Thames 1,3 std 2-15 Oct,
Manchester P, NE, SW, all std 16 Oct - 5 Nov,
Swindon A trans, 2-22 Oct (announced as 16-22 Oct).

Triangles : NW4 std, 134 trans, 881 trans

15 dies used

894/t Muscular Dystrophy Week 2-27 Oct 1967

Ended 22 Oct at some offices as indicated below.

London AA std,   W1 A,E std,

SE 3,6 both std (both announced as trans),

London missort : 71 std.

Blackburn & Accrington trans, 2-22 Oct,   Bolton B trans,
Boston trans,   Cwmbran std (announced as trans),
Goole std,   Harrow & Wembley std (announced as trans),
High Wycombe A std, 2-22 Oct,   Kingston upon Thames 3 std,
Leeds B std,   Luton A std,
Newbury trans (announced as std),   Plymouth A trans,
Preston A trans, 2-22 Oct,   Sittingbourne trans 2 Oct, std by 11 Oct,
Stourbridge trans,   Tamworth trans,   Walsall, and B both trans,
Wisbech std (announced as trans), type 3, type 5 by 28 Oct,

Triangles : 92 trans, 620 trans, KT std

22 dies used

Late uses :
25 Oct Preston A trans (due to end 22 Oct)
28 Oct Cwmbran std, Stourbridge trans
29 Oct Newbury trans

897t National Savings simply grow (third use) 8 Oct - 24 Dec 1967

Carluke (from 9 Oct),   Coatbridge,   Greenock,
Hamilton,   Irvine,   Kilmarnock,
Lanark,   Mauchline.

8 dies used

905/t Sue Ryder Homes (second use) 23-28 Oct 1967

London SW1 D std,

Basingstoke std,   Camberley std,   Cranbrook std,
East Grinstead std (also used exceptionally 16-17 Oct, see E.52),
Haslemere std,   Kidderminster std (announced as trans),
Redditch std, then trans, both see 10.45am 23 Oct,
Saffron Walden std,   Saxmundham std (announced as trans)

Triangles : 669,690

10 dies

Late uses : 29 Oct East Grinstead std, Haslemere std

907/t Sue Ryder Homes (third use) 31 Oct - 6 Nov 1967

London N1 B std,

Andover std,   Barry trans,   Berwick-on-Tweed trans,
Glasgow C std,   Harrow & Wembley std,   Keighley trans,
Kirkcaldy trans,   Leeds B std,   Oban trans,
Sheffield C trans,   Taunton trans,   Trowbridge std,

13 dies used

Late uses :
 7 Nov Andover std
 8 Nov Kirkcaldy trans

909/t Radio-TV Licences 1-30 Nov 1967

There were five sub types of this slogan, shown below as A,B,C,D and G where
sub-type is known; at large offices town dies/slogan dies were not necessarily
used together for the whole period, thus the slogan types used are shown once
for the office. Some offices used the slogan 20-30 Nov, these are not noted.

London D,F,I,T,AA,BB (A and G),   E1, and A(A and G),   EC D,E,G,H(A),
       N1 A,B(A),   NW1 C(A),
       W1 A,B,C(G),   WC D(G),

E 15(A),   N 16(A),   NW 2(?),3(A),10A(A),
SW 11 transposed, 15,16,17,18,19 (all A),
W 2A,B(G),   3(A),5(two)(A),6(G),8(A),

London missort : 6A,75

Altrincham A,B(A),   Barnet types 2 & 5(A),   Birmingham H(G),
Bolton B(G),   Bournemouth-Poole C(A), Bradford A,B(A and B),
Bristol D(A), NDO(A),   Castleford(D),   Dartford(B),
Edgware(A),   Edinburgh C transposed(G),
Epsom(B),   Folkestone(G),
Glasgow 2(Waterloo St)(G)   seen late,
Grays(B),   Guildford(G),   Harrow & Wembley, and A(A),
Hounslow long & short arcs(A), Ilford & Barking(A),
Keighley(B) transposed,   Leeds A,B(B),   Lewes(G),
Morpeth(A),   Newport Mon (G),   Newry(G),
Pontefract(D),   Pontypridd(G),
Reading arcs, no arcs, + (A and G),
Richmond Yorks(D),   Richmond & Twickenham A(A),
Romford & Dagenham B,C,L(A and B),   Scunthorpe(B),
Southall(A),   Swansea, and A(G)(2),   Taunton(A),
Uxbridge(G),   Walsall, and B(G),   Watford(two similar)(A),
Weybridge(A),   Woking(G),   Wrexham(G).

Listed as "about 83 dies used" standard and a further 3 transposed, as above.

Late uses :
 1 Dec   Swansea A, Walsall B
 3 Dec   Lewes
 4 Dec   SW11 transposed
 6 Dec   Weybridge
 8 Dec   W2 A,B
10 Dec   Altrincham A, Bolton B, Wrexham
13 Dec   Edinburgh C transposed
26 Jan 1968 Glasgow 2 (Waterloo St)

913 Save at work (second use)   20 Nov - 9 Dec 1967

London EC B,D,E,F,G,   SW1 A,B,C,D,F,

London missort : 6A

About 10 dies used at 2 offices

916-918 Voters Lists   28 Nov to 12 Dec 1967

A new sub type was used in 1964-66 and again in 1967, listed here shown at the
end of 917 - type 98A. Note there are some transposed uses here, of 917t.
< entries, ie those not recorded but possibly used, are shown by comparison with
the GPO listing for this slogan, and are shown in a separate list at the end.

916 Type 98

London N1 A,B,

Barnsley A,   Bishop Auckland,   Boston,
Canterbury,   Crewe,   Doncaster,
Durham A,   Grantham,   Hereford A,
Kidderminster,   Luton A,   Neath,
Reigate & Redhill types 2 & 5,
Stoke-on-Trent arcs & no arcs.

Listed as "about 20 dies", as shown above.

Late use :
13 Dec Bishop Auckland

917/t Type 98A

London NW1 A,

E 4,7,10,11,15,17,   SE 3,5,6(types 2 & 3),13,15,
SW 2,4,5,9(types 3 & 7),13,17,19,

Aberdeen A,B,   Aldershot,   Bangor Co Down,
Barrow-in-Furness,   Basingstoke,   Blackburn & Accrington,
Burnley,   Burton-on-Trent,   Dumbarton,
Dumfries,   Dunfermline,   Edinburgh NW,
Enniskillen,   Falkirk transposed,
Fareham,   Farnborough,   Galashiels,

Gloucester A,	Harrogate A,	Keighley transposed,
Lancaster & Morecambe A,	Lincoln A,	Loughborough,
Macclesfield,	Newbury transposed,	
Northampton 1,	Northwich,	Nuneaton,
Oldham A,B,	Paisley,	Perth,
Peterborough A,	Preston A,	Reigate & Redhill,
Rochdale,	Rossendale,	Rugby A,
St Helens A,	Stamford,	Stockport A,
Warrington D,	Wigan A,	Workington.

New sub-type :

N 4,7,8,16,17,19,22,	NW 2,6,8,10,10A,11,	W 3,4(types 3 & 7),11,

London missort : 5B (N7) used on normal mail, 37B,60

Aberdeen A,	Andover,	Ashford Kent
Ballymena,	Barry,	Bradford B,
Bridgend,	Bridgnorth,	Bridgwater,
Chelmsford,	Chichester (squat & type 3) transposed,	
Chippenham,	Exeter,	Gainsborough,
Glasgow SEDO,	Halifax,	Hexham,
Hinckley,	Huddersfield,	Lisburn transposed,
Luton B,	Lymington,	Maidenhead,
Maidstone (two similar),	and GB,	Malvern,
Market Harborough,	Northampton 1,2,	Penzance,
Retford,	Rotherham,	St Austell transposed,
Slough,	Stroud,	Wakefield A,
Winchester,	Yeadon,	York.

Listed as "about 115 dies" standard and 6 transposed, as shown above

Early uses :
28 Oct   Stamford
29 Oct   Lincoln A (probably from 28 Oct)
27 Nov   Workington

Late uses :
13 Dec   SE5 shorter arcs
14 Dec   SW4
15 Dec   SW19 shorter arcs
16 Dec   N19
18 Dec   NW2
19 Dec   SE5 longer arcs, SW9
22 Dec   Ashford Kent Gt Britain
23 Dec   SW19 longer arcs
14 Feb 1968   E10

918   Type 98B

Bedford,	Camberley,
Rochester & Chatham,	Windsor.

4 dies used.

Additional offices listed by GPO but not seen - clearly I do not know which type these are, if used at all : E 2,3,6, N 9, Birkenhead, Bury, Cirencester, Harwich, Newton Abbot, Newtownabbey, Portadown, St Andrews, Wallsend.

Others announced but not thought to have used the slogan : Aylesbury, Darlington

925-926/t <u>Post early for Christmas 12-19 Dec 1967</u>

These two designs were not announced at all, thus the dates shown above are merely those of 927/t below. **925** is the old holly design, used standard only at Taunton E 4 Dec. Triangle : 776.

926/t is the Candle design. Two sub-types exist, thin lettering with F over I, thick with F left of I, but these are not distinguished in this list.

E 17,

Aldershot,
Ashton-under-Lyne Gt Britain,
Barnsley A,
Canterbury,
Chester A,
Colwyn Bay,
Enfield,
Godalming,
Ilford & Barking,
Lewes,
Lowestoft,
Mansfield,
Northampton 1,2,3,
Oldham B,
Pontefract,
Rochdale,
St Albans types 2 & 3,
Southall,
Walsall, and C,
Watford (two similar),
Worthing.

Ashford Kent, and Gt Britain,

Barry,
Carlisle A,
Chesterfield,
Croydon, and A,
Epsom,
Gravesend,
Ipswich,
Llandudno,
Maidenhead,
Newport Mon types 5 & 6,
Norwich, and A-1-4,
Penzance,
Reigate & Redhill, and Gt Britain,
Rochester & Chatham,
Sheffield C,
Staines,
Warwick & Leamington Spa 1,
Woking,

Brentwood,
Chesham & Amersham,
Chippenham,
Darlington,
Evesham,
Harrogate,
Keighley transposed,
Llandudno-Colwyn Bay,
Maidstone (two similar),
Newry,
Peterborough A,
Romford & Dagenham C,
Taunton type 3,
Worcester A,

Listed as "about 64 dies standard", and one transposed, as shown above.

Earliest uses :
7 Nov   Lincoln B
3 Dec   Brentwood
9 Dec   Epsom
11 Dec   about 10

Late uses :
20 Dec   about 10
21 Dec   Chippenham, Lewes, Newry, Worthing
22 Dec   Watford
23 Dec   Carlisle A, Northampton 3

927/t <u>Post your Christmas cards 12-19 Dec 1967</u>

London D,F,I,K,T,AA,BB,   E1,   NW1 B,C,   SE1 A,F,
       EC B,D,E,F,G,H,   N1 A,B,   WC C,D,
       SW1 B,C,D,F,   W1 A,B,C,L1,

NW 3,   SE 9,18,   SW 3,7,
W 2A,B,   5(types 3 & 5),6,8 (also dated 15 Dec 1968 in error),12,

London missort : 6A

Aylesbury,
Bexleyheath,
Bishop Auckland,
Bolton A,B,
Bury,
Chelmsford,
Coventry A,
Dewsbury,
Dunfermline,
Enfield,
Falkirk transposed,
Grimsby & Cleethorpes (broken & unbroken town dies), and A,
Guildford,
Haywards Heath,
Hitchin,
Kingston upon Thames 1,3,
Leatherhead,
Luton A,

Bedford,
Birkenhead A,B,
Blackburn & Accrington,
Bromley & Beckenham,
Canterbury,
Chichester transposed,
Crewe,
Dudley B transposed,
Durham A,
Erdington,
Folkestone,
Harrogate A,
Hereford, and A,
Hounslow short arcs,
Lancaster & Morecambe A,
Leeds B,
Macclesfield,

Belfast C,
Birmingham A,G,   ADO,CH,WDO,
Bletchley,
Burnley,
Cardiff A,B,
Colchester transposed,
Dumfries,
Edgware transposed,
Exeter,
Grays,
Harrow & Wembley A, and *,
High Wycombe A,
Ipswich std and transposed,
Leicester A,B,
Manchester S,

Morpeth,	Moseley DO,	Neath,
Newport Mon type 5,	Oxford A,	Paisley,
Perth,	Plymouth, and A,	
Pontefract,	Pontypridd,	Preston A,B,
Reading arcs & no arcs, and +,		Reigate & Redhill (types 2 & 7),
Richmond Yorks,	Richmond & Twickenham A,	Rochdale,
Romford & Dagenham B,L,	Rugby A,	St Albans (types 2 & 3),
St Helens A,B,	Scunthorpe,	Sevenoaks,
Southampton C,	Stafford,	
Stockport A,	Stoke-on-Trent arcs & no arcs,	
Stroud,	Sutton,	Swansea A,
Swindon A transposed, std by 17 Dec,		
Tonbridge,	Uxbridge,	Warrington D,
Watford (two similar),	West Bromwich,	
Weybridge,	Wigan A,C,	Winchester,
Woking,	Wolverhampton no arcs, and A,B,	
Worcester B,	Wrexham,	Yeovil.

Triangles; 190 std, 570 trans

Listed as "about 160 dies" standard, and about 6 transposed, and 1 "both" as shown above

Early uses :
 4 Dec Folkestone
11 Dec Bolton A,B, Bromley & Beckenham, Chichester transposed, Stoke-on-Trent no arcs, Weybridge

Late uses :
20 Dec about 14, including Chichester transposed
21 Dec Bletchley
23 Dec Bishop Auckland
24 Dec Aylesbury

929 Attlee Memorial Appeal 15 Dec 1967 to 12 Jan 1968

London EC F,   WC D,E (E seen 20 Dec only)
- these two offices from 20 Dec only,

Birmingham E,	Bradford B,	Doncaster,
Fylde Coast 1,2,	Glasgow C,	Huddersfield no arcs, and A,
Manchester P,	Swansea, and A.	

10 dies used

932/t Save at work (third use) 1 Jan to 2 March 1968

Bolton B trans,   Croydon trans, and A std,   Ipswich, and A both trans,
Peterborough A,B trans, Plymouth, and A both trans, Preston A,B trans,
Walsall, and B both trans, York std.

Triangle : 620 trans

9 dies used (two at Croydon)

Late use : 3 March Ipswich trans

933/t Diamond Jubilee Ideal Home Exhib 1 Jan to 30 March 1968

London AA std,   EC B std,   N1 A std L 12 Jan, trans by 15 Jan,
    NW 1 B std,   SE1 F std,   SW1 D, later C,

W 2B,C std.   London missort : 75.   Triangles : N1 std and trans

7 dies used

934 Good Templars Centenary (first use) 1-29 Jan 1968

Bourne.   Triangle : 103   1 die used.

936 & 937/t Civil Engineers 150th Anniv (first use) 1-6 Jan 1968

936 - 4 line design - London SW1 B.   1 die used

937/t - 3 line design - Belfast C std,   Cardiff std,

Edinburgh (not use 1 Jan public hol or 10.45am 2 Jan), std in error 2.45pm
2 Jan, trans by 1.15pm 3 Jan.

Triangle : S33 trans

3 dies used

Late uses : 8 Jan Belfast std, Edinburgh C trans

938t National Savings simply grow (fourth use) 8 Jan - 31 March 1968

Dingwall,   Dumbarton,   Fort William,
Greenock,   Paisley,   St Andrews,
Stornoway,   Wick,

8 dies used

Late use : 11 April Fort William

940/t National Eisteddfod 1968 (first use) 15-27 Jan 1968

Barry trans,   Bridgend trans,   Cardiff B std, trans by 18 Jan,
Neath trans,   Pontypridd trans,   Port Talbot trans,
Swansea A trans.

Triangle : 162 std

7 dies used.

943t Save at work (fourth use) 1-29 Feb 1968

Luton A,   1 die used

949/t-950/t I'm backing Britain 9-29 Feb 1968

949/t - short design with lines at right :

London D,F,I,J,K,T,BB,   N1 B,   NW1 A,C,
       SE1 A,   SW1 A,B,C,I,   W1 A,B,C,
       WC D,

NW 3,   SE 5,   W 2A,

Birmingham A,E,G, CH,H,   Bletchley,   Bristol E, NDO both <u>transposed</u>
Chester A,
Edinburgh C std 12 Feb (1.15pm & 2.45pm) then C (E 13 Feb),D, NW all <u>transposed</u>,
Glasgow 2 (Waterloo St), Hitchin,   Maidenhead,
Neath,   Pontypridd,   Swansea, and A,L,
Wrexham.

Triangle : -U-/MtP

About 37 dies used std, 4 transposed, 1 "both"

Late uses :
  1 March W 2B
  2 March Hitchin
  4 March London I
 11 March London J,BB
 19 March Bletchley

950/t - long design with no lines at right :

London EC D,E,F,G,H,

E 15 (two),17(two),   N 16,   NW 10,
SE 9,18,   SW 3,6,11,15,16,17,18(two),19,
W 3,4(types 3 & 7),5(two),6,8,

London missort : 6A

Abingdon,   Aldershot,   Altrincham A,
Ashford Kent,   Ashton-under-Lyne,   Axminster,
Aylesbury,   Ballymena <u>transposed</u>,   Barnet,
Barnsley A,   Bexleyheath,   Birkenhead B,
Birmingham ADO,WDO,   Blackburn & Accrington, Bolton B,

Bradford B,   Burnley,   Burton.on.Trent,
Bury,   Carlisle A transposed,   Chichester transposed,
Crewe,   Dartford,   Dawlish,
Doncaster,   Dumfries,   Dunfermline,
Edgware,   Epsom,   Exeter transposed,
Falkirk transposed,   Farnborough,   Folkestone,
Grays,   Guildford types 3 & 5 transposed,
Halifax,   Harrogate A,   Harrow & Wembley,
High Wycombe A,   Hounslow,   Huddersfield,
Ilford & Barking,   Keighley transposed,   Kingston upon Thames 1,3,5,
Lewes,   Lincoln A,   Morpeth,
Moseley DO,   Newry transposed,   Newton Abbot,
Oxford B,   Pontefract,   Richmond Yorks,
Richmond & Twickenham A,   Rochdale,   Romford & Dagenham B,C,L,
Rugby,   St Albans transposed,   St Helens A,
Scunthorpe,   Slough,   Southall,
Stafford A,   Stoke-on-Trent arcs & no arcs,
Swindon A transposed,   Taunton,   Uxbridge,
Walsall, and B,   Warley B,   Watford,
Weybridge,   Wigan A,   Winchester transposed,
Woking,   Wolverhampton A,B,

plus FPOs, see chapter 10 of "Collecting Slogan Postmarks",

Triangle : 190 trans

About 90 dies used std, 10 dies trans.   Announced but not used : Newport Mon

Early uses :
 7 Feb Lewes
 8 Feb Dartford

Late uses :
 1 March   SW17, Harrogate, Slough
 5 March   W3
 8 March   Pontefract
10 March   Bexleyheath
11 March   Morpeth
13 March   Lincoln A
15 March   SE18
20 March   Ashton-under-Lyne
21 March   Dartford, Taunton
26 March   Bolton B
31 March   SW15
14 April   Newton Abbot
17 April   Weybridge
 5 May 1969 E17 (types 3 & 7)

952/t   Save at work (fifth use)   12 Feb to 30 March 1968

Gillingham std L 14 Feb, trans by ?14 Feb,
Rochester & Chatham std L 14 Feb, trans by 19 Feb, type 2 but type 7 by 6 March,

2 dies used

972/t   Ulster Week in Manchester   26 Feb to 9 March 1968

Manchester A,C,F (two dies) trans,   E,N,S,SE,SW all std,
Salford std,   Wythenshawe std.

Triangle : 498 trans

9 dies used

974t   Tees-side International Eisteddfod   1 March to 30 May 1968

Guisborough,
Redcar Yorkshire, changed to Redcar Teesside from 1 April,
Saltburn-by-Sea.

Triangles : 326,796,004

3 dies used

977/t <u>British Sailors Society 150 years 2-30 March 1968</u>

London SW1 B,C std,   W1 B std,

W 8 std,

Bristol C trans,   Cardiff B std,   Durham A std,
Guildford trans,
Harrow & Wembley std, from 4 March, thought to have been transferred from York,
Leeds A std,   Manchester A,P std,   Southampton C trans,
Windsor std,   York std 2-?3 March only, then Harrow see above.

Triangles : 162 std, 325 trans, 890 std

12 dies used

Late uses : 31 March W8 std
 1 April Harrow & Wembley std
 4 April Manchester P std

980t <u>Save at work (sixth use) 7-30 March 1968</u>

Norwich, and A-1 to 4,

5 dies used

988 <u>Antiques Fair Solihull 17 March to 27 April 1968</u>

Birmingham A,E,G (type 6, later type 3),   Solihull.

Triangle : 75

4 dies used

992/t <u>Check your tyres 24 March to 21 April 1968</u>

Offices marked < have not been reported used but are included in GPO list, and
if used could have been in transposed position.

London AA,   W1 A,K2,   WC D,

E 17,   N 14,17,   NW 9,   SE 4(types 2 & 7),6,22,
SW 7,11,16 and Gt Britain,   W 2A,B,

London missort : 75

Abingdon,   Aldershot,   Alnwick,
Alton,   Altrincham A,   Andover,
Ardrossan,   Armagh,   Ashford Kent,
Ashton-under-Lyne,   Aylesbury,   Ballymena,
Ballymoney,   Banbridge,   Banff,
Bangor Caernarvonshire,   Bangor Co Down,   Barmouth,
Barnet,   Barnsley A,   Barrow-in-Furness,
Basingstoke,   Bathgate,   Beccles,
Bedford,   Belfast A,C,   Birkenhead B,
Bishop Auckland,   Bishop's Stortford,   Blackburn & Accrington,
Blandford Forum,   Bletchley,   Bolton A,B,
Boston,   Bournemouth-Poole C,   Bradford B,
Braintree,   Brentwood,   Bridgnorth,
Bridgwater arcs & no arcs, Bristol E,   Burnley,
Burton.on.Trent,   Camberley,   Camborne-Redruth,
<Carmarthen,   Carrickfergus,   Chelmsford,
Chesham & Amersham,   Chester A,   Chesterfield <u>transposed</u>,
Chippenham,   Chorley (worn die, new one by 17 April),
Cirencester,
Clacton-on-Sea,   Coatbridge & Airdrie A,   Cookstown <u>transposed</u>,
Corby,   Crewe,   Cupar,
Dartford,   Deal,   Dereham,
Dewsbury,   <Diss,   Doncaster,
Downpatrick,   Dumfries,   Dundee A,
Dunfermline,   Dungannon,   East Grinstead,
Edinburgh NW <u>transposed</u>, Enniskillen <u>transposed</u>, std by 18 April,
Evesham,   Fakenham,   Falkirk <u>transposed</u>,
Fareham,   Folkestone,   Forfar,

Frome,
Fylde Coast 1,5,
Gainsborough,
Galashiels,
Glasgow -S- transposed,
Gloucester A,
Godalming std L 25 March, transposed by 1 April,
Grantham,
Halifax,
Halstead,
Hamilton,
Harrogate A,
Harrow & Wembley,
Harwich,
Haslemere,
Haverfordwest,
Hawick,
Hemel Hempstead,
Hereford A,
Hertford,
Hexham,
High Wycombe A,
Hinckley,
Hitchin,
Holywood,
Horsham,
Hounslow,
Ipswich,
Keighley,
Kendal,
Kettering,
Kidderminster,
Kilmarnock transposed,
King's Lynn,
Kingston upon Thames 1,
Kirkcaldy,
Lanark,
Larne,
Leominster,
Lichfield,
Limavady,
Lincoln A std L 16 April, transposed by 19 April, Lisburn,
<Liverpool SD,?SW,
Llandrindod Wells transposed,
Loughborough,
Lowestoft,
Ludlow,
Lurgan,
Luton A,
Maidenhead,
Maidstone two type 3 dies,
Manchester F, S,SE(types 3 & 7),SW,
Mansfield std, transposed by 21 April,
Market Drayton,
Market Harborough,
Melton Mowbray,
Merthyr Tydfil,
Milford Haven,
Minehead,
Montrose,
Morpeth std L 7 April, transposed later, Neath transposed, std by 17 April,
Newbury, and Gt Britain both transposed,
Newcastle Co Down,
Newry,
Newtown,
Newtownabbey,
Newtownards,
Northallerton,
Nuneaton,
Oban,
Oldham A,B,
Omagh,
Oxford B transposed,
Paisley,
Penrith,
Penzance,
Perth,
Peterborough A,
Pontypridd,
Portadown,
<Portmadoc,
Port Talbot,
Preston A,
Pwllheli,
Reading arcs types 2 & 7, and no arcs,
Redditch,
Reigate & Redhill,
Rhyl types 2 & 3,
Richmond Yorks,
Richmond & Twickenham A,
Rochdale,
Romford & Dagenham B,
Rotherham,
Rothesay,
Rugby A,
St Austell,
Scunthorpe,
Sevenoaks,
Sheffield A,
Sittingbourne,
Slough,
Southall,
Southampton A,C,
Spalding,
Stafford A,
Stockport A,
Stowmarket seen late,
Strabane,
Stroud,
Swansea A,
Swindon A,
Taunton,
<Thetford,
Tiverton,
Tonbridge,
Trowbridge transposed,
Uxbridge,
Walsall,
<Warminster,
Warrington A,
Wellington Salop,
Welshpool,
Whitehaven,
Wigan A,
Wimborne,
Winchester,
Wisbech,
Woking,
Wokingham,
Worcester A,
<Workington,
Wrexham,
<Yeovil.

Triangles : 78 std, 544 trans, 569 trans

Listed as about 223 dies used standard, about 17 transposed. Shown above are
about 220 dies including the < entries, 11 transposed and 5 "both".

Late uses :
22 April Ashford Kent, Kilmarnock transposed, Maidstone, Portadown, Southall,
Spalding, Swindon A
23 April Alton, Forfar, Reigate & Redhill, Stowmarket
24 April High Wycombe A, Ludlow
28 April Crewe
29 April Newtownabbey
 1 May Penzance
 3 May Evesham
 8 May Lichfield
 9 May Slough
12 May Brentwood
13 May Richmond Yorks std (see later trans)
22 May Bangor Caernarvonshire std (see later trans)
27 May Aylesbury
12 June Rhyl
18 June Bangor Caernarvonshire transposed (E 30 May)
11 Aug Cirencester
18 Aug Richmond Yorks transposed (E 25 May)
 1 Sep SW7
17 Sep Hounslow short arcs (later long arcs)

23 Sep   Ashton-under-Lyne
25 Sep   Northallerton <u>transposed</u> (E 28 May)(and later as exceptional after Cox)
22 Nov   Worcester A
23 Dec   Hounslow long arcs (E 26 Sep)
17 Feb 1969   Hounslow type 5 no arcs (E 14 Jan 1969, 2 & 7 Jan reported but
17 April 1969   Hounslow type 3 short arcs (E 25 Feb 1969)   which die?)

1009t <u>Devon County Show   18 April to 16 May 1968</u>

Barnstaple,   Exeter, new town die by 15 May,   Newton Abbot.

3 dies used

1012/t <u>Expo Sussex 68   20 April to 20 July 1968</u>

Arundel std 20 April to L 23 April, trans by 12 May to 8 June
(broken frame by last day),
Burgess Hill trans 20 April to 8 June,
East Grinstead trans, broken die ex Arundel, 10 June to 20 July,
Haywards Heath trans 10 June to 20 July,
Lewes std 20 April to 8 June,
Littlehampton std 20 April to L 7 May, trans by 10 May to 20 July,
Newhaven std 10 June to 20 July

Announced but not used : Horsham supposed to be in second batch ie from 10 June,
but "Horsham Festival" in use so die remained at Littlehampton

Triangles : 451 std, 990 trans

4 dies used at 7 offices

<u>Conquer Cystic Fibrosis/National CF Week   22 April to 4 May 1968</u>

1017/t   1967 design used in error :

East Kilbride std seen 23 April, prob continued until replaced by 1018,
Edinburgh C <u>transposed</u> seen 25 April.

1018/t New (correct) design : most offices appear to have started late, mostly
up to 26 April.

London EC F,

W 8,

Abingdon,   Barnsley A,   Barry <u>transposed</u>,
Belfast A,   Blackburn & Accrington, Bolton B,
Bournemouth-Poole ?,   Bradford B,   Bristol C <u>transposed</u>,
Burnley,   Coventry A,   Derby A,
Doncaster,
East Kilbride (see 1017 above), 1968 design by 29 April,
Edinburgh C <u>transposed</u> E 26 April, see 1017t above,
Fylde Coast 5,   Gloucester A,   Guildford,
Hereford A,   Ipswich,   Leeds B,
Leicester B,   Luton std L 30 April, also reported <u>transposed</u>,
Matlock,   Morpeth,   Northampton I,
Nottingham B,   Perth,   Petersfield,
Pontypridd,   Sheffield C,   Southampton C,
Stockport A,   Swindon A,   Warrington A.

Triangle : S70 std

Used standard at about 35 offices, trans at 3, "both" at 1

Late uses :
  5 May   Burnley, Derby A, Sheffield C, Southampton C, Swindon A
  6 May   Ipswich
  7 May   Blackburn & Accrington
  8 May   Bolton B
  9 May   Abingdon
 11 May   Stockport A
 17 June Hereford A

1020t Kent County Show 25 April to 9 July 1968

Canterbury,   Maidstone (two similar town dies).   Triangle :-L-/493

2 dies used

Civil Engineers 150th Anniv (second use)

1023   Belfast C std, 29 April to 4 May - 3-line design
1027   London SW1 B std, 2-6 May - 4-line design
1041t Edinburgh C trans, 13-20 May - 3-line design

1025 Victoria & Albert Museum 29 April to 20 May 1968

London N1 A,B,   SE1 F,   SW1 D,   WC C,D,E,

W 4 types 3 & 7,

Triangle : W4

5 dies used.

1026/t Country Code - safeguard water supplies 1 May to 26 June 1968

Birmingham E std,   Bridgwater std no arcs, arcs die by 13 May,
Bristol B,D(types 2 & 3),E, all std,   Chesterfield trans,
Huddersfield std,   Manchester S std,   North Shields std,
Oldham A,B std,   Romford & Dagenham B,L std,
Swansea, and A,L trans, Wigan A std,   Yeovil std.

12 dies used

1033/t Good Templars Centenary (second use) 6 May to 30 June 1968

Date of use vary as shown below.

Burnley std 6 May - 3 June,
Manchester A,F trans 13 May - 10 June,
Bromley & Beckenham std 2-30 June (type 5, type 3 by 17 June)

Triangle : 498 trans

3 dies used

1034t 125th Suffolk Show 8 May to 4 June 1968

Bury St Edmunds,   Ipswich, and A (2 dies), Lowestoft.

Triangle : 405 trans

4 dies used

1035/t County Show Stafford 8-21 May 1968

Leek std,   Lichfield trans,   Stafford A trans,
Stoke-on-Trent std arcs & no arcs,   Walsall std,
Wolverhampton A,B (2 dies) std.

Triangle : 834 std

7 dies used

1043/t Cancer Research Fund 14-27 May 1968

London F,G std,   EC F std,   N1 A trans,   WC D std,

N 16 trans,   SE 5 trans,
SW 11 trans,16 trans,19 trans,   W 2B std, 5 trans,

Ashford Kent std,   Barnsley A std,   Birmingham G std,
Bradford B std,   Bristol C (types 3 & 5) trans,
Burton.on.Trent std,   Coventry A trans,   Croydon trans,
Doncaster std,   Dudley B trans,   Gloucester A trans,
Leeds B std,   Lincoln B std,   Loughborough std,

Matlock trans,   Oxford B trans,   Peterborough A trans,
Romford & Dagenham B trans,   Rotherham std,   Slough std,
Solihull std,   Sutton Coldfield std,   Tamworth std seen late,
Trowbridge trans,
Walsall trans,   Watford trans,   Winchester trans.

Triangle : -U-/MTP std, 520 trans

About 20 dies used std and 20 trans.

Late uses : 28 May London G std, Tamworth std.

1049/t-1051t Learn to Swim Week Scotland 27 May to 1 June 1968

1049/t is type 692, long die (no lines at right) with 17 waves under Scotland,
1050/t is type 692A, long die (no lines at right) with 15 waves under Scotland,
1051t is type 692B, short die (with lines at right).

Aberdeen A,   type 692 std,
Coatbridge & Airdrie A,   type 692 trans,
Dumfries,   type 692B trans,
Dundee B   type 692A trans,
Dunfermline,   type 692 trans,
Edinburgh C,   type 692A trans,
Falkirk,   type 692 trans,
Glasgow F,   SEDO,   type 692A std, (probably F first day only)
Greenock,   type 692B trans,
Hawick,   type 692 trans,
Inverness,   type 692A trans,
Kirkcaldy,   type 692 trans,
Oban,   type 692 std, trans by 29 May,
Paisley,   type 692 trans,
Perth,   type 692 trans,
Rothesay,   type 692 trans,
Thurso,   type 692 trans,
Wick,   type 692 trans,

Triangles : S70 (type 692 trans), AB (type 692 std)

19 dies used

Late use : 3 June Dumfries (type 692B trans)

1052 The Dairy Festival 28 May to 31 July 1968

London SE1 F,

Birmingham F,G,   Blackburn & Accrington, Bradford B,
Coventry A,   Gloucester A,B,   Nottingham B,
Reading, two old style no arcs die, and one with arcs,
Southampton C,   Stoke-on-Trent arcs & no arcs.

Triangle : 75

10 dies used

Early use : 27 May Blackburn & Accrington

Late use : 4 Aug Reading with arcs

1056/t East of England Show 1 June to 18 July 1968

Bedford std (GPO says 3 dies, but I feel only 2 used, shorter/longer arc seen),
Ely std,
Haverhill std,
Huntingdon std, trans from 7 June (GPO date),
Oakham std L 4 June, trans by 11 June,
Oundle std L 5 June, trans by 12 June,
Peterborough A std L 5 June, trans by 6 June, B std L 4 June, trans by 10 June
(2 dies),
Royston std,
St Ives std L 4 June, trans by 12 June,
St Neots std, trans from 7 June (GPO date),
Stamford std L 9 June, trans by 12 June,
Whittlesey std L 4 June, trans by 13 June.

14 dies used (assuming two at Bedford)

Early uses :
12 May   Huntingdon std
31 May   Peterborough ?B std

1060/t   TUC Centenary 1-22 June 1968

London EC F std,   N1 A std,   NW1 B std,   WC B,D,E std,

W 2A,B(types 2 & 3) std,   London missort : 75 std

Belfast C std,   Bristol C trans, std by 18 June,   Dewsbury std,
Edinburgh B with JUN, then C with JNE by 3 June, both trans,
Glasgow C std,   Gloucester A trans,   Guildford trans,
Morpeth std, trans by 12 June, Oxford A,B trans, Rhondda 1 std,
Scunthorpe std,   Southampton A std,   Stockport A std,
Stoke-on-Trent std.

Triangles : 547C std, 603 trans

21 dies used (assuming 2 at WC and W2)

Late uses :
23 June   Preston A std, Scunthorpe std
24 June   Edinburgh trans, Stockport A std
31 July   Southampton A std

1067t   National Eisteddfod 68 (second use) 10 June to 20 July 1968

Dates of use differ as shown below.

Barry 10 June - 20 July,   Bridgend 24 June - 20 July,
Cardiff B 8-20 July (?die transferred from Merthyr Tydfil),
Merthyr Tydfil 10-20 June,   Neath 10 June - 20 July,
Pontypridd 24 June - 10 July, Port Talbot 10 June - 20 July,
Swansea A 1-20 July.

7 dies used at 8 offices

1073/t   RICS Centenary Year   15-21 June 1968

London F,G std,   EC G std,   N1 B std,
     NW1 announced but not seen,   SE1 A std,
     SW1 D std,   W1 A std,   WC C std,

SW 11 trans,   W 2B std types 2 & 3,

Birkenhead B std,   Birmingham A std,
Bristol NDO std L 17 July, trans by 17 July 4.45pm,
Cardiff B std,   Glasgow SEDO trans,
Halifax std (announced as Leeds),   Leicester B std,
Manchester F std,   Nottingham B std,   Warrington A std.

20 dies used (assuming used at NW1)

Early uses : 14 June W2 B, Bristol NDO, both std

Late uses :
24 June   Warrington A std
28 June   Bristol NDO trans

1085/t   National Savings oaks from acorns 1 July to 13 Sep 1968

Edinburgh C,D (2 dies) trans,   NW,S,W all trans,
Falkirk std in error L 7 July, trans from 9 July (GPO date I think),
Greenock trans,   Hamilton trans.

8 dies used

1096/t   Good Templars Centenary (third use) 15 July to 15 Oct 1968

Dates of use differ as shown below.

London SW1 D std 22 July - 19 Aug,   WC D std 22 July - 19 Aug,

Blackburn & Accrington std 5-25 Aug,   Canterbury trans 15 July - 12 Aug,
Cirencester std 16 Aug - 15 Oct.

Triangles : SW1 std, 84 trans (handstamp triangle added), 204 std

5 dies used

1097t   Civil Engineers 150th Anniv (third use)   15-19 July 1968

London missort die -79- used for stamping normal mail at SW1 trans
(only collectors' covers seen). 1 die used.

1100   People on the move exhib Birmingham 20 July to 2 Aug 1968

Birmingham A,E,G,   ADO,CH,H,WDO,   Moseley DO,   Warley B.

9 dies used

1102/t   United Counties Show   25 July to 7 Aug 1968

Cardigan std (from 31 July),
Carmarthen trans, but std on last day (on collectors' covers anyway!),
Haverfordwest trans (from 30 July).

Triangle : 167 trans

3 dies used

1107/t   New stamps for Scotland   1 Aug to 4 Sep 1968

ALL trans except Bathgate and Glasgow.

Ardrossan,   Bathgate std 10.30am 1 Aug, trans by 11am 1 Aug,
Coatbridge & Airdrie A, Dumbarton,
Dumfries (interrupted for "Civil Engineers" 5-10 Aug), Dundee B,
Dunfermline,   Edinburgh C,D,   Forfar,
Fort William,   Galashiels,
Glasgow F std (type 2, type 3 by 19 Aug),   Hawick,
Kilmarnock,   Kirkcaldy,   Montrose,
Oban,   Paisley,   Perth,
St Andrews.

Triangle : S55 trans

20 dies used

Late use : 17 Sep Bathgate trans

1112t   Civil Engineers 150th Anniv (fourth use)   5-10 Aug 1968

Dumfries (4-line design).   1 die used

1115/t   'for sale' New stamps for Wales and Mon   12 Aug to 4 Sep 1968

Bangor Caernarvonshire trans,
Barmouth std, trans from 23 Aug (GPO date I think),
Barry trans,   Bridgend trans,
Cardiff A std to 15 Aug, trans by 15 Aug (no time recorded for either),
Carmarthen trans,   Haverfordwest trans,   Rhyl trans,
Swansea A std type 5 L 12 Aug 3pm, trans type 3 by 16 Aug, L trans (one die),
(note : the "L trans" refers to die "L", L not here meaning "latest")
Tenby trans.

10 dies used

1120t   Alcan Golf One putt for £22,916 19 Aug to 2 Oct 1968

Dates of use differ as shown below.

Birmingham A,G (2 dies), H, all 19 Aug - 28 Sep,
Southport A 17 Sep - 2 Oct.

Triangle : 75

4 dies used

1122t <u>New stamps for Northern Ireland 19 Aug to 4 Sep 1968</u>

Armagh,	Ballymena,	Belfast A,C,
Coleraine,	Enniskillen,	Londonderry (from 29 Aug),
Newry,	Portadown.	

Triangle : I31

8 dies used.

1126/t <u>Pick an English Worcester 26 Aug - 7 Sep 1968</u>

London G,	EC E,F,	N1 A <u>transposed</u>,	NW1 B,
SE1 A,F,	SW1 D,	WC D,	

SW 11,	W 2B,

London missort : 75

Barnsley A,   Birmingham E,   Blaydon-on-Tyne,
Bolton B,   Bradford B,   Bristol C,
Camberley, and Gt Britain, Canterbury,   Carlisle A,
Chelmsford,   Coventry A,   Doncaster, and A,
East Grinstead <u>transposed</u>, Edinburgh EC <u>transposed</u>
Exeter std 26 Aug, <u>transposed</u> from 27 Aug,   Glasgow C,
Hebburn,   Hemel Hempstead std, <u>transposed</u> by 4 Sep (then late std),
Hereford A,   Huddersfield,   Leeds B,
Leicester B,   Luton A,   Manchester F,
Nottingham B,   Oxford B,   Plymouth A,
Preston A,   Reigate & Redhill,   Richmond Yorks <u>transposed</u>,
St Austell <u>transposed</u>,   Stanley,   Stockport A,
Swansea, and A,   Watford (two similar type 3 town dies) <u>transposed</u>,
Windsor std to 2 Sep, <u>transposed</u> from 3 Sep,   Wolverhampton A,B,
York.

Triangle : 255 std

Listed as "about 41 dies standard, 6 trans and 2 "both"; above listing shows
about 39 dies used standard, 6 transposed, 3 "both"

Announced but not used : London E1 (used at NW1 instead), W1, Cardiff

Early use : 21 Aug Plymouth A std

Late uses :
 8 Sep Hemel Hempstead std again, Swansea A std
16 Sep Wolverhampton B std

1128/t <u>Save at work (seventh use) 26 Aug to 30 Nov 1968</u>

Dates of use differ as shown below.

Blackburn & Accrington std 7 Oct - 2 Nov,
Burnley std 7 Oct - 2 Nov,   Chelmsford std 7 Oct - 2 Nov,
Dewsbury std 4-30 Nov,   Fylde Coast 3,5 std 9 Sep - 5 Oct,
Halifax std 1-30 Sep,   High Wycombe B trans 23 Sep - 19 Oct,
Hitchin std 23 Sep - 19 Oct   Kingston upon Thames 1,7 trans 21 Oct - 16 Nov,
Lincoln A std 28 Oct - 9 Nov,   Maidstone trans 21 Oct - 16 Nov,
Nottingham B,C std 23 Sep - 19 Oct, Nuneaton (types 3 & 5) std 7 Oct - 2 Nov,
Oldham A,B std 9 Sep - 5 Oct,   Pontypridd std 9 Sep - 5 Oct,
Redditch trans 26 Aug - 21 Sep,   Rotherham A std 23 Sep - 19 Oct,
Stockport A,B std 9 Sep - 5 Oct,   Wakefield A,B std 4-30 Nov,
Wigan A std 7 Oct - 2 Nov,   Yeovil std 26 Aug - 21 Sep,

21 dies used

Late uses :
 6 Oct Fylde Coast 3 std, Stockport A std (both due to end 5 Oct)
16 Oct Oldham A std (due to end 5 Oct)
 5 Nov Wigan A std (due to end 2 Nov)

1130/t-1131/t <u>Good Templars Centenary (fourth use) 1 Sep to 30 Oct 1968</u>

Dates of use differ as shown below.

1130/t Unframed design :

Birmingham E,F std 2-30 Sep,
Gloucester std 1 to L 14 Sep, trans by 17 to 29 Sep,
Hinckley std 2-30 Sep,   Leeds C std 30 Sep - 30 Oct,
Lincoln A std 2-30 Sep,   Mitcham std 3-30 Sep,
Sutton std 2-30 Sep,   Swindon A trans 1-29 Sep,
Tewkesbury std 3 to L 18 Sep, trans by 3 to 30 Oct,
Wallsend std 1 Sep - 30 Oct.

Triangles : 513 (h/s) std, 788 std, 959 std

10 dies used

Late use : 19 Nov Tewkesbury trans

1131/t Framed dedign :

SW 7 trans 2 to L 23 Sep, std by 24 to 30 Sep,
Manchester F trans 5-30 Sep.

London missort : 10 trans and std.

2 dies used

1133 <u>Human Rights Year 2 Sep to 26 Oct 1968</u>

London F,G,T,BB (4),   E1, and A (2),   EC B,D,E,F,G,H (6),
       N1 A,B (2),   NW1 A,C (2),   SW1 A,B,C,D (4),
       W1 A,1B,C,L2,M2 (4), WC D (1),

SW 11 (1),   W 2A (1).

London missorts : 6A,75

Triangle : W2

Estimated 27 dies used at 10 offices (numbers in brackets above are estimates)

1137/t <u>Leukaemia Research Fund 8 Sep - 7 Dec 1968</u>

Dates of use differ as shown below.

Aberdeen B std 1 Oct - 30 Nov,
Bradford B std 8-30 Sep, and A,B std 31 Oct - 10 Nov,
Derby A trans 1 Nov - 7 Dec,
Fylde Coast 1,2,3,5 (two "5" dies, diff layouts) std 1 Oct - 30 Nov,
Norwich A-1,2,3,4 (4 dies) trans 1 Oct - 30 Nov,
Southampton C,D std 1 Oct - 30 Nov,
Swansea A types 3 & 5, L std (L 10 Oct though GPO said L not used after 16 Sep),
8 Sep - 28 Oct,

10 dies used

1143 <u>Caravan & Camping Exhibition 28 Sep to 16 Nov 1968</u>

London G,H,BB,   E1 A,   NW1 B,   SE1 A,F(types 3 & 7),
       SW1 C,

W 2A,B.   London missort : 75

7 dies used

Late use : 18 Nov London G

1144/t Pick an English Cox 30 Sep to 12 Oct 1968

London F,   EC B,   N1 B,   NW1 A,
    SE1 A,   SW1 D,   WC D,

SW 11 (two similar),   W 2A,C.

London missort : 75

Aberdeen A,   Berwick-on-Tweed std 7 Oct, transposed by 10 Oct,
Bishop Auckland,   Bristol E transposed,
Camberley,   Canterbury,   Carlisle B,
Chester B transposed,   Chesterfield,   Colchester,
Coventry A,   Driffield,   East Grinstead transposed,
Edinburgh C,D both transposed,   Exeter transposed,
Fakenham,   Glasgow C,   Hemel Hempstead Gt Brit,
Hereford A,   Hexham,   Lancaster & Morecambe A,
Loughborough,   Louth transposed,   Manchester F,
Northallerton,   Oxford,   Plymouth A transposed,
Preston B,   Reigate & Redhill,   St Austell transposed,
Southport B,   Walsall,   Watford transposed,
Wellington Salop transposed,   Windsor.

Listed as 37 offices std and 11 trans, as shown above

Announced but not used : London E1 (but NW1 instead), W1, Leicester, West
Bromwich, Worksop.

Late uses :
14 Oct London F, Chesterfield
16 Oct Lancaster & Morecambe A
- also Glasgow C which continued and joined up with 1178 in Nov

1145/t Muscular Dystrophy Week 30 Sep to 27 Oct 1968

London T std,   EC F std,   SE1 2V,3V,V2 std,

Basingstoke std,   Bedford std,   Birmingham G std,
Bolton B std,   Bristol D types 2 & 3 trans,
Cardiff B trans,   Chorley std,   Croydon std,
Dartford std,   Derby std L 14 Oct, trans by 16 Oct,
Dewsbury std,   Durham A std,   Edinburgh D trans, from 13 Oct
Glasgow F std,   Kingston upon Thames 1,3 std, Luton A,B std,
Nottingham B,C std,   Stoke-on-Trent arcs & no arcs std,
Warrington A,C,D std.

22 dies used

Announced by GPO but not reported used : Edinburgh NW

Late use : 3 Nov Edinburgh D trans

1146t National Savings - let Glasgow flourish 30 Sep to 20 Dec 1968

Glasgow E3, N (type 5) and -N (type 2), NW,
Glasgow.S. L 5 Oct, -S- by 8 Oct, SEDO,SW,W,W3

8 dies used

Late use : 6 June 1969 Glasgow E3

1149 Ulster Week in Leicester 30 Sep to 12 Oct 1968

Leicester A,B,C (3 dies), Ashby-de-la-Zouch,   Coalville,
Oakham,   Wigston.

7 dies used

1150/t Newcastle Students Charities Week 30 Sep to 2 Nov 1968

Newcastle upon Tyne A,B (new B no arcs town die by 3 Oct)(2 dies) std,
North Shields std,
South Shields trans (types 2 & 3 town dies)(one slogan die).

4 dies used

Late use : 3 Nov North Shields std

1152/t Radio-TV Licences 1 Oct to 30 Nov 1968

Except for one office this campaign ran 1-30 Oct, but in addition used at Dundee 1-30 Nov.
There were five sub types of this slogan, shown below as A,B,C,D and G where sub-type is known; at large offices town dies/slogan dies were not necessarily used together for the whole period, thus the slogan types used are shown once for the office. < entries are those announced thought likely to have used the slogan.

London F,G,J,AA (A),   EC G (A),   W1 K1(?),

SE 3(B),5(A and B),6(A and C),15(A),18 types 2 & 3(A),

<Abingdon,   Aldershot(A),   Altrincham A(A),
Ashford Kent(G) transposed, Ashton-under-Lyne(B), Aylesbury(A),
<Barnet,   Barnsley A,B(C),   Bexleyheath(A),
<Birkenhead,   Birmingham A,E,F(A and B), ADO(G),CH(B),H(G),WDO(B),
Blackburn & Accrington(C), Bletchley(A),
Bolton A,B(G) std L 4 Oct, transposed 7 Oct (then std again),
Borehamwood(G) transposed L 10 Oct, std by 25 Oct,   Bournemouth-Poole C(A),
Bradford B(B),
Bristol A(B) transposed, NDO(A) std L 7 Oct, transposed from 8 Oct,
Bromley & Beckenham(G), Burnley(C),
Burton.on.Trent & Burton-on-Trent (A),
<Bury,   Carlisle A,B(C) transposed,
Castleford(D),   Chesterfield(A),   Chichester(A) types 3 & 7,
Crewe(A),   Darlington(D),   Doncaster A(A),
Dumfries (D)types 2 & 5 transposed,
Dundee A(D) transposed used 1-30 Nov,   Dunfermline(G) transposed,
Edgware(A) transposed,   Edinburgh C(D) transposed, W(G) transposed,
Enfield(A and G)(2),   <Epsom,   Falkirk arcs & no arcs(D) transposed,
Farnborough(A)(announced as Dartford),   Feltham(G),
Folkestone(A) transposed, Glasgow 2 (Waterloo St)(D) transposed,
Gloucester A,B(A),   Gravesend(G),   <Grays,
Greenock(G) transposed,
Guildford types 3 & 5(B and G) std L 8 Oct, transposed by 16 Oct,
Halifax(A),   Harpenden(G), Harrogate A, and Gt Brit(B) transposed
Harrow & Wembley, and A and *(A,B and D),   Hatfield(A),
Haverfordwest(G),   <Hayes,   Hemel Hempstead, & Gt Brit(G),
<Hoddesdon,   Huddersfield(A),
Ilford & Barking(B),   <Keighley,   Kingston upon Thames 3(G),
Leatherhead(G),   Lewes(G) transposed,   Lincoln A,B(A),
Maidenhead(C) transposed,
Manchester C(A)(types 3 & 5), S(D),SE(A),SW(types 3 & 7)(A),
Morpeth(A),   Moseley DO(B),   Neath(D),
Newry(G),   Newton Abbot(D) transposed, Northwood(G),
Peterborough A(A),   Pinner(G),   Pontefract(D),
Pontypridd(D),   Potters Bar(G),   Preston A(B),
Rhondda 1 (used at Pontypridd)(D),   Richmond Yorks(D),
Richmond & Twickenham A(A),   Rochdale(C),
Rochester & Chatham types 2,3 & 7(A and B) transposed,
Rugby A(B),   St Albans (two)(A and G), St Helens A,B(B and C),
Salford(B),   Scunthorpe(B),   Sidcup(G),
Slough(B),   Southall (two)(G),
Stockport A(A),   Sutton (types 3 & 5)(B), Swindon A,B(A),
Taunton(B) transposed,   Trowbridge(A),   Uxbridge(G),
Walsall(two similar)(G), Waltham Cross(A),   Warley B(B),
Welwyn Gdn City A(G),   Weybridge(B),   Wigan A,B(C) std & transposed,
Winchester (two)(A and B) transposed,
Wolverhampton arcs & no arcs, and B(C and D) transposed,
Wrexham(G),   York(A).

Listed as "about 130 dies used" standard and a further 30 transposed,

Announced but not thought to have been used : London N1, SE1, SW11, W2, Hounslow, Stafford, Woking.

Early use :
 5 Aug Folkestone std L 12 Sep, but trans by 1 Oct.

Late uses :
31 Oct Birmingham CH,WDO
 1 Nov St Albans
 4 Nov Potters Bar
 5 Nov Blackburn & Accrington, Wigan B

```
 6 Nov  Pontypridd, Richmond & Twickenham A
 8 Nov  Ilford & Barking
11 Nov  Harrogate GB transposed
19 Nov  Chichester (type 7), Northwood, Richmond Yorks
20 Nov  Taunton GB transposed
22 Nov  Slough arcs (used again later)
26 Nov  Chichester type 3
27 Nov  Newton Abbot transposed
 2 Dec  Bletchley, then Exceptional Use after 20 Dec
 3 Dec  Neath
 8 Dec  Taunton transposed
 9 Dec  Ashton-under-Lyne, then Exceptional Use after 20 Dec
16 Dec  Gravesend
17 Dec  Slough no arcs (E 4 Dec)
22 July 1969  Slough arcs (E 18 Dec)
```

1177/t Pick an English Conference 11-23 Nov 1968

London F,	EC F,H,	N1 B,	NW1 C,
SE1 A,	SW1 A,	WC C,	

SW 11 (two),   W 2A,B,

London missort : 75

Barnsley B,	Birmingham F,	Bolton B,
Bradford B,	Bristol Γ transposed,	Camberley,
Canterbury,	Cardiff B transposed,	
Carlisle B, and B Gt Brit,	Chelmsford,	Coventry A,D,
Darlington,	Doncaster (two),	
East Grinstead transposed,	Exeter transposed,	Hereford B,
Huddersfield A,	Ipswich transposed,	Keighley,
Leicester B,	Luton B,	Manchester P,
Nottingham A,D,	Oxford 2,	Plymouth A transposed,
Pontefract transposed,	Preston B,	Reigate & Redhill,
St Austell transposed,	Sheffield B,	Stockport B,
Swansea A,	Watford std L 14 Nov, transposed by 19 Nov,	
Windsor,	Wolverhampton,	York.

About 40 offices used standard, 8 transposed and 1 "both".

Announced but probably not used : London E1, W1, Leeds

```
Late uses :
24 Nov  Camberley, Chelmsford, Huddersfield A, York
25 Nov  W 2B, St Austell transposed
26 Nov  Preston B, Reigate & Redhill
27 Nov  London F
12 Dec  Stockport B
14 Dec  Stockport A
```

1178/t Pick an English Cox 11-23 Nov 1968

Although not announced, it appears the Scottish offices had a preference for apples rather than pears, using the Cox slogan rather than Conference.

Aberdeen A std,   Edinburgh B,C trans,   Glasgow C std,

but Glasgow C appears to have been in continual use since 1144

1181/t-1183 Voters Lists 28 Nov to 12 Dec 1968

A new sub type was used in 1964-67, and was used again in 1968 as here shown at the end of 1182 - type 98A.

1181/t Type 98

London N1 A,B,

SE 3,5,6,13,15,

Bishop Auckland,	Darlington,	Durham A,
Edgware transposed,	Kidderminster,	Maidenhead,
Pontefract,	Reigate & Redhill,	

Listed as "about 14 dies" standard and 1 transposed, as shown above.

Exercise D1: What was your childhood like? – contd.

Name: **Date:**

10. What did you like least about your childhood?	
11. What is your most important memory?	
12. Can you remember being held by your mother/father to comfort you?	
13. Did you every feel severely or persistently rejected as a child by your mother/father? If YES, why do you think your parents behaved that way?	
14. Did you have anything special in your childhood i.e. a toy, or place to visit?	
15. Who was the most important person in your childhood?	
16. Can you remember an occasion when you were very happy?	
17. Can you remember an occasion when you were very sad?	
18. Can you remember a time when you were very angry?	→

Exercise D1: What was your childhood like? – contd.

Name: **Date:**

19. How did you see yourself as a child, i.e. well behaved, naughty?	
20. How did your parents react i.e. did you get treats?	
21. What sort of things did you get into trouble for?	
22. How did your parents deal with this behaviour?	
23. When you were a child, were you ever: a) Physically abused? b) Neglected? c) Sexually abused? d) Emotionally abused?	
24. What can you remember about primary school?	
25. How did you get on at school?	
26. What did you dislike at school?	
27. Was there anyone special to you at school? i.e. teacher, friend.	

Exercise D2: What was it like as a teenager?

Name: **Date:**

1. What can you remember about being a teenager?	
2. How did you get on with your parents?	
3. Did you have difficulties with your parents?	
4. How did you get on with your brothers/ sisters?	
5. Did the relationship between yourself and your family change during your teens? If so, how?	
6. What did you most like about your teens?	
7. What did you least like about your teens?	
8. What was your most important memory?	
9. Did you attend High School regularly? If not, why not?	→

Exercise D2: What was it like as a teenager? – contd.

Name: **Date:**

10. Did you change schools at any time?	
11. Did you enjoy school?	
12. What exams, if any, did you pass?	
13 Did you ever truant from school?	
14. Did you get into trouble at school? If yes, how were you punished?	
15. How did your parents discipline you?	
16. How did you feel about this?	
17. How would you describe your teenage years? Were you: a) involved in drugs? b) involved with alcohol? c) ever in trouble with the police? d) Did you have psychiatric treatment as a teenager?	→

Exercise D2: What was it like as a teenager? – contd.

Name: **Date:**

18. Who were your friends at school?	
19. Who was your favourite teacher and why?	
20. When did you first have a girlfriend/ boyfriend?	
21. Describe this relationship?	
22. How did your parents feel about this?	
23. Did you finish school?	
24. What did you do when you left school? i.e. get a job/college?	
25. At what age and why did you leave home?	
26. How did your parents feel about you leaving home?	

Exercise D3: Previous relationships?

Name: **Date:**

1. When/how did you meet?	
2. What attracted you to each other?	
3. Did you live together/marry?	
4. How long together?	
5. What did each of your families think of each other?	
6. How did you spend your time together?	
7. Was it easy to talk to each other?	
8. What did you tend to agree/disagree about?	
9. What happened if you disagreed, did this ever lead to violence?	→

Exercise D3: Previous relationships? – contd.

Name: **Date:**

10. Did you have children in this relationship?	
11. Did you usually agree/disagree on how to bring the children up?	
12. How much time did you spend with the children and each other? What did you enjoy doing most?	
13. Who made the decisions about money, children, going out, etc.?	
14. When/why did the relationship deteriorate?	
15. How did you feel about this?	

NB If there are children from this relationship refer to Section A – Pregnancy/preparation for birth, Exercises A7, 8, 9 and 10.

Exercise D4: Children from previous relationships living in the household

Name: **Date:**

1. Names and ages of children?	
2. Were they living with you when they were young?	
3. Did anybody help you look after them and who?	
4. Did the children ever stay with anyone else?	
5. What sort of things did the children enjoy doing most?	
6. What did you enjoy doing with them?	
7. What did you dislike doing with them?	
8. What did you dislike about being a parent?	

Exercise D5: Children from previous relationships not living in the household?

Name: **Date:**

1. What are the names and ages of your children?	
2. When did you last see them?	
3. Where were you living when they were young?	
4. Did anyone help you look after them?	
5. Who looked after them? Fed them Got up in the night Changed their nappies Bathed them Put them to bed Played with them Took them to school Disciplined them	
6. Did the children ever live or stay with anyone else?	
7. What sorts of things did the children enjoy doing most?	
8. What did you enjoy doing with them?	
9. What did you dislike doing with them?	

→

Exercise D5: Children from previous relationships not living in the household? – contd.

Name: **Date:**

10. What did you like about being a parent?	
11. What did you dislike about being a parent?	
12. When did your social worker begin to express concerns?	
13. Why do you think this was?	
14. How did you feel when the children first went into foster care?	
15. How often did you see them during this time?	
16. How did you feel when you were told they would be adopted?	
17. How do you feel about the situation now?	
18. Do you blame anyone?	

Exercise D6: Past support networks/others who gave support

Name: **Date:**

1. Was there family support/who?	
2. Did you have friends/neighbours who offered support?	
3. What kind of support was offered?	
4. Did this support stop and if so why?	
5. Did you have/know anyone with whom you could discuss worries/concerns with?	
6. Did you know anyone with whom you shared good times or good experiences with?	

Exercise D7: Present relationship

Name: **Date:**

1. Are you currently married? Living together?	
2. How long have you been together?	
3. How did you meet?	
4. What attracted you to each other?	
5. What did each of your families think of your relationship?	
6. Are there children from this relationship? Who are they? (Refer to History of Pregnancy in Exercise A10)	
7. Are there any other children living in this household? (i.e. stepchildren)	→

Exercise D7: Present relationship – contd.

Name: **Date:**

8. How much time do you spend talking to each other? What about? Children/yourselves/problems/other.	
9. Is it easy to talk to each other? Would you like to talk more?	
10. What do you tend to agree about? What do you tend to disagree about?	
11. Do you usually agree or disagree about the children and how to bring them up? What do you disagree about?	
12. Who makes the decisions about money, children, going out, other?	
13. What happens if you disagree? Does this ever lead to violence between you both? What happens to the children if this happens?	
14. How much time do you spend together with no children/other people? What do you most enjoy doing together?	→

Exercise D7: Present relationship – contd.

Name: **Date:**

15. What would you change about your relationship?	
16. Do you think it will last? A long time? A moderate time? A short time?	
17. Who makes the rules? Does anyone break them? What rules are there?	
18. Describe your family life	
19. Do you intend to have more children?	

Exercise D8: Example of a part completed ecomap

Name: **Date:**

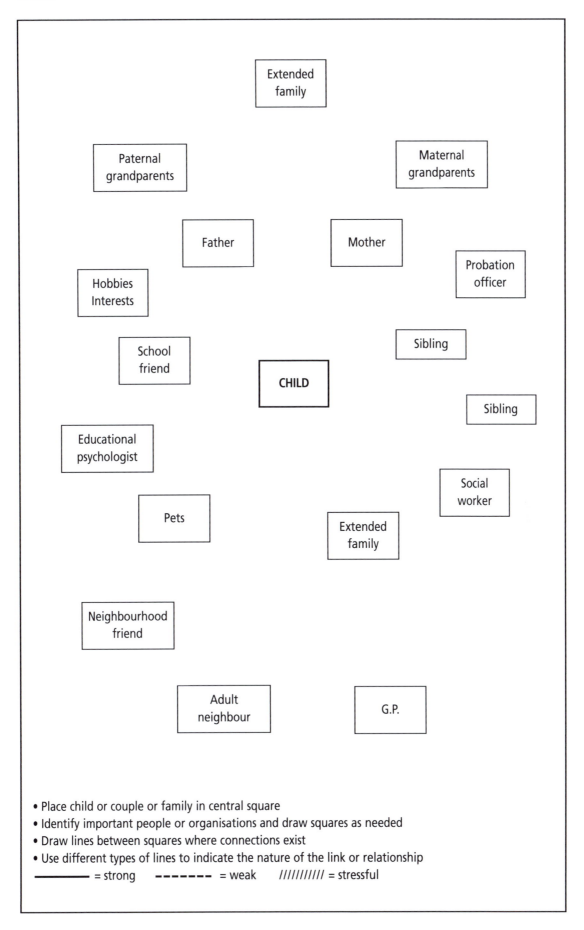

- Place child or couple or family in central square
- Identify important people or organisations and draw squares as needed
- Draw lines between squares where connections exist
- Use different types of lines to indicate the nature of the link or relationship
  - ——————— = strong   – – – – – – = weak   /////////// = stressful

Exercise D9: Present support

Name: **Date:**

1. Do I know other people who I can depend upon in a crisis?	
2. Do I know other people who I feel close to e.g. a friend?	
3. Do I know other people who can recognise my strengths and make me feel valued/ good?	
4. Do I know other people who will challenge me and make me face things I need to face?	
5. Do I know other people with whom I can discuss my worries/concerns?	
6. Do I know other people who I can share my good times and good experiences with?	

Exercise D9: Present support

Exercise D10: Good things/bad things in my life

Name: **Date:**

	Good things in my life	Bad things in my life
Which are a result of my own actions		
Which are a result of things outside my control		

Exercise D11: Personal ladder scale

Name: **Date:**

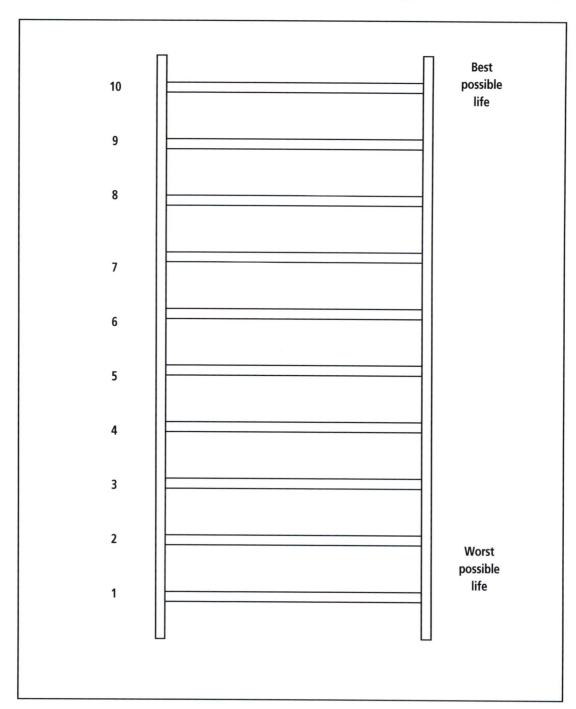

Exercise D12: Best thing about my family

Name: **Date:**

The best thing about my family

The best thing that has happened in the last five years

How others see my family

How I would like my family to be

Our family motto for life is

Exercise D13: Present personal situation

Name: **Date:**

1. How would you describe yourself in: a) Appearance b) Personality c) Feelings about yourself	
2. What do you think are your strengths and weaknesses? a) As a person b) As a partner/husband/wife c) As a parent	
3. Are you employed? If so, what is your job?	
4. Do you like your job? Why? Would you like to change it?	
5. How many jobs have you had since you left school?	
6. If you are not working – when did you last work? What was the job and why did you leave? How long had you been there?	
7. Do you think you will find another job? If so, when?	→

Exercise D13: Present personal situation – contd.

Name: **Date:**

8. What are the best and worst aspects of not working?	
9. How do you financially support yourself?	
10. How would you describe your relationship now between your parents and yourself?	
11. How would you describe your relationship now between your brothers and sisters and yourself?	
12. How would you describe your physical and mental health now?	
13. Are you currently receiving or have you recently received treatment for the above? Please specify.	
14. Where appropriate: a) Who looks after you when you are ill? b) How does your illness affect your ability to look after your children? c) What arrangements have you made for the care of the children when you are ill? d) What affect does your illness have on your children?	→

Exercise D13: Present personal situation – contd.

Name: **Date:**

15. What is your usual mood?	
16. How do you think you react to stressful situations?	
17. When do you lose your temper? Describe a situation at home that might result in you losing your temper?	
18. What do you do when you lose your temper?	
19. How does this affect a) Your partner? b) Your children?	
20. Do you think you have a problem with a) Drink? b) Drugs? Please describe	
21. Does anyone else think you have a problem with drink/drugs? i.e. spouse/ partner H.V. GP etc. What do they think the problem is?	→

Exercise D13: Present personal situation – contd.

Name: **Date:**

Ask Questions 22-30 of those parents where drink/drugs is known or suspected to be a problem	
22. Who looks after you when you have been drinking/using drugs?	
23. Does your drinking/drug taking occur: a) In your home? b) Away from your home?	
24. How often do other people involved with drinking/drug taking come to your house?	
25. How often has there been any fighting/violence in the house as a result?	
26. What arrangement have you made for the care of the children while you are under the influence of drink or drugs?	
27. Do the children know you have a drink/drugs problems? How do they know?	
28. Have the children seen you drink/taking drugs?	
29. Is there evidence of drink/drugs around the house?	
30. What effect do you think your drinking/drug taking has on the children?	→

Exercise D13: Present personal situation – contd.

Name: **Date:**

31. Have you ever been in trouble with the police? Do you have any convictions? (Please specify) (Practitioners should, following a response from the parents, comment on its accuracy compared with information you have been given.)	
32. Have you ever been to prison?	
33. Are you currently waiting to go to court for any matter?	
34. Are you currently subject to any court order/injunction or parole?	
35. Are you currently on probation?	
36. If any of the above applies, what effect do you think this has on the children?	

Exercise D14: Parents' perception of current causes for concern

Name: Date:

1. What at this stage do you think are the problems experienced by the child or areas of concern about their upbringing?
 	
  a) Injury/physical abuse
 	
  b) Neglect
 	
  c) Sexual abuse
 	
  d) Emotional abuse
 	
  e) Marital/family conflict/violence
 	
  f) Physical/behavioural problems exhibited by the child	

2. Could you give an example of the problems as you see them? (Then the social worker can share an example from their perspective.)	
3. How serious do you think the problem is?	
4. Which do you think is the most serious of problems? (Then compare with the social worker's view.)	
5. How did the problems come to light? When was this?	
6. How did the problems come about? (This should explore who or what is thought to be responsible.)	→

Exercise D14: Parents' perception of current causes for concern – contd.

Name: **Date:**

7. Who is concerned now and why?
 	
   a)   Parents
 	
   b)   Other family member
 	
   c)   Health Visitor
 	
   d)   GP
 	
   e)   Teacher
 	
   f) Social worker	

8. What do you think will happen if things do not get changed?	
9. Why do you think that will happen?	
10. What do you think you need to do to change your current situation?	

Aim

The purpose of this section is to assess the client's level of self-esteem and confidence. You may be able to link this to past experiences and will be able to identify what areas need developing if self-esteem is to increase.

Preparation

You need to check out if the client can read or not. If not you may wish to read questions out on some exercises or avoid these exercises altogether.

By using the Rosenberg and adjective tests that are provided here, you can actually measure clients' self-esteem. This may be useful to do at the start of the programme and again at the end of the programme. You can check the results against your observations at the centre.

Explain to your client before you start, what you are doing and why!

N.B. Some clients do not promote their concept of 'self' but are more concerned with a common or family identity. It may be detrimental to a client from such a cultural background to be involved in promoting self-confidence if they are expected to function and be accepted within their family. You may need to consult someone else on this subject.

Guidance notes on exercises

Exercise E1: About me

Encourage the client to tick the relevant boxes.

Pick out relevant points for discussion with your client.

When making notes on the session you should be able to comment on self-esteem/relationships/mood/trust and decision making.

Exercise E2: Draw yourself

You will need a blank sheet of paper and a range of coloured pencils/crayons representing the various possible skin colours of the clients.

Encourage the client to draw themselves and then discuss why they have drawn themselves as they have.

Exercise E3: Strengths checklist

Encourage the client to complete this exercise by allocating a number for each question.

Summarise the session and make a note of conclusions.

Exercise E4: Describe yourself

Ask the client to pretend they are describing themselves to someone who does not know them. Get them to complete the exercise sheet.

Discuss what they have written and pick out significant points. If it is very derogatory you may need to offer some positive comments before the session ends.

Exercise E5: Adjective chart

Encourage the client to tick the words they feel apply to them. It may be helpful to read each one and explain what it means. At the end you may want to pick out significant words for discussion or you may want to assess their current level of self-esteem.

Count how many odd numbers and how many even numbers they have ticked. Show this as a ratio e.g. 18:6 means 18 odd numbers ticked and 6 even numbers ticked which can be broken down into 3:1. The higher the ratio of odd numbers to even numbers, the higher the self-esteem.

In the example above self-esteem is not too low, but would benefit from a boost.

Some clients may struggle to tick any words indicating that they have little notion of 'self'.

N.B. The score of an individual fluctuates and over a period of time may show a significant change.

Exercise E6: Rosenberg self-esteem scales

Encourage the client to tick the appropriate boxes.

Work out the score and inform the client of the findings.

The score will fluctuate and over a period of time may change significantly.

A score of 28 or more would indicate a good self-esteem.

Scoring

Question No.	Strongly Agree	Agree	Disagree	Strongly Disagree
1	4	3	2	1
2	1	2	3	4
3	4	3	2	1
4	4	3	2	1
5	1	2	3	4
6	1	2	3	4
7	4	3	2	1
8	1	2	3	4
9	1	2	3	4
10	4	3	2	1

Exercise E7: Personal profile

Give the client a blank piece of paper.

They may write or draw, or they may want you to write it for them. Explain carefully what goes in each section. If they have written on it copy it down on to A4 paper.

Summarise what you have learnt and check that the client agrees.

Make a note on the E7 summary sheet.

Exercise E8: Basic human rights

The worker should tell the client what human rights are, and then should ask the client to list what they feel their rights are.

A list of basic human rights is shown on the Exercise sheet E8. The worker can use it in whichever way seems most appropriate in drawing out the client's views on their rights.

Exercise E1: About me

Name: **Date:**

Questions Tick your answers	Sometimes	Rarely	Never	Often	Very often
People listen to me when I share my troubles					
I take care of my appearance					
I am clean and tidy					
I talk about myself a lot					
I discuss myself with others					
I like myself					
Men like me					
Women like me					
I talk to my children					
I talk at my children					
I enjoy being a parent					
I like my mother					
I like my father					
I like my husband/cohabitee/boyfriend					
I like my sisters					
I like my brothers					
I make friends easily					
I have lots of friends					
I enjoy my friends company					→

Exercise E1: About me – contd.

Name: **Date:**

Questions Tick your answers	Sometimes	Rarely	Never	Often	Very often
I help my friends when they are in trouble					
I find it easy to talk to men					
I find it easy to talk to women					
I find it easy to talk to officials					
I enjoy meeting new people					
I look people in the eye when I talk to them					
I am confident when talking to others					
I have a temper					
I can keep my temper under control					
I can stand up for my rights without getting angry					
I feel confident when I am in public places					
I have the same views as my parents on all issues					
I am patient when things go wrong					
I get into a lot of arguments					
I admit when I am in the wrong					
I find it easy to say sorry					
I can accept it when I am picked on					
I own up when I have done something wrong					
I have a routine and keep to it					→

Exercise E1: About me – contd.

Name: **Date:**

Questions Tick your answers	Sometimes	Rarely	Never	Often	Very often
I am always on the last minute					
I can make decisions					
I share decision making					
I do not like making decisions					
I can disagree and say what I think when necessary					
I avoid making decisions					
I worry unnecessarily					
I think crying is a weakness					
I let people know when I am happy					
I let people know when I am sad					
I let people know when I am angry					
I think showing any emotion is weak					
I trust others					
I find touching my children easy					
I find touching my husband/cohabitee/boyfriend easy					
I like touching					

At this moment in time I am feeling:

Happy – Sad – Angry – Frustrated – Lonely

Depressed – Isolated – Loving – Good

Exercise E2: Draw yourself

Name: **Date:**

```



                            Exercise E2: Draw yourself
```

The National Curriculum in England (cont.)

Programme of Study	Book 1A	Book 1B	Book 2	Book 3	Book 4	Book 5	Book 6
Compound words		Unit 25	Unit 1, 12	Unit 25		Unit 15	Unit 16
Common exception words	Unit 1, 3, 10, 11, 12, 13, 14	Units 16, 18, 19, 20, 23 and 26	Unit 1–6, 9, 11, 12, 18, 20, 22, 27	Unit 2, 4, 7, 12, 13, 21	Unit 8	Unit 20, 21	Unit 4, 8, 12, 20, 23, 25, 27
YEAR 2							
Pupils should be taught to:							
Spell by							
Segmenting spoken words into phonemes and representing these by graphemes, spelling many correctly							
Learning new ways of spelling phonemes for which one or more spellings are already known, and learn some words with each spelling, including a few common homophones							
Learning to spell common exception words	Unit 1, 3, 10–14	Unit 16, 18, 19, 20, 23, 26	Unit 1–6, 9, 11, 12, 18, 20, 22, 27	Unit 2, 4, 7, 12, 13, 21	Unit 8	Unit 20, 21	Unit 4, 8, 12, 20, 23, 25, 27
Learning to spell more words with contracted forms			Unit 25	Unit 15		Unit 15	Unit 27
Learning the possessive apostrophe (singular)			Unit 19	Unit 11	Unit 21		
distinguishing between homophones and near-homophones			Unit 1, 2, 11, 12, 27	Unit 16 , 18	Unit 22	Unit 19	Unit 17
Add suffixes to spell longer words, including ment, ness, ful, less, ly			Unit 13, 24	Unit 14 (full, ness, ment, less) Unit 22 (ly)	Unit 8 (ly) Unit 15 (less, ness, ment, ly)	Unit 1, 2, 13, 26	Unit 4, 5, 14
Apply spelling rules and guidance, as listed in English Appendix 1							
write from memory simple sentences dictated by the teaher that include words using the GPCs, common exception words and punctuation taught so far.							
APPENDIX							
The /dʒ/ sound spelt as ge and dge at the end of words, and sometimes spelt as g elsewhere in words before e, i and y			Unit 7	Unit 10		Unit 27	Unit 25
The /s/ sound spelt c before e, i and y			Unit 6	Unit 3			Unit 15, 25
The /n/ sound spelt kn and (less often) gn at the beginning of words			Unit 2	Unit 4		Unit 7	Unit 15
The /r/ sound spelt wr at the beginning of words			Unit 22	Unit 26		Unit 7	Unit 15
The /l/ or /əl/ sound spelt –le at the end of words			Unit 18	Unit 5			
The /l/ or /əl/ sound spelt –el at the end of words			Unit 18	Unit 5			

Programme of Study	Book 1A	Book 1B	Book 2	Book 3	Book 4	Book 5	Book 6
The /l/ or /əl/ sound spelt –al at the end of words			Unit 18	Unit 5			
Words ending –il			Unit 18	Unit 5			
The /aɪ/ sound spelt –y at the end of words	Unit 12		Unit 20				
Adding –es to nouns and verbs ending in consonant-letter–y			Unit 20	Unit 7		Unit 4, 5	Unit 1
Adding –ed, –ing, –er and –est to a root word ending in –y with a consonant before it	Unit 12	Unit 17	Unit 28 Unit 21 (Resource Book)	Unit 8 (er, est) Unit 9 (ing)		Unit 1	Unit 5
Adding the endings –ing, –ed, –er, –est and –y to words ending in –e with a consonant before it			Unit 21	Unit 5, 9, 14 (ing, ed), Unit 6 (y)	Unit 27	Unit 1	Unit 4
Adding –ing, –ed, –er, –est and –y to words of one syllable ending in a single consonant letter after a single vowel letter	Unit 7, 8	Unit 17	Unit 21	Unit 4, 9 (ing, ed)	Unit 2, 19, 27	Unit 1, 2	
The /ɔː/ sound spelt a before l and ll, e.g. ball			Unit 13	Unit 2	Unit 18	Unit 17	Unit 5
The /ʌ/ sound spelt o, e.g. mother			Unit 14				
The /iː/ sound spelt –ey, e.g. donkey			Unit 20			Unit 24	Unit 1
The /ɒ/ sound spelt a after w and qu			Unit 23	Unit 11			
The /ɜː/ sound spelt or after w			Unit 11				
The /ɔː/ sound spelt ar after w			Unit 6, 23	Unit 11			
The /ʒ/ sound spelt s			Unit 26	Unit 23, 13	Unit 9, 12		
The suffixes –ment, –ness, –ful, –less and –ly			Unit 24	Unit 14	Unit 8 (ly), Unit 15 (less, ness, ment, ly)	Unit 1, 2, 13, 26	Unit 4, 5
Contractions			Unit 25	Unit 15		Unit 15	Unit 27
The possessive apostrophe (singular nouns)			Unit 19	Unit 11	Unit 21		
Words ending in –tion			Unit 26	Unit 12	Unit 11, 24		
Homophones and near-homophones			Unit 1, 2, 11, 12, 27	Unit 16, 18	Unit 22	Unit 10, 16, 19	Unit 17, 11
Common exception words	Unit 1, 3, 10–14	Unit 16, 18–20, 23, 26	Unit 1–6, 9, 11, 12, 18, 20, 22, 27	Unit 2, 4, 7, 12, 13, 21	Unit 8	Unit 20, 21	Unit 4, 8, 12, 20, 23, 25, 27

The National Curriculum in England (cont.)

Programme of Study	Book 1A	Book 1B	Book 2	Book 3	Book 4	Book 5	Book 6
YEAR 3 AND YEAR 4							
Pupils should be taught to:							
use further prefixes and suffixes and understand how to add them (Appendix 1)	Unit 4, 6, 7, 8	Unit 17	Unit 13, 15, 21, 24, 26, 28	Unit 12, 13, 19, 20, 21, 23	Unit 1, 6, 7, 10, 13–15, 17, 18, 24, 25, 27	Unit 1, 2, 9, 14, 15, 20, 21, 26	Unit 3, 4, 5, 20, 21
spell further homophones			Unit 1, 2, 11, 12, 27	Unit 16, 18	Unit 1, 22	Unit 10, 16, 19	Unit 17, 11
spell words that are often misspelt (Appendix 1)	Unit 1, 3, 10, 11, 12, 13, 14	Unit 16, 18–20, 23, 26	Unit 1–6, 9, 11, 12, 18, 20, 22, 27	Unit 2, 4, 7, 13, 21	All units	All units (Unit 27)	All units (Unit 13)
place the possessive apostrophe accurately in words with regular plurals [for example, girls', boys'] and in words with irregular plurals [for example, children's]					Unit 21		
use the first two or three letters of a word to check its spelling in a dictionary			Unit 1, 2, 9, 22, 27	Unit 28	Unit 5, 28		Unit 3, 18, 28 (and throughout)
write from memory simple sentences, dictated by the teacher, that include words and punctuation taught so far.							
APPENDIX							
Adding suffixes beginning with vowel letters to words of more than one syllable		Unit 17	Unit 13, 28	Unit 5, 8	Unit 10, 19, 24, 25, 27	Unit 9, 14, 20	Unit 4
The /ɪ/ sound spelt y elsewhere than at the end of words				Unit 18			
The /ʌ/ sound spelt ou, e.g. trouble				Unit 17	Unit 5		
More prefixes, e.g. In–, sub–, super–		Unit 27	Unit 13, 15	Unit 20, 21	Unit 6, 7, 13, 14, 18, 27	Unit 1, 2, 9, 14, 15, 20, 21, 26	Unit 3–5, 20, 21
Suffix –ation			Unit 26 (tion)	Unit 12	Unit 11		Unit 4
Suffix –ly			Unit 24	Unit 22	Unit 8	Unit 13	Unit 5
Words with endings sounding like /ʒə/ or /tʃə/, e.g. treasure			Unit 26	Unit 23	Unit 3, 9		
Endings which sound like /ʒən/, e.g. confusion			Unit 26	Unit 13	Unit 12, 24		
The suffix -ous, e.g. poisonous				Unit 19	Unit 10	Unit 20	
Endings which sound like /ʃən/, spelt –tion, –sion, –ssion, –cian, e.g. musician			Unit 26 (tion)	Unit 12 (tion), Unit 13 (sion)	Unit 11, 12		Unit 20
Words with the /k/ sound spelt ch (Greek in origin), e.g. chemist				Unit 17	Unit 5		

The National Curriculum in England (cont.)

Programme of Study	Book 1A	Book 1B	Book 2	Book 3	Book 4	Book 5	Book 6
Words with the /ʃ/ sound spelt ch (mostly French in origin), e.g chef				Unit 18	Unit 16		
Words ending with the /g/ sound spelt –gue and the /k/ sound spelt –que (French in origin), e.g. antique					Unit 16		Unit 10
Words with the /s/ sound spelt sc (Latin in origin), e.g. science				Unit 17	Unit 5	Unit 7	Unit 10
Words with the /eɪ/ sound spelt ei, eigh, or ey, e.g. eight				Unit 18		Unit 23	Unit 23
Possessive apostrophe with plural words					Unit 21		
Homophones and near-homophones			Unit 1, 2, 11, 12, 27	Unit 16, 18	Unit 1, 22	Unit 10, 16, 19	Unit 17, 11
YEAR 5 AND YEAR 6							
Pupils should be taught to:							
use further prefixes and suffixes and understand the guidance for adding them	Unit 4, 6–8	Unit 17	Unit 13, 15, 21, 24, 26, 28	Unit 12, 13, 19, 20, 21, 23	Unit 1, 6, 7, 10, 13-15, 17, 18, 24, 25, 27	Unit 1, 2, 9, 14, 15, 20, 21, 26	Unit 3, 4, 5, 20, 21
spell some words with 'silent' letters, e.g. knight, psalm, solemn			Unit 22	Unit 4, 17	Unit 5	Unit 7	Unit 8, 15 (silent letters) Unit 11, 24, 25, 27 (unstressed letters)
continue to distinguish between homophones and other words which are often confused				Unit 16, 18	Unit 22	Unit 19	Unit 17
use knowledge of morphology and etymology in spelling and understand that the spelling of some words needs to be learnt specifically, as listed in Appendix 1						Throughout	Throughout
use dictionaries to check the spelling and meaning of words			Unit 1, 2, 9, 22, 27	Unit 2, 12, 17, 18, 20, 21, 28	Unit 5–7, 9, 11, 13, 14, 16–19, 24, 26, 28	Unit 2, 3, 6–8, 14–17, 19, 23, 27	Unit 28 and throughout
use the first three or four letters of a word to check spelling, meaning or both of these in a dictionary				Unit 28	Unit 5, 28	Unit 7, 14 and throughout	Unit 3, 18, 28 and throughout
use a thesaurus						Unit 28	

The National Curriculum in England (cont.)

Programme of Study	Book 1A	Book 1B	Book 2	Book 3	Book 4	Book 5	Book 6
APPENDIX							
Endings which sound like /ʃəs/ spelt –cious or –tious, e.g. gracious				Unit 19 (cious)		Unit 20	
Endings which sound like /ʃəl/						Unit 21	Unit 14
Words ending in –ant, –ancel–ancy, –ent, –encel–ency					Unit 25	Unit 9	
Words ending in –able and –ible						Unit 9	
Words ending in -ably and -ibly						Unit 14	
Adding suffixes beginning with vowel letters to words ending in –fer						Unit 15	Unit 3
Use of the hyphen						Unit 23	Unit 23
Words with the /iː/ sound spelt ei after c						Unit 16	Unit 12
Words containing the letter-string ough						Unit 7	Unit 8, 11, 15, 24, 25, 27
Words with 'silent' letters (i.e. letters whose presence cannot be predicted from the pronunciation of the word)				Unit 4 (b and k) Unit 17 (o, h and c)	Unit 5		
Homophones and other words that are often confused, e.g. aloud / allowed, serial / cereal, complement / compliment, affect / effect, draft / draught			Unit 1, 2, 11, 12, 27	Unit 16, 18	Unit 1, 22	Unit 16, 10, 19	Unit 17, 11

Scotland: Curriculum for Excellence

Nelson Spelling provides a carefully structured course for teaching spelling to children in Primary 1–7. The course is designed to build children's competence and confidence as they progress. Children are taught spelling strategies including understanding morphology and etymology, as well as adding to their store of tricky words, homophones, and frequently misspelt words. The Scope and Sequence charts of each book give a detailed breakdown of the spelling concepts covered in each unit.

Year group	Primary 1	Primary 2	Primary 3	Primary 4	Primary 5	Primary 6	Primary 7
Nelson Spelling resources	Workbook Starter A Workbook Starter B	Pupil Book 1A Pupil Book 1B Workbook 1A Workbook 1B	Pupil Book 2 Workbook 2A Workbook 2B	Pupil Book 3	Pupil Book 4	Pupil Book 5	Pupil Book 6 Revision Book
	Teacher's Book 1 for Starter Level and Books 1A, 1B & 2			Teacher's Book 2 for Books 3, 4, 5 & 6			
	Resources and Assessment Book for Starter Level and Books 1A, 1B & 2			Resources and Assessment Book for Books 3 & 4		Resources and Assessment Book for Books 5 & 6	
Scotland Curriculum for Excellence levels Note: this level guidance is approximate	**First** **Writing – Tools for writing** • using knowledge of technical aspects to help my writing communicate effectively within and beyond my place of learning *I can spell the most commonly-used words, using my knowledge of letter patterns and spelling rules and use resources to help me spell tricky or unfamiliar words.* **LIT 1–21a**				**Second** **Writing – Tools for writing** • using knowledge of technical aspects to help my writing communicate effectively within and beyond my place of learning *I can spell most of the words I need to communicate, using spelling rules, specialist vocabulary, self-correction techniques and a range of resources.* **LIT 2–21a** *(Continuing to Third: I can use a range of strategies and resources and spell most of the words I need to use, including specialist vocabulary, and ensure that my spelling is accurate.* **LIT 3–21a)**		

Wales: Foundation Phase Language, Literacy and Communication Skills Area of Learning and Key Stage 2 English Programme of Study

Nelson Spelling provides a carefully structured course for teaching spelling to children in Years R–6. The course is designed to build children's competence and confidence as they progress. Children are taught spelling strategies including understanding morphology and etymology, as well as adding to their store of tricky words, homophones, and frequently misspelt words. The Scope and Sequence charts of each book give a detailed breakdown of the spelling concepts covered in each unit.

Year group	Reception	Year 1	Year 2	Year 3	Year 4	Year 5	Year 6
Nelson Spelling resources	Workbook Starter A Workbook Starter B	Pupil Book 1A Pupil Book 1B Workbook 1A Workbook 1B	Pupil Book 2 Workbook 2A Workbook 2B	Pupil Book 3	Pupil Book 4	Pupil Book 5	Pupil Book 6 Revision Book
	Teacher's Book 1 for Starter Level and Books 1A, 1B & 2			Teacher's Book 2 for Books 3, 4, 5 & 6			
	Resources and Assessment Book for Starter Level and Books 1A, 1B & 2			Resources and Assessment Book for Books 3 & 4		Resources and Assessment Book for Books 5 & 6	
Writing accurately Handwriting, Grammar, Punctuation and Spelling	**Learners are able to:** • discriminate between letters • distinguish between upper- and lower-case letters and show an awareness of full stops • use correct initial consonant by beginning to apply phonic knowledge • begin to use spelling strategies such as sound symbol correspondence and oral segmentation with support such as clapping sounds in vowel-consonant and vowl-consonant-vowel-consonant words • use spelling support such as phonic mats, flashcards and other resources • use familiar and high frequency words in writing	**Learners are able to:** • spell some words conventionally, including consonant-vowel-consonant and common digraphs, e.g. *th*, *ck* • use spelling strategies such as sound–symbol correspondence and segmenting • use spelling support such as picture dictionaries, spelling mats and other resources • spell high-frequency words correctly	**Learners are able to:** • use spelling strategies such as segmenting, simple roots and suffixes, e.g. *-ing*, *-ed* • use knowledge of syllables to spell polysyllabic words • use a dictionary • spell high-frequency words correctly	**Learners are able to:** • spell plural forms, e.g. *-s*, *-es*, *-ies* • use past tense of verbs consistently, e.g. consonant *doubling before -ed* • use strategies including knowledge of word families, roots, morphology and graphic knowledge to spell words, e.g. *most common polysyllabic words* • spell all high frequency words correctly	**Learners are able to:** • use punctuation [...] apostrophes for omission, e.g. *it's (it is)* • use strategies including knowledge of word families, roots, morphology, derivations and graphic knowledge to spell words, e.g. *words with more complex patterns*	**Learners are able to:** • use the full range of punctuation to guide the reader in complex sentences, e.g. [...] *apostrophes for possession* • use a variety of strategies to spell words with complex regular patterns, e.g. *exercise, competition*	**Learners are able to:** • use strategies to spell correctly polysyllabic, complex and irregular words

17

Wales: Foundation Phase Framework for Children's Learning for 3 to 7-year-olds in Wales and English in the National Curriculum for Wales

Year group	Reception	Year 1	Year 2	Year 3	Year 4	Year 5	Year 6
Nelson Spelling resources	Workbook Starter A, Workbook Starter B	Pupil Book 1A, Pupil Book 1B, Workbook 1A, Workbook 1B	Pupil Book 2, Workbook 2A, Workbook 2B	Pupil Book 3	Pupil Book 4	Pupil Book 5	Pupil Book 6, Revision Book
	Teacher's Book 1 for Starter Level and Books 1A, 1B & 2			Teacher's Book 2 for Books 3, 4, 5 & 6			
	Resources and Assessment Book for Starter Level and Books 1A, 1B & 2			Resources and Assessment Book for Books 3 & 4		Resources and Assessment Book for Books 5 & 6	

Foundation Phase Framework for Children's Learning for 3 to 7-year-olds in Wales

Writing: Skills
The Foundation Phase should enable children to enjoy experimenting with written communication and to make progress in their ability to:
• develop their ability to spell common and familiar words in a recognisable way.

Foundation Phase Outcome 5
Simple words are usually spelled correctly, and where there are inaccuracies, the alternative is phonically plausible.

Foundation Phase Outcome 6
Spelling is usually accurate.

Key Stages 2–4
English in the National Curriculum for Wales

Broad lines of progression in the level descriptions for writing
Use of skills in writing:
Important early understanding of spelling relates to letter strings and sound–symbol relationships (Level 1). Pupils then build on this understanding to spell increasingly complex words (Levels 2 to 5). Independence in spelling is seen in pupils' ability to spell unfamiliar words (Level 6 to Exceptional Performance), and to check what they write.

Writing: Skills (6.)
Pupils should be given opportunities to communicate in writing and to:
• develop and use a variety of strategies to enable them to spell correctly

Attainment target 3: Writing (Level 2)
Simple, monosyllabic words are usually spelled correctly, and where there are inaccuracies the alternative is phonetically plausible.
Attainment target 3: Writing (Level 3)
Spelling is usually accurate, including that of common, polysyllabic words.
Attainment target 3: Writing (Level 4)
Spelling conforms to regular patterns and is generally accurate.
Attainment target 3: Writing (Level 5)
Words with complex regular patterns are usually spelled correctly.
Attainment target 3: Writing (Level 6)
Spelling is generally accurate, including that of irregular words.

Northern Ireland: Levels of progression in Communication across the curriculum: Primary (Levels 1–5)

Nelson Spelling provides a carefully structured course for teaching spelling to children in Primary 1–7. The course is designed to build children's competence and confidence as they progress. Children are taught spelling strategies including understanding morphology and etymology, as well as adding to their store of tricky words, homophones, and frequently misspelt words. The Scope and Sequence charts of each book give a detailed breakdown of the spelling concepts covered in each unit.

Year group	Primary 1	Primary 2	Primary 3	Primary 4	Primary 5	Primary 6	Primary 7
Nelson Spelling resources	Workbook Starter A, Workbook Starter B	Pupil Book 1A, Pupil Book 1B, Workbook 1A, Workbook 1B	Pupil Book 2, Workbook 2A, Workbook 2B	Pupil Book 3	Pupil Book 4	Pupil Book 5	Pupil Book 6, Revision Book
	Teacher's Book 1 for Starter Level and Books 1A, 1B & 2			Teacher's Book 2 for Books 3, 4, 5 & 6			
	Resources and Assessment Book for Starter Level and Books 1A, 1B & 2		Resources and Assessment Book for Starter Level and	Resources and Assessment Book for Books 3 & 4		Resources and Assessment Book Books 5 & 6	
Framework for Literacy Development	Foundation Stage		**Key Stage 1** — Pupils are expected to reach Level 2 by the end of Key Stage 1. There is also an expectation that they will progress by at least one level between each Key Stage.		**Key Stage 2** — Pupils are expected to reach Level 4 by the end of Key Stage 2. There is also an expectation that they will progress by at least one level between each Key Stage.		
Levels of progression in Communication across the curriculum: Primary (Levels 1–5) • talk about, plan and edit work • write with increasing accuracy and proficiency.	By the end of Y1	Progressing towards KS1	Level 1/2	Level 2	Level 3	Level 4	Level 4/5
	Most children should: begin to problem-solve how to write words through beginning to apply sound-symbol correspondence, using familiar words to make new words or finding words in the environment	**Most children should:** show increased independence when writing words by applying sound-symbol correspondence, making analogies and accessing words from a range of sources	**Pupils can:** (Level 1) write words using sound-symbol correspondence (Level 1) write personal and familiar words. **In a limited and specified range of forms, pupils can:** (Level 2) spell and write common and familiar words recognisably	**In a range of forms, for different audiences and purposes, pupils can:** (Level 2) spell and write common and familiar words recognisably	**In a range of specified forms and for specified audiences and purposes, pupils can:** (Level 3) make improvements to their writing (Level 3) spell and write frequently used and topic words correctly	**In a range of forms, for different audiences and purposes, pupils can:** (Level 4) check writing to make improvements in accuracy and meaning (Level 4) use accurate grammar and spelling on most occasions	**In a range of forms, for different audiences and purposes, including in formal situations, pupils can:** (Level 5) redraft to improve accuracy and meaning (Level 5) use accurate grammar and spelling

Northern Ireland: Key Stages 1 And 2 Areas of Learning – Language and Literacy

Year groups	Primary 1	Primary 2	Primary 3	Primary 4	Primary 5	Primary 6	Primary 7
Nelson Spelling resources	Workbook Starter A Workbook Starter B	Pupil Book 1A Pupil Book 1B Workbook 1A Workbook 1B	Pupil Book 2 Workbook 2A Workbook 2B	Pupil Book 3	Pupil Book 4	Pupil Book 5	Pupil Book 6 Revision Book
	Teacher's Book 1 for Starter Level and Books 1A, 1B & 2			Teacher's Book 2 for Books 3, 4, 5 & 6			
	Resources and Assessment Book for Starter Level and Books 1A, 1B & 2			Resources and Assessment Book for Books 3 & 4		Resources and Assessment Book for Books 5 & 6	
Language and Literacy	**Foundation Stage**		**Key Stage 1** Pupils are expected to reach Level 2 by the end of Key Stage 1. There is also an expectation that they will progress by at least one level between each Key Stage.		**Key Stage 2** Pupils are expected to reach Level 4 by the end of Key Stage 2. There is also an expectation that they will progress by at least one level between each Key Stage.		
	Writing Children should be enabled to: • begin to problem-solve how to write using sound-symbol correspondence as the first strategy		**Writing** Children should be enabled to: • use a variety of skills to spell words in their writing • spell correctly a range of familiar, important and regularly occurring words		**Writing** Children should be enabled to: • use a variety of skills to spell words correctly		

TEACHING SPELLING

Do we need to teach spelling?

One of the most vigorous debates in education has been, as Dr Margaret Peters once famously put it, whether spelling is 'caught or taught'. Can children learn to spell just by being exposed to words in print, or should they be taught to spell in a discrete and structured way? Some children develop spelling skills through reading, but research has shown that even 'careful' readers need some structured input in order to gain full mastery of spelling.

Is there one correct way, or 'best' way to teach spelling, and do we need to teach spelling pro-actively at all? If so, what are the main aspects of language that a teacher who wants to create a balanced spelling programme should take into account and encourage? The following pages seek to answer these questions.

A whole-school policy

A whole-school policy will give clarity and consistency for staff and children and it is important that it is discussed, agreed and 'signed-up to' by all the staff. Such an agreed policy document should address:

- the agreed spelling philosophy and strategy
- the use of structured course materials
- other spelling support materials in each classroom and work area
- the role of parents
- supporting children with particular spelling needs, including intensive spelling recovery programmes.

The place of memory

Memory

- visual memory
- auditory memory
- devices to stimulate and train memory

Visual memory

Serial probability

Most adults can hold large numbers of visual patterns in their memory. Despite the huge number of possible variations, most of us are able to recognise when a particular string of letters doesn't 'look right'. This is known as 'serial probability' and is an important component in learning to spell. It is developed more quickly if children are systematically taught the common phonemically regular patterns, to which they can add, in an organised way, the less frequent or irregular occurrences.

We can help children develop their memory by organising and categorising information. This is especially important for young children who do not have significant experience of the printed word.

Auditory memory

Sound discrimination

Researchers such as Westward have shown that for many children, visual memory alone is not enough. He has shown that, for many children, the ability to discriminate through hearing is equally as important as visual discrimination.

Working on sound/symbol relationships in a phonic programme to underpin early reading can have the spin-off benefit of helping with visual and auditory memory. Both *Letters and Sounds: Principles and Practice of High Quality Phonics* and the National Curriculum in England (2014) recognise this.

Poor visual and aural memory

For some children, visual and auditory memory develops slowly. For these children, grouping words with similar letter strings and sounds can be especially useful. Teachers will have their own ways of helping children with poor memories, but the key is probably not to demand too much and risk discouraging them. Most children will achieve greater success if the memorising is little and often.

Devices to stimulate and train memory

The handwriting/spelling link

As long ago as the 1940s, the spelling guru Professor Fred Schonell stressed that the 'visual, auditory and articulatory elements must be firmly cemented in writing'. This was supported by Margaret Peters in her research, and has been confirmed by many teachers since. Not only can the use of handwriting help to reinforce the spelling of groups of words with similar letter strings, but the handwriting practice offered is, in itself, also a valuable and useful activity. Spelling and handwriting are excellent bedfellows.

'Handwriting' does not have to mean a smooth joined style, although the sooner children can join the better, as it will help them hold patterns of letter strings in their mind. At the very beginning, when working with single letters and sounds, making letters in the air as well as on paper can be a useful method of memory stimulation and 'programming'. Equipment such as plastic letters and sandpaper letter shapes can be useful too.

Look, Say, Cover, Write, Check

A well-tried and effective device to help children memorise individual and groups of words is 'Look, Say, Cover, Write, Check'. Each of the *Nelson Spelling* Pupil Books has a flap on the front cover. Children should use the flap to cover the word list (though they should realise that it is far more effective to try to learn just a few of the words at a time, not the whole list). Once children are familiar with the 'Look, Say, Cover, Write, Check' technique, they can use it for the early, frequently-used but irregular words, such as *was*, *said* and *they*.

Mnemonics

The use of handwriting and 'Look, Say, Cover, Write, Check' are the main approaches to aid the development of memory, but others, such as the use of mnemonics can be used too. Mnemonics can have useful, if limited, applications especially with those one-off problem words – remembering the cess pit in the middle, means you'll never again misspell 'ne*cess*ary'!

The place of understanding

Structural understanding

- phonographical awareness
- word morphology
- etymology
- syllabification
- semantics and syntax

Phonographical awareness

44 phonemes but 26 graphemes!

English has 44 sounds (phonemes) variously represented by 26 letters (graphemes). Most English words are spelled as they sound, so learning the grapheme-phoneme correspondences gives a solid foundation on which to build. There is a growing body of evidence that children progress faster in reading and other language skills if they follow a structured phonics programme from the earliest stages.

Rhyme and analogy

Reading (decoding) and spelling (encoding) are best planned in parallel. Research by Goswami and Bryant on rhyme and alliteration, found that whilst reading and spelling seem to develop independently in the first two years, thereafter a change occurs and the two processes definitely seem to facilitate one another. As they note:

It is probably a short intellectual step from knowing that 'light', 'fight', 'sight' and 'tight' all end in the same sound, to understanding that that is why they all share a common spelling pattern.

Equally fascinating and significant is what Bryant found when working with Bradley. They clearly established that sensitivity to rhyme and alliteration in 4 and 5-year-old non-readers correlates closely with spelling ability three or more years later. A well-planned and carefully structured phonics programme will benefit not only younger children but older ones too. Older children who need additional support with reading often benefit from a structured and organised phonemic emphasis on spelling.

Word morphology

Roots and affixes

Morphology is concerned with the parts of the word that carry meaning, most commonly roots or stems, and their relevant suffixes and prefixes. Understanding how the 'bits fit together' improves children's chances of spelling a word correctly. The word *unnecessary* is notoriously difficult to remember, but realising that it is composed of the root *necessary* and the prefix **un** will help clear the first hurdle.

When children are learning the rules of English spelling, it will help them to understand the morphology of the words in question. For example, to understand how to spell the adverb *happily*, it helps to know that it comprises the frequently used suffix **ly** and the root *happy*, in which the **y** has followed the rule and been changed to an **i**.

An understanding of morphology can also help with spelling compound words and contractions. Many words used by young writers are compound (e.g. *sometimes, something, outside, football* and *birthday*) or contractions (e.g. *don't* and *didn't*). Once children are clear about how these words are constructed from their 'base' words, then problems of remembering where to put the apostrophe and which letters are omitted begin to melt away.

Etymology

A living language

A long history of language influxes since the Anglo-Saxon era has led English to develop into the form we speak and write today. Latin (together with its own Greek influences) had been introduced with the Romans and subsequently many other language 'importations' have come to contribute to our modern English words and spelling. Not only is this fascinating for children to discover, but a recognition of the impact of the specific letter strings on our spelling, such as **phy** from Greek, can also be helpful.

Syllabification

Useful chunks

Morphology and syllabification are different from one another. Whilst morphology relates to meaning, syllabification relates to the speech 'impulses' of a word. The two should not be confused, for they can be, and very often are, quite different. A good example is the word *development*. Morphologically the word comprises the root *develop* and the suffix **ment**. However, when split into speech impulses, or syllables, it might be split *de/vel/op/ment*.

Both morphology and syllabification play an important part in *Nelson Spelling*, but it helps to be aware of the important distinction between them. Syllables often comprise useful 'chunks' of words that children can recall more easily than strings of individual letters.

Semantics and syntax

Significance of meaning

An awareness of semantics and syntax (word meaning) becomes significant in such contexts as deciding between old favourites such as the homophones *their* and *there*, and later in whether or when to spell *practice* with a **c** or an **s**.

Some other issues

As many teachers know, most children enjoy working in an environment where spelling is supported and taught, but it is important to strike a sensible balance to make best use of pupils' and teachers' time. A school spelling policy needs to take account of a spelling scheme, the supporting resources, and the clear recognition by the children of when accurate spelling matters and when it is less important.

Working through the carefully graded sequence of units in *Nelson Spelling* will provide a sound foundation, but it is also important to sensitively correct errors in children's work, and take the opportunity they present for diagnosis and further teaching. You will also want to have spontaneous spelling lessons, for example picking up on a particular letter string, or words connected to a theme or subject.

The role of the teacher

In a busy classroom, it is impossible to supply every child with 'spellings' at the moment of need. Children therefore need to see their teacher as a support and 'partner'.

Correcting errors and public presentation

When you look at children's draft pieces of work, you should acknowledge positively any reasonable attempts at spelling. This is the time to correct any errors, because you also need to make it clear that quality control matters when writing for public presentation. The definition of 'going public' needs to be understood by everyone, and will certainly include work for display, and in any books which will potentially have an audience, such as other pupils, parents, other teachers, inspectors and school governors. You will need to encourage children to take pride in well-presented work.

Looking for patterns of difficulty

It is important to be constantly alert to patterns of spelling difficulty. If a type of error recurs, you might want to give children the appropriate unit in *Nelson Spelling*, even if this happens to be out of sequence. Alternatively, you might prefer to provide a list of similar words with the same letter pattern for the child to learn and practise. For most patterns, these lists can be found in the Supporting word lists given in each unit in this Teacher's Book.

Frequently occurring difficulties are regularly highlighted as a result of the end of key stage assessments which, for example, have noted:

At KS1 (age 7) children need to:

- distinguish between long and short vowels in single syllable words
- identify separate phonemes in words of different length
- apply knowledge of visual patterns as well as phonics to attempt unfamiliar words
- understand how adding endings to words can affect the spelling of the word stem, e.g. **ing**, **ed**, **er**
- learn to spell common words where there are different ways of representing the vowel digraphs, e.g. *brake, break*
- learn how to analyse words of more than one syllable using knowledge of morphemic structure.

At KS2 (age 11) it was noted that children should:

- use their knowledge of word roots to ensure the correct spelling of unstressed vowels, e.g. *vanish/vaneshing; injure/injered*
- learn ways to check their accuracy when using prefixes and suffixes, e.g. check pronunciation of *swimming/swiming, regardless/regardles*.

Supporting independent spelling

Wall displays

We should constantly be seeking to help children achieve independence in spelling. 'Spelling support' should be a permanent feature of every writing area in every classroom or work area. Especially for younger age groups, it is useful to provide word lists, probably on the wall, of difficult words which have a high frequency. Lists of such words are given on pages 26–27 of this book. Word lists from other subjects across the curriculum can also be posted on the wall. The wall display might also feature one or more of the letter patterns which have been the focus of *Nelson Spelling* units recently studied.

Dictionaries and thesauruses

Dictionaries, word books and thesauruses will be useful for many children, but they will only be effective if children are confident and competent in using them. *Nelson Spelling* gives some opportunities for basic dictionary skills, but there is no substitute for constant practice, especially when a child or group has a few minutes to spare.

Using computers

If children are using a computer programme that has a spell-checking facility, they must use it to check the spellings. Not all errors will have been remedied, but most will - and children will have picked up the right attitude to spelling accurately. Word processing can also be used as an extension to other spelling reference resources.

Home-school links

As with reading, spelling is one of the areas where home support can enhance the effectiveness and speed of learning. Great care is needed when briefing parents: one-to-one support can be invaluable, but too much pressure of the wrong sort can become counter-productive.

Taking spellings home

Each unit in *Nelson Spelling* has a Words to Learn list, which relates closely to the pupil book pages. We recommend that children take copies of the words home to learn and that they should be tested regularly so that a pattern and purpose can become established. Without this checking and testing, the drive to learn the spellings will lose its momentum.

Some schools allow children to take home the pupil books, each unit of work potentially providing a self-contained 'homework' package. Again this should only be done if properly explained beforehand, and then monitored.

On-going support

Other ways in which parent support can be helpful in an on-going way include:

- calling attention to other words that have a similar letter string to those recently practiced – especially in environmental print contexts
- always being available to write down words needed in the course of written work at home – then testing it using the 'Look, Say, Cover, Write, Check' method
- praising good effort in spelling, especially if the error is a phonemically 'reasonable' attempt, before correcting any error
- playing spelling games, such as finding small words within longer words and collecting as many words as possible with a given letter string.

KEY SPELLING RULES

The majority of spelling rules can most immediately be understood from an appreciation of morphology (roots, suffixes and prefixes, contractions, compound words, plural constructions) and etymology (origins, meanings, foreign words). These are progressively introduced, developed and revised alongside the teaching of the regular patterns sound/letter correspondences.

The following list, whilst not exclusive, represents for the benefit of the teacher the main useful rules. It is suggested that these might be introduced in particular circumstances with individual children, though on occasions it may be appropriate to build a class or group lesson around a particular rule.

The only sure rule is that nearly every spelling rule has its exceptions! Nevertheless, as a knowledge of rules can improve the odds of spelling a word correctly, they certainly have their place.

General rules

1. **q** is never written without **u** (queen).

2. No English words end with **v** and very few end with **i** or **j**.

3. 'ee' or 'i' sounds at the end of a word are usually represented by **y**.

4. The /k/ sound after a short vowel is written **ck** (except multisyllable words ending in **ic**).

5. **i** comes before **e** (when the sound is 'ee') (piece), except after **c** (receive; ceiling; receipt) or when the sound is not 'ee' (eight; reign; heir).

6. If nouns and verbs are formed from the same root the noun usually ends in **ce** and the verb in **se** (e.g. practice/practise; advice/advise; licence/license).

Making plurals

1. To make the plural form of most nouns, we just add **s** (goat/goats; shop/shops).

2. To make a plural if the noun ends with **s**, **x**, **sh** or **ch** we add **es** (bus/buses; bush/bushes).

3. To make the plural if the noun ends in a consonant + **y**, we change **y** to **i** and add **es** (baby/babies).

4. To make the plural of a noun that ends in a vowel + **y**, we just add **s** (day/days).

5. To make the plural of a noun that ends in **f** or **fe**, we normally change the **f** or **fe** to **v** and add **es** (wolf/wolves; wife/wives).

6. To make the plural of a noun that ends in **o**, we normally add **es** (hero/heroes; volcano/volcanoes), unless it ends in **oo**, or is a music word, or is a shortened form (cuckoo/cuckoos; cello/cellos; photo/photos).

Using suffixes

1. To add a suffix when a word ends with **e**: drop the **e** if the suffix begins with a vowel or is **y** (ice/icing/icy) keep the **e** if the suffix begins with a consonant (wake/wakeful). Some exceptions: true/truly; argue/argument; due/duly.

2. To add a suffix **able** or **ous** to a word that ends in **ce** or **ge**, retain the **e** to keep the **c** or **g** soft (notice/noticeable; manage/manageable; outrage/outrageous).

3. To add a suffix to a short word, or a word where the last syllable is stressed, look at the letter before the last:

   - if it's a single vowel we normally double the last letter before adding the suffix (hop/hopping/hopped; transmit/transmitter).

   - if it's not a single vowel we normally just add the suffix (sing/singing; read/reading; profit/profited).

Note: **w**, **x** and **y** are never doubled.

4. To add a suffix when a word ends with **y** (that sounds 'ee'), change the **y** to an **i** before adding the suffix (ugly/ugliness).

5. **ul** or **il** at the end of a word only have one **l** (spoonful; until).

6. **able** is a five-times more frequent suffix than **ible**, especially if the antonym (opposite) begins with **un** (reliable/unreliable; resistible/ irresistible).

Using prefixes

1. To add a prefix – just do it! (un+sure/unsure; mis+spelt/misspelt; im+moral/immoral). Don't adjust for double letters!

2. **al** at the beginning of a word only has one **l** (also; always).

WORD FREQUENCY TABLES

Several tables indicating the frequency of words used by children have been researched, but a certain amount of care needs to be given to their application in the context of writing and spelling.

The more useful lists in the current context are those that have been specifically derived from the words children write or speak, such as those produced by Dee Reid and Bridie Raban. Not surprisingly there is a fair degree of correlation between such lists as these and the lists based on the words children read, such as that produced by Masterson, Stuart, Dixon and Lovejoy (Children's Printed Word Database, 2003), the 'Key Words' of McNally and Murray and the 'Basic Word List' of Dolch, subsequently revised and updated. However, there are also some differences, so for obvious reasons this course has been more alert to the words children use in their writing than in their reading. Nevertheless, the influences of all these lists will be seen in the selections made. The divergences between the lists tend to be more pronounced in the later stages. As is demonstrated in the following charts, the early stages lists of words required for reading and writing are reasonably similar.

The selection of words is also driven in part by the words required for schools in England to teach, as listed in the National Curriculum for English (2014).

12 words represent 25% of all words read by early readers

Eleven of these twelve words are also to be found in the top 20 words used in writing, with only *that* falling outside.

The numerals denote the position in the *Word for Word* writing frequency tables below.

'Regular'		'Irregular'	
and	1	a	3
in	10	he	8
is	19	I	4
it	7	of	16
that	34	the	2
		to	5
		was	6

The next 20 words represent approximately a further 10% of all words read.

Note: The majority fall within the top 50 required for writing.

'Regular'	'Irregular'
as 79	all 42
at 43	be 72
but 27	are 49
had 18	for 30
him 51	have 38
his 37	one 26
not 46	said 17
on 15	so 24
	they 13
	we 9
	you 23

These two charts demonstrate that teaching by focusing on these words, in terms both of reading and spelling, will have been time very well spent.

There are other useful lists, devised with a didactic purpose. Two notable examples which have helped inform the selection of words used in *Nelson Spelling* are those based on the work of Schonell, and subsequently revised, and the Morris-Montessori Word List, created from the linguistically-based *Phonics 44* system devised by Dr Morris.

Nelson Spelling is linguistically structured and developmental, and the course has been so arranged to ensure that most of the early words required in writing are covered in the first units, especially at Levels 1 and 2. Inevitably, though, there are some words that need to be addressed slightly earlier than they would naturally appear in the sequence of spelling patterns and spelling word families in the course.

The 50 words most frequently written by 7/8-year-olds:

and	was	went	of	she	one	with	go	saw	not
the	it	my	said	when	but	day	his	all	like
a	he	they	had	you	me	out	have	at	very
I	we	then	is	so	up	that	came	her	are
to	in	on	got	there	for	some	were	home	get

The next 200 words most frequently written by 7/8-year-olds:

him	do	tree	long	another	ear	cave	suddenly
down	after	over	looked	heard	things	trees	wind
back	what	again	too	king	witch	woke	dinner
mum	as	yes	thought	more	something	never	find
them	dog	from	by	playing	know	tried	sad
because	off	us	walk	fire	think	best	run
put	see	boy	cat	white	give	bit	turned
into	people	away	upon	garden	story	dark	clothes
will	two	this	who	nice	walked	end	football
did	come	old	way	friends	castle	always	top
man	our	found	dragon	don't	didn't	baby	wanted
little	school	lived	red	oh	food	boat	why
time	once	play	round	take	opened	lot	sunflower
big	if	girl	mummy	hair	park	wood	around
house	door	told	well	three	giant	daddy	bird
called	ran	fell	where	help	gone	green	head
would	no	morning	gave	here	room	it's	sea
dad	next	started	lots	how	sister	lady	thing
their	took	other	want	played	asked	soon	gold
has	good	water	friend	eyes	blue	fair	hole
can	an	your	children	shop	or	its	walking
be	about	am	make	balloon	outside	men	ever
could	night	first	tea	black	bad	Mr	let
going	name	just	through	Christmas	brother	only	lost
bed	made	now	car	look	sleep	snowman	mother

If, in addition to working through the units in Levels 1 and 2, the following groups of words are taught, the pupils will systematically have covered all the 250 most frequently used words by 7/8-year-olds by the end of Level 1.

1	2	3	4	5	6	7
story	mummy	eyes	who	asked	castle	tried
baby	daddy	clothes	where	after	giant	opened
lady	little		were	never	people	
only	dinner				because	8
	suddenly					snowman
						sunflower

STARTER LEVEL

As we all know too well, decoding skills for reading and encoding skills for writing/spelling develop at different rates. Nevertheless, the core of the early encoding skills required for the development of competency in spelling fit alongside a synthetic phonics approach to reading. These Starter Level workbooks provide a secure structure and are sequenced to complement the work children will have undertaken for their letter-sound recognition work.

The Starter workbooks can be used and paced according to class, group or individual requirements. Some schools might choose to use them for take-home work.

Workbook Starter A Scope and Sequence

Page	Focus
2	s
3	t
4	p
5	a
6	i
7	n
8	m
9	d
10	cvc words
11	cvc words
12	g
13	o
14	c
15	k
16	cvc words
17	cvc words
18	ck
19	e
20	u

Page	Focus
21	r
22	cvc words
23	cvc words
24	h
25	b
26	f/ff
27	l/ll
28	ss
29	cvc words
30	cvc words
31	j
32	v
33	w
34	x
35	y
36	z/zz
37	q/qu
38	High-frequency words
39	High-frequency words

Workbook Starter B Scope and Sequence

Page	Focus
2	ch
3	ch
4	sh
5	sh
6	ng
7	th
8	ai
9	ai
10	ee
11	ee
12	igh
13	igh
14	oa
15	oa
16	oo (long)
17	oo (long)
18	oo (short)
19	oo (short)
20	ar

Page	Focus
21	ar
22	or
23	or
24	ur/ ure
25	ur/ ure
26	ow
27	ow
28	oi
29	oi
30	ear
31	ear
32	air
33	air
34	er
35	er
36	a-e
37	i-e
38	o-e
39	u-e

Book 1A Scope and Sequence

Unit	Pupil Book Focus	Pupil Book Extra	Pupil Book Extension	Workbook Focus	Workbook Extra	Resource Book Focus	Resource Book Extension
1	**letters** ordering letters	identify missing letters in letter strings	ordering words by initial letter	initial letters of words	identifying initial letters of objects	join the dots in alphabetical order	making cvc words; alphabetical order
2	**short a e i o u** medial vowels in cvc words	writing rhyming patterns	copying *and* pattern; writing *and* words	medial vowels in cvc words	identifying cvc words within words	matching cvc words; simple cvc rhyming	cvcc endings: cloze activity; rhyming patterns
3	**sh th** initial and final digraphs	simple cloze activity	word quiz	matching words to pictures	identifying words in a picture	*sh* patterns; rhyming patterns	*sh* + *ing* and *ed*
4	**ck nk** adding *ack eck ink unk* to make words	*ick ock uck ank ink* patterns;	adding *ing* to *eck, ock, ick* & *ink* words	matching words to pictures	identifying rhyming words	identifying *ck/nk* words; rhyming words	rhyming patterns; vowels; cloze activity
5	**ch tch** initial and final positions	sorting jumbled letters into words	listing words; simple cloze activity	matching words to pictures	identifying words in a picture	*ch* patterns; *ch* word fan ; word matching	word building; *which* & *watch*
6	**s es** key word matching	*s* plurals	*es* after *s, x, sh* and *ch* (plurals and 3rd person singular)	matching key words to pictures	cloze activity	copying simple plurals	plurals with both *s* and *es*
7	**ing ed er** word matching with *ing*	adding *ing/ed/er*	final letter doubling with *ing*	matching words to pictures	choosing words to match pictures	adding *ing*	sentences with *ing;* final letter doubling rule
8	**er est** key word matching	adding *er* to create comparative	adding *est* to create superlative	matching key words to pictures	cloze activity based on a picture	matching words with pictures	letter patterns; word fans
9	**ll ff ss zz** key word matching; adding ing	copying target words	making plurals	matching key words to pictures	identifying and writing rhyming words	copying words; rhyming patterns	adding *ed* and *ing*
10	**a-e ai ay** a-e word matching	*ail aid ain* rhyming	*ay* quiz	matching words to pictures	cloze activity	*a-e* patterns; rhyming patterns	word matching; cloze activity
11	**ee ea ie e-e** key word matching	*ie* and *e-e* with *ee* sound wordsearch	matching words to pictures and adding *ing*	matching key words to pictures	identifying and writing rhyming words	*ee ea* words; rhyming patterns	word matching; cloze activity
12	**i-e ie igh y** key word matching	word matching with *ing*	'magic' e altering the sound of medial vowels; *-ve* endings	matching key words to pictures	identifying words in a picture	writing words; rhyming patterns	matching words to pictures; key exceptions: *live, give, like*
13	**oa o-e oe ow** copying and finding target words	*oke oast oes ow* rhyming families	long *o* word puzzle	matching key words to pictures	choosing words to match pictures	writing words; rhyming patterns	word sums; cloze activity: *one, gone & some*
14	**oo u-e ue ew** key word matching	word sums	sorting words by *ew oot ue* patterns	word matching	cloze activity	writing words; rhyming patterns	word fan; writing sentences

The darker cells introduce statutory material for this year group in the National Curriculum for England.
The paler cells denote revision of a topic covered in previous years.

Book 1B Scope and Sequence

Unit	Pupil Book Focus	Pupil Book Extra	Pupil Book Extension	Workbook Focus	Workbook Extra	Resource Book Focus	Resource Book Extension
15	*y* endings key word matching	finding root words	cloze activity	word matching	cloze activity	writing words; word sums	word fan; word matching; sentence writing
16	*ar* key word matching	building words with word sums	*ar ark art* rhyming families	word matching	identifying rhyming words	*ar & ark* patterns; rhyming words	cloze activity; key exceptions : *are, care, fare*
17	*oi oy* key word matching	*oi oy* wordsearch	word matching with *ing*	word matching	cloze activity	*oil oin oint oise oy* patterns; rhyming words	word sums; word matching; sentence writing
18	*ear ea* key word matching; *ear* words in a sentence	target word quiz	cloze activity	word matching	identifying words in a sequence of letters	word matching; rhyming words	word matching; cloze activity
19	*er ir ur* key word matching; sentence writing	sorting words by *er ir ur* patterns	*er ir ur* wordsearch	word matching	identifying target words in a picture	word fan; word matching	completing words; writing clues; word puzzle
20	*ou ow* selecting rhyming key words	important *ou* words	sorting long/short *ow* words	word matching	identifying rhyming words	word sums; word matching	completing words; key exceptions; cloze activity
21	*or ore aw au* key word matching; finding target words	cloze activity	target word quiz	word matching	cloze activity	word matching; completing words; rhyming words	crossword puzzles
22	*air ear are* key word matching	sorting words by *air ear are* patterns	building words	word matching	choosing a word to match a picture	*air are* patterns; word sums	cloze activity; quiz
23	*oo* (short) key word matching; sentence writing	*ook ood* patterns	building words with word sums	key word matching	identifying rhyming words	*ook oon* patterns; copying *oo* words	word sums; sorting by rhyme patterns
24	**days of the week** simple questions based on *Solomon Grundy* nursery rhyme	cloze activity on origins of names of days of week	quiz on origins of names of months	ordering days of the week	writing simple diary entries for each day	days of the week quiz activity	ordering months; sorting jumbled letters into words
25	**compound words syllables** key word matching	building compound words	dividing words into syllables	key word matching	completing compound words	word sums with picture clues	compound word puzzle; sentences; syllables
26	*wh ph* key word matching	target word quiz	building compound words	word matching	cloze activity	*wh ph* letter patterns; word sums; word matching	word matching; writing questions with *wh*
27	*un* beginnings key word matching	finding root words	using *un* prefix to create antonyms	word matching	identifying target words in a picture	un words; word matching	word fan; word matching
28	**alphabet** identifying missing letters; quiz on letter position	putting letters in alphabetical order	putting words in alphabetical order	writing the alphabet in capital letters	alphabetical order quiz	identifying initial letters of words	putting letters and words in alphabetical order

LEARNING TARGETS

Pupil Book: Focus
to identify the next letter in the alphabet

Pupil Book: Extra
to identify missing letters in letter strings

Pupil Book: Extension
to identify the initial letter of words

Workbook: Focus
to identify the initial letter of key words

Workbook: Extra
to identify the initial letter of objects seen in pictures

Resource sheet: Focus
to practise identifying the order of letters in the alphabet

Resource sheet: Extension
to focus awareness on the vowel letters; to undertake initial letter alphabetical ordering of three-word groups

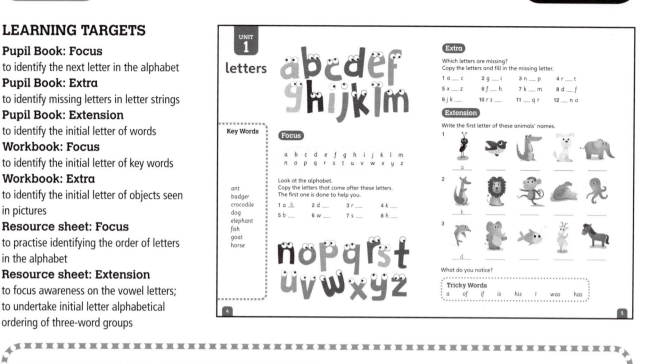

BACKGROUND NOTES AND SUGGESTIONS

The unit gives an opportunity to revise earlier work on the alphabet and the sounds that letters commonly represent. However, this unit enables the teacher to focus work on the names (as opposed to the phoneme represented) of each letter.

The children will enjoy the classic, simple alphabet songs. This sort of activity will be good preparation for the work, which in many cases will need significant support, and even to be undertaken orally. Also, make use of alphabet friezes, play simple card games involving letter/picture matching.

Another popular activity with a group of children is to help them arrange themselves in a line according to the alphabetical ordering of their first names and then their surnames.

Pupil Book answers

Focus

1 b	2 e
3 s	4 l
5 c	6 x
7 t	8 i

Extra

1 a b c	2 g h i
3 n o p	4 r s t
5 x y z	6 f g h
7 k l m	8 d e f
9 j k l	10 r s t
11 p q r	12 m n o

Extension

1 a b c d e
2 k l m n o
3 d e f g h

The children should notice that the words are in alphabetical order as determined by their initial letter.

Workbook answers

Focus

1 **b**adger	2 **h**orse
3 **f**ish	4 **c**rocodile
5 **d**og	6 **g**oat
7 **a**nt	8 **e**lephant

Extra

1 t	2 d	3 p
4 f	5 b	6 z
7 s	8 g	9 m
10 a	11 w	12 i

Resource sheet answers

Focus

The children join the dots to make the picture of an owl and a cat.

Extension

A 1 hat hit hot hut
   2 bed bad bid bod bud
   3 bag beg big bog bug
   4 bat bet bit but
   5 put pat pet pit pot
   6 hum ham hem him

B 1 ant boy cat
   2 axe bag cup
   3 apple banana carrot
   4 fan man ran
   5 bad had sad
   6 dish fish wish

Supporting word lists

The following lists of simple cvc rhyming words will be useful in working with the children on arranging words in alphabetical order according to initial letters. (More extensive lists are available in Unit 2.)

bad Dad had mad pad sad
an can fan man Nan pan ran van

bet jet let met net pet set vet wet yet
bed fed led red wed

bin din fin pin sin tin win
dip hip nip pip sip zip

hop lop mop pop top
bog cog dog fog hog jog log

but cut gut hut jut nut rut
bug dug hug jug mug rug tug

LEARNING TARGETS

Pupil Book: Focus

to complete simple cvc words with mixed medial vowels

Pupil Book: Extra

to collect and write short words with common letter sequences

Pupil Book: Extension

to sort, copy and use words with the common **and** letter pattern

Workbook: Focus

to complete simple cvc words with mixed medial vowels

Workbook: Extra

to identify simple cvc words in longer words

Resource sheet: Focus

to differentiate simple cvc letter sequences

Resource sheet: Extension

to complete a simple cloze activity using **ell**, **ill** and **oll** words; to identify and sort **ell**, **iss**, **uff**, **iff** and **ess** words

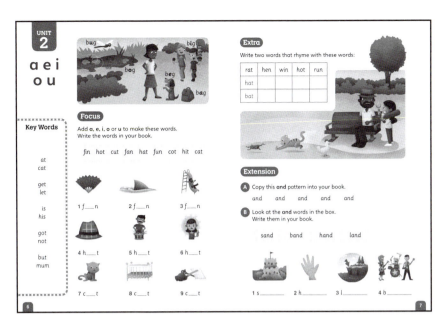

BACKGROUND NOTES AND SUGGESTIONS

All the key words in this revision unit are high-frequency words, so particular attention might usefully be devoted to ensuring these are thoroughly mastered.

As well as focusing on simple cvc pattern words, the Extension activities include short vowel **ll**, **ff** and **ss** words.

Pupil Book answers

Focus

1 fan	**2** fin	**3** fun
4 hat	**5** hit	**6** hot
7 cat	**8** cot	**9** cut

Extra

Teacher to check individual answers

Extension

1 sand **2** hand **3** land **4** band

Workbook answers

Focus

1 man	**2** cat	**3** fan
4 bed	**5** leg	**6** ten
7 hit	**8** fin	**9** bin
10 box	**11** dog	**12** hot
13 fun	**14** sun	**15** cut

Extra

1 pen	**2** car
3 hen	**4** cat
5 hut	**6** men
7 ten	**8** pan

Resource sheet answers

Focus

Ⓐ bed tap cup

Ⓑ cat mat pat
ten men hen
dog log fog

Extension

Ⓐ Jill/Bill and Bill/Jill huffed and puffed their way to the top of the hill. The school bell rang down in the village. They peeped through the door of the old mill. Suddenly, the top step gave way and Jill fell down. What a loud yell she gave! She was not hurt, but she broke her new doll.

Ⓑ

tell	kiss	puff	cliff	mess
well	hiss	huff	stiff	less
sell	miss	gruff	sniff	dress

Supporting word lists

bad Dad had mad pad sad
am jam Pam Sam
an can fan man Nan pan ran van
bap cap gap lap map nap rap
sap tap yap
at bat cat fat hat sat mat rat pat
bag gag hag lag nag rag sag tag wag
and band hand land sand
*was have
bet met jet let net pet set vet wet yet
bed fed led wed Ted red
peg beg keg leg
hen ten men pen den Ben
mend send
went sent tent bent dent rent lent vent
yes yet
*he me we

it bit fit hit lit pit sit wit
is his
bin din fin pin sin tin win
bid did hid kid lid rid
big dig fig jig rig wig
bib rib
mix fix

dip sip nip zip pip hip
ill bill fill hill kill mill pill till will
*give live

top hop mop lop pop
dog bog fog log jog cog hog
got hot rot lot tot cot jot not pot
box fox
cod nod rod
cock dock lock mock rock sock
*to do no go so

up cup pup sup
but cut gut hut jut nut rut
Mum hum rum sum
bun fun gun run sun
us bus
bug hug mug jug rug dug tug
rub cub tub
buck duck luck muck suck tuck
*put upon

bell fell sell tell well yell
ill bill fill hill kill mill
pill till will
doll
gull hull

LEARNING TARGETS

Pupil Book: Focus
to complete simple ccvc and cvcc words with
an initial or final **sh** or **th** digraph

Pupil Book: Extra
to undertake a simple cloze activity using
words with an initial or final **sh** or **th** digraph

Pupil Book: Extension
to match **sh** or **th** words and clues

Workbook: Focus
to match **sh** or **th** words and pictures

Workbook: Extra
to identify **sh** and **th** words in a picture

Resource sheet: Focus
to copy **sh** words and match rhyming words

Resource sheet: Extension
to add inflectional endings to **sh** words

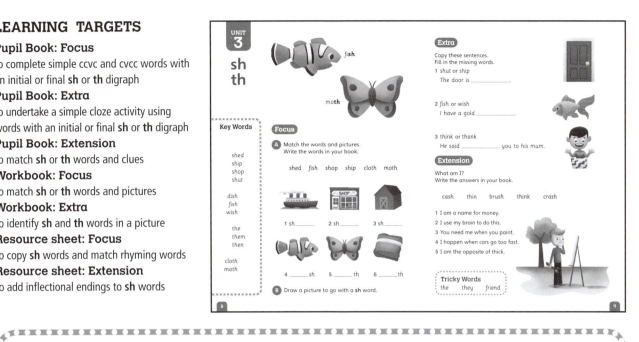

BACKGROUND NOTES AND SUGGESTIONS

Children get real satisfaction from mastering these 'early' consonant digraphs, which lend themselves to numerous games and word-collecting activities.

It is worth giving special attention to *shall* and *wash*, two significant **sh** words, both of which have an irregular feature at this level.

th has two pronunciations, as may be deduced from the grouping of the words in the *Supporting word lists*. However the difference rarely causes confusion with spelling.

When sounding both **sh** and **th**, help the children to avoid introducing an 'intrusive' vowel – both **sh** and **th** sounds are made by allowing air to pass gently from the mouth; they are not pronounced **sher** or **ther**. If this can be established it helps later when children are sounding words to themselves to support their attempts at spelling an unfamiliar word.

Pupil Book answers

Focus

A 1 ship   2 shop   3 shed
    4 fish   5 moth   6 cloth

B Teacher to check individual answers

Extra
1 shut   2 fish   3 thank

Extension
1 cash   2 think   3 brush
4 crash   5 thin

Workbook answers

Focus
1 shed   2 shelf   3 ship
4 dish   5 fish   6 rash
7 moth   8 sixth   9 thin
10 shop   11 cloth   12 shell

Extra
shed, ship, dish, shell, fish, moth,
cloth, shelf

Resource sheet answers

Focus
A Children should copy the letters
and words.

B sip - ship
hop - shop
sell - shell
self - shelf
hut - shut
hot - shot

Extension
A mashing   mashed
brushing   brushed

B *happening now*   *happened yesterday*
dashing   dashed
splashing   splashed
fishing   fished
crashing   crashed
crushing   crushed
smashing   smashed

Supporting word lists
sh-
sham shall shack
shed shelf shell
shin ship shift
shop shot shock
shut

-sh
ash bash cash dash gash lash mash
rash sash (wash)

mesh
dish fish wish
cosh posh
hush rush
two-letter blend +sh
clash flash slash crash smash splash
flesh fresh
swish
blush flush plush slush brush crush

th
the them then
there their
than that this

thin thing think
thick thrill
throb
thud thumb thump
thrust thank

th
with
depth
fifth sixth tenth width
moth cloth

LEARNING TARGETS

Pupil Book: Focus

to complete simple words, selecting either the **ack** or **eck**, or the **ink** or **unk** letter sequences

Pupil Book: Extra

to match words with the target patterns to objects in a picture

Pupil Book: Extension

to match **ink**, **eck**, **ock** and **ick** words to complete present tense verbs

Workbook: Focus

to match target pattern words to pictures

Workbook: Extra

to identify rhyming words

Resource sheet: Focus

to copy and identify **ck** and **nk** words

Resource sheet: Extension

to identify rhyming words;
to add the medial short vowel letters to **ck** and **nk** words

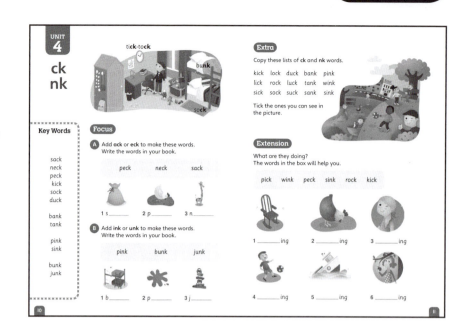

BACKGROUND NOTES AND SUGGESTIONS

Interchanging the vowel (e.g. *pack peck pick puck*) is a useful way of helping the children recognise the short vowel component of the word. As a group or class activity, try finding how many word groups of this type can be made.

ck and **nk** are useful for practising inflectional endings as they do not require modification, the **ing** or **ed** simply being added. Also, a useful discussion can be had on what **ing** or **ed** added to a word tells us (about the tense of the verb).

Sometimes it can be hard for children to know when to use **c**, **k** or **ck**. The /k/ sound is spelt as **k** before **e**, **i** and **y**. The **ck** and **nk** spellings are usually found at the end of a root word.

Pupil Book answers

Focus

(A) **1** sack   **2** peck   **3** neck

(B) **1** bunk   **2** pink   **3** junk

Extra

kick, duck, bank, pink, lick, rock, wink, sick, sock, suck, sank, sink

Extension

1 rocking   **2** pecking   **3** winking
4 kicking   **5** sinking   **6** picking

Workbook answers

Focus

1 sack   **2** duck
3 neck   **4** junk
5 bunk   **6** sink
7 kick   **8** ink
9 sock   **10** tank
11 peck   **12** bank

Extra

1 back, sack, pack
2 neck, deck, peck
3 bank, tank, sank
4 duck, luck, suck
5 pink, wink, sink

6 lock, rock, sock
7 lick, sick, kick
8 bunk, sunk, junk

Resource sheet answers

Focus

(A) back peck kick rock
bank sink tank sunk

(B) lick sock sink tank

Extension

(A) sank - bank
link   - sink/rink
suck   - duck
pink   - sink/rink
sack   - back
rock   - sock

(B) **1** suck   **2** pink
3 sank   **4** pick
5 bank   **6** wink
7 neck   **8** lock
9 tank   **10** rank

(C) **1** pink   **2** bank   **3** sank
4 suck   **5** neck

Supporting word lists

back lack pack rack sack tack
deck neck peck
kick lick pick sick tick wick
dock lock rock sock
duck luck muck suck tuck

bank rank sank tank
ink link mink pink rink sink wink
bunk junk sunk

LEARNING TARGETS

Pupil Book: Focus
to match **ch** and **tch** words to pictures

Pupil Book: Extra
to rearrange jumbled letters to make **ch** and **tch** words

Pupil Book: Extension
to introduce the letter pattern **tch**;
to practise the **tch** spelling pattern using a cloze activity

Workbook: Focus
to match **ch** and **tch** words to pictures

Workbook: Extra
to identify **ch** and **tch** words in a picture

Resource sheet: Focus
to practise using the initial **ch** in a word fan

Resource sheet: Extension
to complete words using the given consonant digraphs; to learn the 'special words' *which* and *watch*

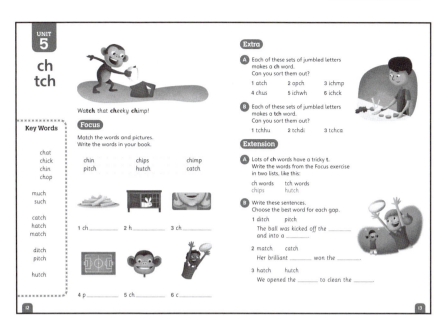

BACKGROUND NOTES AND SUGGESTIONS

Two longer words, not included in the activities but worth teaching at this stage because of their relatively high frequency are *children* and *Christmas*.

Pupils may spot that *Christmas* has a silent **h**; the initial **ch** does not operate as a consonant digraph.

tch is common for the phoneme normally spelt **ch** when following a single vowel letter (e.g. c*a*tch). Important exceptions to this are *rich, which, such, much*.

When sounding **ch** (and **th** and **sh** digraphs also), help the children to avoid introducing an 'intrusive' vowel. The **ch** sound is made by allowing air to pass gently from the mouth; they are not pronounced **cher**. If this can be established it helps later when children are sounding words to themselves to support their attempts at spelling an unfamiliar word.

Pupil Book answers

Focus

1 chips	**2** hutch	**3** chin
4 pitch	**5** chimp	**6** catch

Extra

A 1 chat 2 chop 3 chimp
    4 such 5 which 6 chick

B 1 hutch 2 ditch 3 catch

Extension

A
ch words	**tch** words
chips	hutch
chin	pitch
chimp	catch

B 1 The ball was kicked off the <u>pitch</u> and into a <u>ditch</u>.
  2 Her brilliant <u>catch</u> won the <u>match</u>.
  3 We opened the <u>hatch</u> to clean the <u>hutch</u>.

Workbook answers

Focus

1 chimp	**2** chin
3 chop	**4** hutch
5 match	**6** pitch
7 chest	**8** patch

9 chips	**10** itch
11 catch	**12** chick

Extra

chin, chimp, hutch, catch, chick, chop, match, chips

Resource sheet answers

Focus

A Children should copy the letter pattern.

B chat chick chip chill chin chop chimp chuck

chick chip chin chimp

Extension

A 1 chum   2 ship
    3 thin   4 chimps
    5 throne   6 rich
    7 fishing 8 sheet
    9 moth   10 teeth

B Teacher to check children's spelling of the special words 'which' and 'watch'.

Teacher to check children's sentences using the special words 'which' and 'watch'.

Supporting word lists

ch
chap chat
chest check chess
chin chip chit chill chick chimp chop
chug chum chuck chunk

ch
rich
much such

tch
batch catch hatch match patch
snatch scratch
fetch sketch stretch
itch ditch hitch pitch stitch
switch
hutch crutch

nch
finch pinch
bench drench trench
bunch lunch munch punch
*which witch watch

LEARNING TARGETS

Pupil Book: Focus
to match key words ending in **s** and **es**
to pictures

Pupil Book: Extra
to secure the basic plural form by adding **s**

Pupil Book: Extension
to form plural nouns by adding **es** to words
with a final **s**, **x**, **sh** or **ch**

Workbook: Focus
to match key words ending in **s** and **es**
to pictures

Workbook: Extra
to complete a simple cloze activity using **s**
and **es** plurals

Resource sheet: Focus
to recognise plural words

Resource sheet: Extension
to make the plural of nouns that end with **s**,
x, **sh** or **ch**

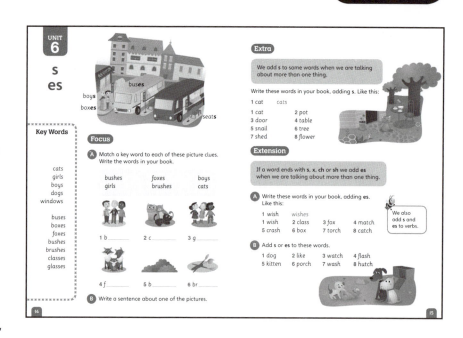

BACKGROUND NOTES AND SUGGESTIONS

The correct formulation of plurals is an important skill for spelling. Fortunately, the vast majority of words conform to a few basic rules and 'sub-rules'. These are introduced here and in later units and then revised throughout the course as opportunities lend themselves.

In this unit, the rules addressed are:

- most nouns, including those that end in **e**, simply add **s**
- for words that end with **s**, **x**, **ch** or **sh** add **es**

For some children at this stage it will be easier to learn that if the plural ends with an extra 'beat' then it is probably spelt with an **es** rather than a simple **s**, e.g. compare *cats* and *cat/ches*.

You might wish to discuss the fact that adding **s** or **es** can make a plural noun and/or a third-person singular verb, e.g. two rocks (noun); she rocks (verb).

Pupil Book answers

Focus

A 1 boys   2 cats   3 girls   4 foxes   5 bushes   6 brushes

B Teacher to check individual answers

Extra

1 cats   2 pots   3 doors   4 tables   5 snails   6 trees   7 sheds   8 flowers

Extension

A 1 wishes   2 classes   3 foxes   4 matches   5 crashes   6 boxes   7 torches   8 catches

B 1 dogs   2 likes   3 watches   4 flashes   5 kittens   6 porches   7 washes   8 hutches

Workbook answers

Focus

1 dogs   2 boys   3 bushes   4 buses   5 windows   6 brushes

7 girls   8 boxes   9 cats   10 glasses   11 foxes

Extra

1 The girl plays with the boys.
2 My teacher lost her pens.
3 The balls are put in boxes.
4 The foxes ran after the ducks.
5 The roads are busy with buses.
6 You pick berries from bushes.

Resource sheet answers

Focus

A dogs girls boys

B cats boxes brushes trees cars buses

Extension

1 dogs   2 buses   3 rakes
4 peaches   5 ants   6 foxes
7 hills   8 brushes   9 ducks
10 glasses   11 trees   12 matches
13 fingers   14 sixes   15 bounces
16 arches   17 lips   18 dishes
19 rivers   20 boxes

Supporting word lists

Words that take s
There are a great number, including:
game table pen cup pond book
school teacher

Some words that take es
ash bush glass inch watch brush dish
kiss tax box grass pass bus gas
sandwich fox class

Some words ending in vowel + y
donkey monkey key day display toy
delay ray boy valley trolley chimney
turkey journey abbey alley jockey

LEARNING TARGETS

Pupil Book: Focus

to match present tense **ing** verbs to pictures

Pupil Book: Extra

to write present (**ing**) and past (**ed**) tenses of the same verbs and use **er** to make nouns

Pupil Book: Extension

to write verbs which require final consonant to be doubled before inflectional ending is added

Workbook: Focus

to match present tense **ing** verbs to pictures

Workbook: Extra

to choose present tense **ing** and **ed** verbs to match pictures

Resource sheet: Focus

to add **ing** to a selection of verbs

Resource sheet: Extension

to add **ing** to a selection of verbs before using them in sentences; to practise doubling the final letter before adding **ing**

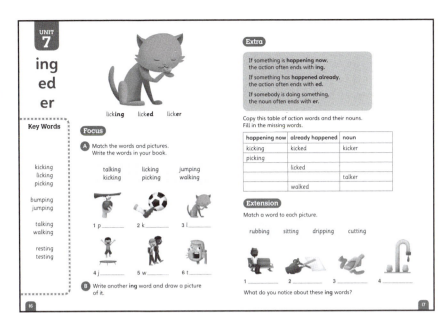

BACKGROUND NOTES AND SUGGESTIONS

In this unit the focus is on the letter pattern **ing** when it forms an inflectional ending (as opposed to the consonant digraph **ng** as in words like *bang*). When introducing the concept, try to avoid using root verbs that require modifications when adding **ing** e.g. dropping the final **e** as in *race/racing*, or where the final consonant needs to be doubled, e.g. *shop/shopping*. However, the notion of final consonant doubling is introduced in the Extension sections. (Note, this occurs in short words when the last letter is a single consonant following a short vowel.) If the verb ends in two consonant letters the suffix is simply added on.

Pupil Book answers

Focus

A 1 picking 2 kicking 3 licking
    4 jumping 5 walking 6 talking

B Teacher to check individual answers

Extra

happening now	already happened	noun
kicking	kicked	kicker
picking	picked	picker
licking	licked	licker
talking	talked	talker
walking	walked	walker

Extension

1 sitting 2 cutting
3 rubbing 4 dripping

Workbook answers

Focus

1 jumping 2 resting
3 kicking 4 talking
5 lifting 6 bumping
7 picking 8 nesting
9 walking 10 helping
11 mending 12 licking

Extra

jumping
dusted
walking
picking
milked
sending
panting
splashed

Resource sheet answers

Focus

jumping walking talking licking
kicking sleeping eating

Extension

A jumping dusting splashing
    falling licking

B 1 hopping 2 mopping
    3 slipping 4 shopping
    5 clapping 6 running
    7 dripping 8 trotting
    9 swimming 10 trapping

Supporting word lists

Some words to which ing/ed can be added without modification:

act acting pant panting camp camping
land landing stand standing
help helping melt melting bend bending
mend mending send sending
milk milking film filming lift lifting
limp limping list listing
sulk sulking hunt hunting
bump bumping dump dumping
jump jumping dust dusting rust rusting
grunt grunting

Some words to which ing/ed can be added after doubling the final consonant:

bat batting fan fanning pat patting
tap tapping wag wagging clap clapping
flap flapping plan planning slap slapping
grab grabbing get getting let letting
peg pegging set setting wed wedding
dig digging fit fitting hit hitting
rip ripping sip sipping sit sitting
tip tipping win winning clip clipping
flip flipping slip slipping drip dripping
grin grinning trim trimming trip tripping
swim swimming hop hopping
jog jogging mop mopping nod nodding
rob robbing sob sobbing blot blotting
flop flopping plot plotting slot slotting
drop dropping trot trotting but butting
cut cutting hug hugging rub rubbing
run running plug plugging
drum drumming

LEARNING TARGETS

Pupil Book: Focus
to match **er** and **est** words to pictures

Pupil Book: Extra
to create comparative (**er**) words from a range of root words

Pupil Book: Extension
to create superlative (**est**) words from a range of root words

Workbook: Focus
to match **er** and **est** words with pictures

Workbook: Extra
to identify the picture that matches particular comparatives and superlatives

Resource sheet: Focus
to match **er** and **est** words with pictures

Resource sheet: Extension
to complete word fans adding the suffixes **er** and **est**

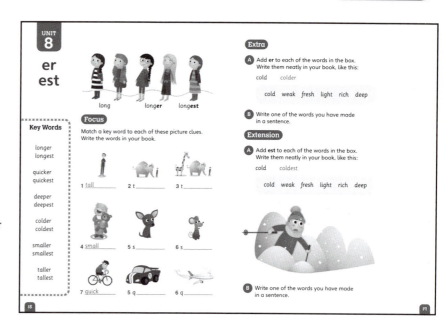

BACKGROUND NOTES AND SUGGESTIONS

For the majority of words, where the adjective ends in two consonant letters, when forming the comparative (**er**) or superlative form (**est**) we just add the suffix (*quicker, quickest*). However, for most words ending in **e** we drop the **e** before adding the suffix (e.g. *later, latest*).

For most short words containing a single short vowel before the final consonant, we double the final consonant (e.g. *bigger, biggest*).

For words ending in **y** we change **y** to **i** before adding the suffix (e.g. *chillier, chilliest*).

It might be possible to extend this work with a few of the children by considering that there are many important exceptions when forming these comparing words, e.g. *good, better, best; far, farther, farthest*. Also, perhaps consider what happens to such base words as *curious, sensible, intelligent* i.e. we use *more* and *most*.

Pupil Book answers

Focus

1 tall	2 taller	3 tallest
4 small	5 smaller	6 smallest
7 quick	8 quicker	9 quickest

Extra

A
cold	colder
weak	weaker
fresh	fresher
light	lighter
rich	richer
deep	deeper

B Teacher to check individual answers

Extension

A
cold	coldest
weak	weakest
fresh	freshest
light	lightest
rich	richest
deep	deepest

B Teacher to check individual answers

Workbook answers

Focus

1 long	2 longer	3 longest
4 small	5 smaller	6 smallest
7 deep	8 deeper	9 deepest
10 tall	11 taller	12 tallest
13 quick	14 quicker	15 quickest

Extra

1 Jess is taller. Meg is tallest.
2 Lucy has longer hair. Meg has the longest hair.
3 Lucy is colder. Jess is coldest.
4 Jess has a smaller bag. Lucy has the smallest bag.

Resource sheet answers

Focus

high	higher	highest
clean	cleaner	cleanest
long	longer	longest
cold	colder	coldest

Extension

A Children should copy the letter pattern.
shorter slower taller deeper higher

B Children should copy the letter pattern.
shortest slowest tallest deepest highest

Supporting word lists

Words simply taking the suffix er or est
straight quick deep weak light cold long proud dull tall rich small

Words with short single vowels
thin fat big hot glum flat sad red

Words with a final e
nice fine wise safe late tame brave rude ripe close

Words with a final y
happy cranky hilly milky frilly chilly floppy spotty fussy dusty lazy crazy rainy sleepy easy greasy icy mighty bony smoky stormy noisy

LEARNING TARGETS

Pupil Book: Focus
to match target double-letter words
to pictures;
to practise adding **ing** to these words

Pupil Book: Extra
to practise writing significant
double-consonant words

Pupil Book: Extension
to practise adding **s** or **es** to these words
to form plural nouns

Workbook: Focus
to match target double-letter words
to pictures

Workbook: Extra
to identify and write rhyming words

Resource sheet: Focus
to copy and write rhyming words

Resource sheet: Extension
to add inflectional endings to words

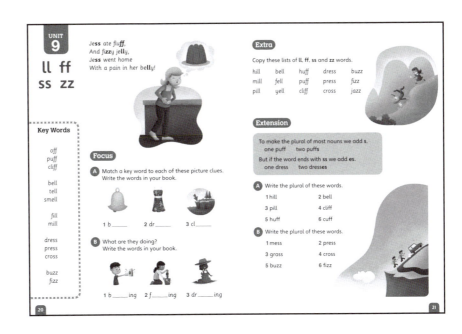

BACKGROUND NOTES AND SUGGESTIONS

There is, of course, no immediately obvious phonological reason for young writers to recognise the need to write a double letter, though it can be explained that double letters representing /f/, /l/, /s/, /z/ and /k/ sounds generally follow short (as opposed to 'long') vowel sounds in short words. There are some exceptions, such as *bus, yes, if*.

Two moderately important words that include **ll** also have an unexpected long vowel – *pull, full*.

A useful discussion can be had on what **ing** or **ed** added to a word tells us.

Pupil Book answers

Focus

A 1 bell   2 dress   3 cliff

B 1 buzzing   2 filling   3 dressing

Extra

Teacher to check the copied words

Extension

A 1 hills   2 bells
    3 pills   4 cliffs
    5 huffs   6 cuffs

B 1 messes   2 presses
    3 grasses   4 crosses
    5 buzzes   6 fizzes

Workbook answers

Focus

1 cliff   2 off
3 puff   4 smell
5 bell   6 tell
7 press   8 dress
9 cross   10 mill
11 fill

Extra

1 mill	hill
2 press	dress
3 sell	bell
4 sniff	cliff
5 hiss	kiss
6 moss	cross
7 cuff	puff
8 drill	frill

Resource sheet answers

Focus

A hill   cliff   ill   dress
    kiss   sniff   mess   doll

B bell   cliff   dress

Extension

A drilled kissed sniffed milled dressed
    1 kissed   2 dressed
    3 milled   4 drilled
    5 sniffed

B drilling   drilled
    kissing   kissed
    sniffing   sniffed
    milling   milled
    dressing   dressed

Supporting word lists

ff
off toff toffee
biff cliff stiff sniff
buff cuff huff puff fluff gruff stuff

ll
bell fell sell tell well yell
spell smell swell
ill bill fill hill kill mill pill till will
drill frill grill skill spill still swill
doll
gull hull skull
*full pull

ss
ass lass mass
less mess bless dress press stress
hiss kiss miss
boss moss toss floss gloss cross
fuss

LEARNING TARGETS

Pupil Book: Focus
to match key words with the pattern **a-e**
to pictures

Pupil Book: Extra
to copy and match words with the **ail**, **aid**
and **ain** letter sequences to a picture

Pupil Book: Extension
to identify words containing the **ay**
vowel digraph

Workbook: Focus
to match words with the pattern **a-e**
to pictures

Workbook: Extension
to complete a simple cloze activity using **ay**,
ai and **a-e**

Resource sheet: Focus
to copy a selection of target words and write
rhyming words

Resource sheet: Extension
to use **ai**, **a-e** and **ay** words to match picture
clues and fill gaps in sentences

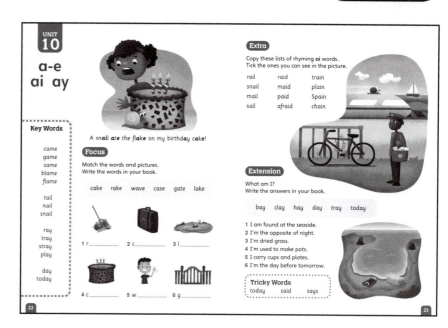

BACKGROUND NOTES AND SUGGESTIONS

This unit introduces the **modifier** (or 'magic') **e**. Here it is in the context of the **a-e** digraph and is linked to the other long **a** graphemes representing this phoneme, namely **ai** and **ay**.

Both **ai** and **ay** words often appear as components of compound words, and therefore this unit is a useful opportunity to begin to introduce work on compound words generally, returned to more fully in Unit 25.

One of the more significant letter patterns associated with the vowel digraph **ai** is **air**. This is part of the focus of Unit 22 in Pupil Book 1B.

English words hardly ever end with **v** (except *spiv*), so if a word ends with that sound the letter **e** needs to be added e.g. *have*.

Pupil Book answers

Focus

1 rake	2 case	3 lake
4 cake	5 wave	6 gate

Extra
rail, train, snail, mail, sail, chain

Extension

1 bay	2 day	3 hay
4 clay	5 tray	6 today

Workbook answers

Focus

1 cake	2 flame
3 gate	4 case
5 game	6 wave
7 snake	8 lake
9 plate	10 rake
11 spade	12 shake

Extra
1 The red team won the <u>game</u>.
2 Mum hit the <u>nail</u> with the hammer.
3 I <u>play</u> with my friend.

4 Can I <u>stay</u> for lunch?
5 The dog has a long <u>tail</u>.
6 The candle has a <u>flame</u>.
7 I <u>paid</u> for the sweets.
8 I love <u>cake</u>!

Resource sheet answers

Focus

Ⓐ game name cake rake wave save

Ⓑ game cake wave rake

Ⓒ cake save flame

Extension

Ⓐ spade rain crane snake
flame plane hay snail

Ⓑ We can't <u>play</u> our <u>game</u> in the
<u>rain</u> <u>today</u>.
We will <u>have</u> to <u>play</u> indoors <u>today</u>.
The <u>rain</u> must stop soon!

Supporting word lists

ace face lace race
place grace trace space
age cage page rage wage stage

blade spade
blame flame shame
brake flake stake shake snake
brave slave grave shave
crane plane
blaze graze
grape shape
crate grate plate slate
chase
aid aim

maid mail main
paid pail pain plain
raid rail rain

aid laid maid paid raid
bail fail hail jail mail nail pail rail sail tail
wail rail Braille frail trail snail
sail nail snail
bay day hay jay lay may pay ray say way
lay clay play
ray bray tray stray spray
way sway
stay

LEARNING TARGETS

Pupil Book: Focus
to select key words that match the pictures

Pupil Book: Extra
to find words in a wordsearch puzzle in which the **ee** sound is represented by **ie**

Pupil Book: Extension
to match **ee** and **ea** words to pictures and add **ing**

Workbook: Focus
to select key words that match the pictures

Workbook: Extra
to identify and write rhyming words

Resource sheet: Focus
to copy a selection of target words and write rhyming words

Resource sheet: Extension
to use **ee** and **ea** words to match picture clues and fill gaps in sentences

BACKGROUND NOTES AND SUGGESTIONS

The **ee** and **ea** vowel digraphs are extremely common in the words young children read and write. They therefore warrant a little extra time and attention. They are also ideal digraphs to support revision of the consonant digraphs. The **ie** and **e-e** digraphs are also introduced here.

Whilst one of the main objectives of this unit is words with the simple **ea** sound, it should be noted that other **ee** sound/letter correspondences will be covered in Pupil Book 2, Units 2 and 20.

Pupil Book answers

Focus

1 bee	2 tree	3 seed
4 sea	5 eat	6 pea

Extra

chief brief field grief thief

Extension

1 sleeping	2 bleeding
3 cleaning	4 weeding
5 screaming	6 eating
7 teaching	8 meeting

Workbook answers

Focus

1 bee	2 tree	3 weed
4 tea	5 meat	6 pea
7 seed	8 feed	9 see
10 sea	11 eat	12 sleep

Extra

1 seed	weed
2 pea	sea
3 eat	meat
4 sleep	sheep
5 feet	sweet
6 cream	dream
7 meal	seal
8 tree	bee

Resource sheet answers

Focus

Ⓐ bee tree seed weed pea tea
eat meat

Ⓑ tree seed eat pea

Ⓒ bee weed tea

Extension

Ⓐ feet eel meal see
sleep seat dream steam

Ⓑ 1 The <u>seat</u> was so soft I quickly went to <u>sleep</u>.
2 We went to the <u>beach</u> where I dipped my <u>feet</u> in the <u>sea</u>.
3 I had a cup of <u>tea</u> and <u>pea</u> soup for my dinner.
4 We have <u>been</u> to <u>see</u> our new puppy.

Supporting word lists

bee fee see free tree
eel feel heel peel reel steel
deed feed need seed weed
bleed breed greed speed tweed
been keen seen green
deep jeep keep peep seep weep
sleep creep steep sheep
feet meet fleet sleet tweet sweet sheet
leek week

see seed seek seen seem
bee beef been
fee feel feet

+ing
feeding needing seeding weeding
bleeding speeding
peeping weeping sleeping creeping
seeping feeling meeting

pea sea tea flea
eat beat heat meat neat peat teat
bleat treat cheat
bean jeans lean mean clean
beam seam team gleam cream dream
steam scream stream
deal heal meal peal seal veal steal
beak leak teak freak speak sneak
tweak streak
bead lead read plead
heap leap reap cheap
each beach peach reach teach
bleach preach
east beast feast least yeast
heave leave weave
sea seal seam seat
tea teak team teat
pea peal peat peak
leaf leak lean leap leach

*please heard

LEARNING TARGETS

Pupil Book: Focus
to match key words to pictures

Pupil Book: Extra
to match present tense verbs to pictures

Pupil Book: Extension
to demonstrate how the addition of a modifying ('magic') e alters the sound of the medial vowel

Workbook: Focus
to match key words to pictures

Workbook: Extra
to identify and write words found in a picture

Resource sheet: Focus
to copy a selection of target words and write rhyming words

Resource sheet: Extension
to identify and name picture clues incorporating the three main representations of the long i vowel; to practise using the two common exceptions: *live* and *give*

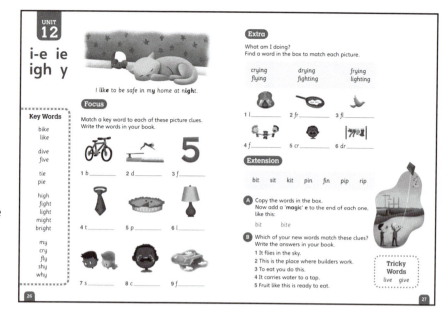

BACKGROUND NOTES AND SUGGESTIONS

igh is traditionally thought of as being one of the trickier vowel graphemes, but unlike many others it has no phonemic variations, and thus once mastered can be very satisfying for the children to use.

Pupils who have done prior work on vowels can be directed to the significance of this group of words, in which one of the representations of the phoneme has no vowel letter other than the 'semi-vowel' **y**. The point can be made that whenever it stands as a vowel, it takes the place of an **i**, usually 'long' (*my*, *cry*) – though not always (*gym*).

The Extension Resource activity demonstrates a simplified version of the spelling rule:

- to make the plural of a noun that ends in a consonant **+y**, change **y** to **i** and add **es** (*fly*, *flies*)

When teaching *live*, *give* (Tricky Words) it is worth explaining that English words hardly ever end with **v** (except *spiv*), so if a word ends with that sound the letter **e** needs to be added.

Pupil Book answers

Focus
1 bike	2 dive	3 five
4 tie	5 pie	6 light
7 shy	8 cry	9 fly

Extra
1 lighting	2 frying	3 flying
4 fighting	5 crying	6 drying

Extension
A
bit bite	sit site
kit kite	pin pine
fin fine	pip pipe
rip ripe	

B
1 kite	2 site	3 bite
4 pipe	5 ripe	

Workbook answers

Focus
1 five	2 bike	3 dive
4 fight	5 light	6 high
7 fly	8 cry	9 shy
10 pie	11 tie	12 bright

Extra
sky, light, dive, bike, fight, fright, fly, bride

Resource sheet answers

Focus
A pipe five hide line wipe

B nine kite bike bite

C dive hide hive nine

Extension
A
pie	bride	smile	light
fight	fly	slide	tie

Children should copy the words.

B
1 I *live* with Mum and Dad over the shop.
2 I hope Dad will *give* me a lolly.
3 I *like* lollies.
4 I shall *give* Dad a big hug!

Supporting word lists

ice dice mice nice rice
slice price spice twice splice
spike strike
spite sprite
stile while smile
spine swine twine shine
glide slide bride pride
crime grime prime slime
tripe swipe
drive

by my
fly sly
cry dry fry try
sky spy sty shy
type style

high sigh thigh
fight light might night right sight tight
light blight flight slight
right bright fright
brighten frighten lighten tighten

LEARNING TARGETS

Pupil Book: Focus
to find and copy **oa**, **o-e** and **ow** words

Pupil Book: Extra
to sort words by the letter sequences **oke**, **oast**, **oes** and **ow**

Pupil Book: Extension
to introduce words with the 'long o' phoneme represented by **o**

Workbook: Focus
to match key words to pictures

Workbook: Extra
to choose and copy words to match pictures

Resource Sheet: Focus
to copy a selection of target words and write rhyming words

Resource Sheet: Extension
to complete word sums involving **oa**, **o-e**, **oe** and **ow**; to learn the 'special words' *one*, *gone* and *some*

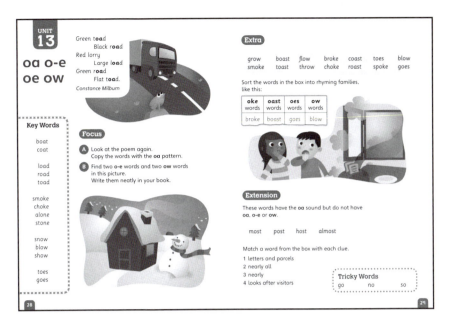

BACKGROUND NOTES AND SUGGESTIONS

It is worth focusing on the modifier ('magic') **e** situation where there is no intervening consonant, e.g. *doe*. Draw parallels with **ie** and **ue** endings.

The phoneme is often represented by a single **o**, notably in some frequently used 'special' words, e.g. *most, almost, cold*. The important **old** letter string is the subject of the Extension Resource for this unit.

The key feature of most words which have the ending **ow** is that it represents the long **o** phoneme (as in *rose*), rather than the regular **ow** sound (as in *cow*).

Some children will be able to appreciate that the bottom group of words in the *Supporting words lists* have the long **o** sound because they are all (except *own*) past tense and their root words have a final (long) **ow**.

Note: The digraph **oa** is rare at the end of an English word.

Pupil Book answers

Focus

Ⓐ toad   road   load

Ⓑ smoke   stone   (alone)   snow   blow

Extra

broke	boast	goes	grow
smoke	coast	toes	flow
choke	toast		blow
spoke	roast		throw

Extension

1 post   2 most
3 almost   4 host

Workbook answers

Focus

1 road   2 coat
3 toad   4 smoke
5 stone   6 alone
7 snow   8 blow
9 show   10 toes
11 goes

Extra

toad	snow	smoke	toast
row	window	throne	goat

Resource sheet answers

Focus

Ⓐ joke pole cone stone note

Ⓑ nose rose rope cone

Ⓒ rose bone hole rope

Extension

Ⓐ1	joke	2	woke	3	smoke
4	spoke	5	boat	6	goat
7	float	8	throat	9	toast
10	roast	11	low	12	mow
13	blow	14	flow	15	snow
16	show	17	goes	18	toes

Children should copy the special words.

Ⓑ 1 gone   2 some
3 one   4 one, gone

Supporting word lists

bone cone lone tone zone
stone scone throne
code rode strode
dope hope mope rope slope grope
dole hole mole pole role vole stole home
coke joke poke woke yoke
broke bloke spoke smoke choke
hose nose pose rose close prose
chose those
note tote vote drove
robe globe probe
froze
doe foe hoe toe
*one gone come some
oats boat coat goat moat float throat
stoat bloat
coal foal goal shoal
foam roam
coax hoax
load road toad
loan moan groan

bow low mow row sow tow know
blow flow glow slow crow grow stow
snow show throw
arrow barrow harrow marrow narrow
bellow fellow yellow elbow
billow pillow willow widow window
minnow
follow hollow
burrow furrow tomorrow sorrow sparrow
shadow shallow swallow
rainbow crossbow hedgerow
own sown blown flown grown shown
thrown known

LEARNING TARGETS

Pupil Book: Focus
to match the key words to pictures

Pupil Book: Extra
to complete word sums, combining target
vowels with other word elements

Pupil Book: Extension
to sort words into letter pattern families

Workbook: Focus
to match words to pictures

Workbook: Extra
to complete a simple cloze activity

Resource sheet: Focus
to copy a selection of target words and
write rhyming words

Resource sheet: Extension
to build **ew** words by completing a word fan

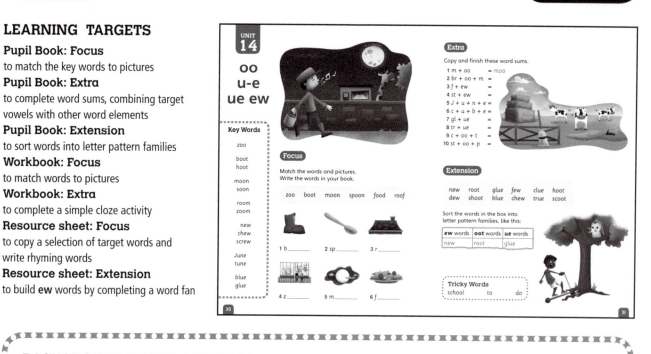

BACKGROUND NOTES AND SUGGESTIONS

In received pronunciation, **oo** represents three different vowel sounds (as in *moon, book, door*). This unit focuses on the first of these, which is the most common and which relates to the graphemes **u-e**, **ue** and **ew**; the other two groups are dealt with elsewhere: **oo** (as in *book*) in Pupil Book 1B, Unit 23.

A frieze of a herd of cows, each with a long **oo** word, can be effective.

Very few words end in **oo**, though those that do (e.g. *zoo, moo*) will be familiar to younger children. If words end in the /oo/ sound it is more likely that they will be spelt **ue** or **ew**.

The **ew** vowel digraph is often found associated with the letter **r**, as can be observed in the *Supporting word lists* below.

Pupil Book answers

Focus

1 boot	2 spoon	3 roof
4 zoo	5 moon	6 food

Extra

1 moo	2 broom	3 few
4 stew	5 June	6 cube
7 glue	8 true	9 coot
10 stoop		

Extension

new	root	glue
dew	scoot	clue
few	hoot	blue
chew	shoot	true

Workbook answers

Focus

1 moon	2 food	3 pool
4 room	5 boot	6 roof
7 tool	8 zoo	9 root
10 broom	11 spoon	12 stool

Extra

1 I play a <u>tune</u> on my <u>flute</u>.
2 The <u>tube</u> of <u>glue</u> was full.
3 The <u>moon</u> will be seen <u>soon</u>.
4 Watch your <u>boot</u> on that <u>root</u>!
5 I have lost the <u>new screw</u>.
6 You need to <u>chew</u> the <u>stew</u>!

Resource sheet answers

Focus

Ⓐ dune duke flute tube cute

Ⓑ June tune tube cube

Ⓒ tune cube flute dune

Extension

Ⓐ new few dew blew grew screw
chew threw

Ⓑ new blew screw chew
Teacher to check individual answers

Supporting word lists

boo moo too zoo shoo
boom doom room zoom bloom gloom
broom groom
boot coot loot hoot root toot
shoot scoot
food mood brood
fool pool tool spool stool
hoof roof proof
hoop loop scoop snoop swoop stoop
droop
moon noon soon spoon
boo boom boot
hoof hoop hoot
roof room root
June dune tune prune

lute cute flute brute
duke fluke
rule
use fuse
rude nude
cube tube
blue clue glue true

yew dew few mew new stew
chew blew flew
brew crew drew grew
screw threw shrew

Check-Up 1

1 cat	**2** hand	**3** fish	**4** duck
5 chick	**6** hutch	**7** buses	**8** licking
9 dress	**10** snail	**11** bee	**12** fight
13 boat	**14** moon	**15** screw	**16** blue

Extension

Teacher to check individual answers

LEARNING TARGETS

Pupil Book: Focus

to match **y** adjectives to pictures

Pupil Book: Extra

to look for root words and other smaller words in **y** adjectives

Pupil Book: Extension

to complete a cloze activity using **y** adjectives

Workbook: Focus

to match **y** adjectives to pictures

Workbook: Extra

to complete a simple cloze activity based on a picture

Resource sheet: Focus

to complete word sums and match target words to pictures

Resource sheet: Extension

to complete a word fan and match target words to pictures

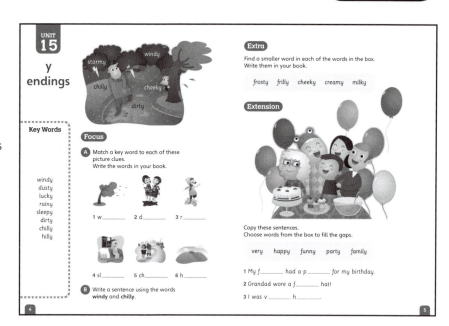

BACKGROUND NOTES AND SUGGESTIONS

This unit introduces the notion that nouns can be changed into adjectives by adding **y.** For a few children it might also begin to be appropriate to introduce the notions that:

- if the letter before the last is a single vowel then double the last letter (*muddy*)
- if the word ends in **e**, drop the **e** before adding the **y** (*slime, slimy*).

For most children these rules will be introduced later in the programme.

Pupil Book answers

Focus

A 1 windy   2 dirty   3 rainy
    4 sleepy   5 chilly   6 hilly

B Teacher to check individual answers

Extra

frosty: frost   sty
frilly: frill   rill   ill   I
cheeky: cheek   he
creamy: cream   ream   am
           Amy   my   a
milky: milk

Extension

1 family, party
2 funny
3 very, happy

Workbook answers

Focus

1 hilly   2 messy
3 sleepy   4 chilly
5 frosty   6 windy
7 frilly   8 cloudy
9 rainy   10 croaky
11 dirty   12 smelly

Extra

1 a <u>happy</u> man
2 a <u>sleepy</u> cat
3 a <u>cloudy</u> sky
4 a <u>dirty</u> dog
5 a <u>smelly</u> bin
6 a <u>frilly</u> skirt
7 a <u>chilly</u> girl
8 a <u>rusty</u> bike

Resource sheet answers

Focus

A sleepy   rainy   dirty   lucky

B chilly   windy   cloudy   moody
    dusty   rocky

    windy   moody   cloudy   chilly

Extension

A dirty   frilly   lucky   creaky   sleepy
    stormy   rainy   windy   grumpy

B dirty   sleepy   rainy   windy
    Teacher to check individual sentences

Supporting word lists

cranky flashy scratchy messy smelly
rocky frosty lucky dusty rusty rainy
brainy milky risky frilly windy chilly
fussy sleepy cheeky leafy creaky creamy
mighty croaky moody sooty salty stormy
hardy marshy dirty cloudy
dotty bossy foggy spotty chatty muddy
tubby runny funny sunny nutty furry
lazy hazy crazy wavy easy icy slimy
bony rosy smoky stony noisy greasy

LEARNING TARGETS

Pupil Book: Focus
to use **ar** to complete key words to match pictures

Pupil Book: Extra
to complete word sums including the **ar** vowel digraph

Pupil Book: Extension
to introduce the letter sequences **ark** and **art**

Workbook: Focus
to match words with pictures

Workbook: Extra
to identify rhyming words

Resource sheet: Focus
to practise **ar** and **ark** patterns and words and sort words by letter patterns

Resource sheet: Extension
to undertake a cloze activity using ar words; to introduce the 'special' words *are*, *care* and *fare* as exceptions

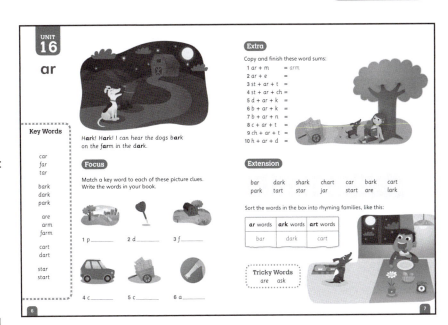

BACKGROUND NOTES AND SUGGESTIONS

The Extension Resource includes work on the **are** sound (as in *care*). This is an important 'exception' to begin to be aware of, and will be covered in more depth in Unit 22 and later in Book 2, Unit 12.

The Extra 'word sums' activity can also lead to looking for words inside words. (e.g. *barn*). Also, some children will enjoy making rhyming couplets (e.g. 'Twinkle, twinkle little star').

Pupil Book answers

Focus

1 park	**2** dart	**3** farm
4 car	**5** cart	**6** arm

Extra

1 arm	**2** are
3 start	**4** starch
5 dark	**6** bark
7 barn	**8** cart
9 chart	**10** hard

Extension

ar words	ark words	art words
bar	dark	cart
car	shark	chart
jar	bark	tart
are	park	start
star	lark	

Workbook answers

Focus

1 farm	**2** bark
3 jar	**4** card
5 cart	**6** scar
7 arm	**8** park
9 harp	**10** dark
11 car	**12** scarf

Extra

1 bar	car	jar
2 dark	mark	bark
3 arm	farm	harm
4 start	dart	art
5 card	hard	yard
6 barn	yarn	darn
7 harp	carp	sharp
8 star	scar	far

Resource sheet answers

Focus

A Children should copy the letter patterns and words.

B
jar	park
car	dark
bar	bark
far	lark
tar	
star	

Extension

A "Let's go for a ride in the <u>car</u>," said Mum.
"We can go to the <u>park</u> or the <u>farm</u>."
"It's not <u>far</u> to the <u>farm</u>," said Cara, "and we can ride on the horse and <u>cart</u>."

"We must get back before it gets <u>dark</u>," said Dad.

B Mum waved and said, "Take <u>care</u> when you <u>are</u> crossing the road, and make sure you have the money for your bus <u>fare</u>."

Supporting word lists

bar car far jar tar star scar
ark bark dark lark mark park
shark spark
arm farm harm
art cart dart part tart start smart
barn darn yarn
card hard lard yard
harp scarp sharp
scarf
harsh marsh
ark arm art
bar bark barn
car card cart
dark darn dart
hard harm harp
*are care fare

LEARNING TARGETS

Pupil Book: Focus
to match key words and pictures

Pupil Book: Extra
to find **oi** and **oy** words hidden in a wordsearch

Pupil Book: Extension
to match and use target words, including suffix **ing**, with pictures

Workbook: Focus
to match words and pictures

Workbook: Extra
to complete a simple cloze activity using **oi** and **oy** words

Resource sheet: Focus
to practise **oil**, **oin**, **oint**, **oise** and **oy** letter sequences and related words

Resource sheet: Extension
to complete word sums using the **oi** and **oy** graphemes

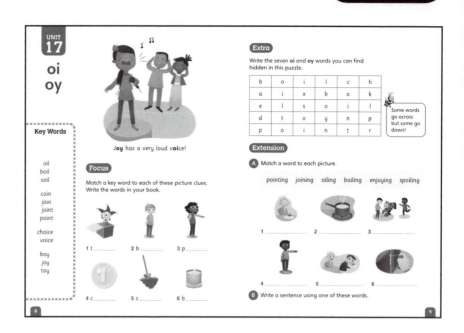

BACKGROUND NOTES AND SUGGESTIONS

The vowel sound represented by **oi/oy** never appears as the letter pattern **oi** at the end of a word. **oy** appears frequently in a medial position if preceding a suffix (e.g. *joyful*) or exceptionally in *groyne*, *royal*.

Pupil Book answers

Focus

1 toy	**2** boy	**3** point
4 coin	**5** soil	**6** boil

Extra

boil toy boy soil coin oil point

Extension

A   **1** enjoying   **2** boiling   **3** joining
    4 pointing   **5** spoiling   **6** oiling

B Teacher to check individual answers

Workbook answers

Focus

1 boy	**2** point
3 voice	**4** toy
5 joint	**6** joy
7 boil	**8** soil
9 coil	**10** oil
11 noise	**12** coin

Extra

1 The kettle began to <u>boil</u>.
2 I <u>join</u> hands with my sister.
3 I can hear Mrs Jones's loud <u>voice</u>!
4 <u>Point</u> to your sister, Anil.
5 My <u>toy</u> is broken.
6 I found a <u>coin</u>.
7 The dogs make a lot of <u>noise</u>.
8 What a lovely baby <u>boy</u>!

Resource sheet answers

Focus

A soil   boil   coin   noise   boy   toy

B joint   coin   boy   boil

C oil   join   point   toy

Extension

A   **1** join   **2** coin   **3** joint
   4 point   **5** boil   **6** soil
   7 coil   **8** spoil   **9** voice
  10 choice   **11** joint   **12** spoilt
  13 moist   **14** boy   **15** toy
  16 joy

B boy   toy   voice   point
   Teacher to check individual sentences

Supporting word lists

join joint joist
soil spoil spoilt
oil boil coil soil toil spoil
coin join
joint point
hoist joist moist
voice choice
noise poise

boy joy toy ploy
groyne

LEARNING TARGETS

Pupil Book: Focus
to match key words with pictures
Pupil Book: Extra
to answer clues to find target words
Pupil Book: Extension
to complete a cloze activity using target words
Workbook: Focus
to match key words with pictures
Workbook: Extra
to identify words within a sequence of letters
Resource sheet: Focus
to match key words with pictures;
to recognise rhyming words
Resource sheet: Extension
to match key words with picture clues and missing words in sentences

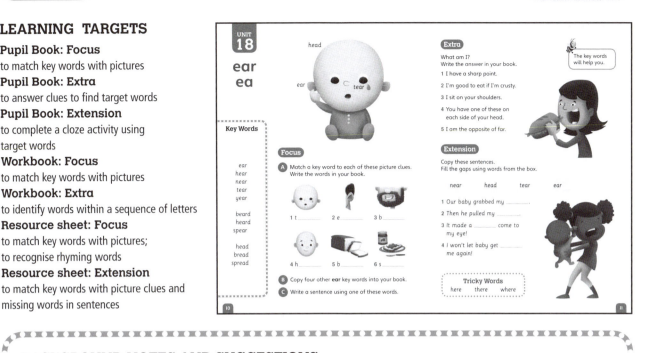

BACKGROUND NOTES AND SUGGESTIONS

Some children will find the auditory distinction between **ea** (*beach*) and **ear** (*year*) difficult at this stage. For such children it is better to focus more specifically on trying to differentiate between the straightforward 'regular' long **ea** (*tea*) and the 'irregular' short **ea** (*head*) words. These can be collected individually or in groups. More work on these sound/letter pattern correspondences follows later in the course in Pupil Book 2, Units 8 and 12.

There is a significant number of irregular **ea** words, falling into two groups, as shown. Some teachers may choose to use the device of describing the **a** in the first group as silent, though purists may object to this approach.

Pupil Book answers

Focus
A 1 tear 2 ear 3 beard
4 head 5 bread 6 spread

B Teacher to check individual answers

C Teacher to check individual answers

Extra
1 spear 2 bread 3 head
4 ear 5 near

Extension
1 head 2 ear 3 tear 4 near

Workbook answers

Focus
1 ear 2 year 3 beard
4 spread 5 bread 6 head
7 hear 8 tear 9 near

Extra
1 tear 2 head
3 spread 4 ear
5 beard 6 year
7 clear 8 bread

Resource sheet answers

Focus
A ear bread tear

B ear near year
head bread spread
clear smear spear

Extension
A beard year tear spear
thread ear spread head

B My dad looks odd. He has a messy beard and his ears stick out!
When he eats bread the crumbs fall into his beard.
The crumbs get spread everywhere.
Also he can hear very well so I can't sneak up on him!

Supporting word lists
dead head lead read
bread dread tread stead
thread spread
breadth instead bedspread

ear dear fear gear hear
near rear tear year
clear smear spear
beard

LEARNING TARGETS

Pupil Book: Focus
to match key words to pictures, and associated activity

Pupil Book: Extra
to sort words into letter pattern families

Pupil Book: Extension
to practise the key words in a wordsearch

Workbook: Focus
to match words to pictures

Workbook: Extra
to label a picture with **er**, **ir** and **ur** words

Resource sheet: Focus
to complete an **ur** words word fan;
to write **er**, **ir**, **ur**, words with pictures

Resource sheet: Extension
to select **ur**, **ir** or **er** to complete words in a range of contexts

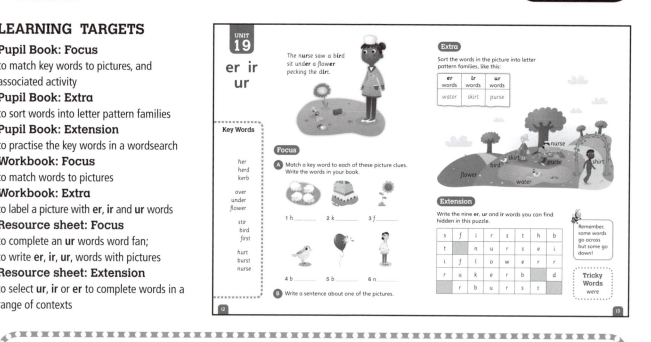

BACKGROUND NOTES AND SUGGESTIONS

This unit introduces another group of frequently occurring **r** vowel sounds. Purists will observe that phonemically the medial **er** in the words listed above and the final **er** are different vowel sounds, the latter being a schwa vowel, and sounding more as a grunt (similar to the word *a*). Nevertheless, most teachers find the grouping of the medial and final **er** letter pattern rarely causes problems and is usually helpful.

A useful spin-off with work on the final **er** pattern is that children can work on double-letter patterns that may be causing problems, similar to those listed in the *Supporting word lists*.

Whilst it is not a vowel digraph which appears very frequently, several of the words in which **ir** does occur are used quite frequently by children.

The **ur** vowel digraph occurs quite often (see also Pupil Book 2, Unit 9), but in spelling acquisition its most significant context is in the suffixes **sure** and **ture** (see Book 3, Unit 23).

Pupil Book answers

Focus

(A) 1 herd   2 kerb   3 flower
     4 bird   5 burst   6 nurse

(B) Teacher to check individual answers

Extra

water   skirt   purse
flower   shirt   nurse
            bird

Extension

flower   her   kerb   nurse   fur
burst   first   bird   stir

Workbook answers

Focus

1 herd   2 kerb   3 letter
4 bird   5 skirt   6 stir
7 burst   8 hurt   9 nurse
10 shirt   11 flower   12 fur

Extra

Teacher to check individual answers

Resource sheet answers

Focus

(A) burn   turn   curl   hurt
    nurse   burst
(B) curl   hurt   nurse
    burst   turn   burn

Extension

(A) 1 purse   2 first
   3 picture   4 herd
   5 treasure   6 dirty
   7 singer   8 curve

(B) Teacher to check individual answers

(C) after   driver   vulture   enter
nurse   third   under   reader
ever   shirt

Letters in tinted boxes make the word *adventures*.

Supporting word lists

her herd
herb kerb verb
fern stern
jerk perk
perm term germ
nerve serve swerve
perch

There are numerous examples of words with final er. Here are a few which also have either tt or pp patterns:

letter litter better trotter potter spotter
gutter butter sitter fitter hitter
slipper hopper zipper shopper chopper
supper clipper trapper stopper

fir sir stir
bird third
dirt flirt skirt shirt
firm
swirl twirl
first thirst
chirp
birth mirth
fire hire wire shire tired
urn burn turn churn
fur
curl hurl
hurt
surf turf
urge surge
curse nurse purse
curve
burnt
burst
nature future
picture puncture
texture mixture
sculpture scripture
structure fracture
denture adventure
furniture
measure treasure pleasure

LEARNING TARGETS

Pupil Book: Focus
to select rhyming words from the key word list

Pupil Book: Extra
to practise the frequent **ou** special words:
you your our should could would

Pupil Book: Extension
to sort a selection of **ow** words according to
their phonemes

Workbook: Focus
to match words with pictures

Workbook: Extra
to identify and copy rhyming words

Resource sheet: Focus
to complete **ou** and **ow** word sums and
match words to pictures

Resource sheet: Extension
to use **ou** and **ow** words to answer a puzzle;
to use the 'special' words *our, hour, thought*
and *through* in a cloze passage

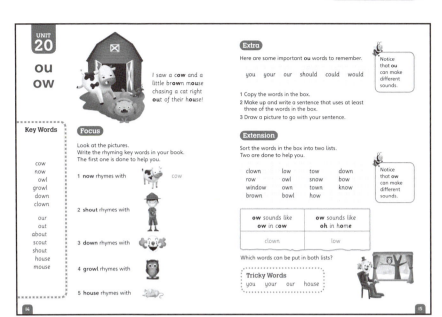

BACKGROUND NOTES AND SUGGESTIONS

The focus of this unit is words with the simple **ow** sound (as in *cow*) and **ou** sound (as in *out*). However, the Pupil
Book Extension section introduces the two main phonemes represented by **ow**; teachers wishing to take this further
with some pupils will find support in Pupil Book 2, Unit 10.

ou is an important letter pattern, though perversely the most frequent significant words using **ou** are phonemically
'irregular'. (See Pupil Book 2, Unit 10.)

The opportunity lends itself with the frequently occurring word *house* to consider the concept of compound words.
It can be fun to see how many compound words can be collected over a period of time which include a particular
word, like *house*.

An important 'special' word is *know*, and this can provide an opportunity to begin to introduce 'silent' letters, in
particular silent **k**. Silent letters are tackled more systematically from Pupil Book 2, Unit 22.

Pupil Book answers

Focus

1 cow	**2** scout	**3** clown
4 owl	**5** mouse	

Extra
Teacher to check individual answers

Extension

clown	low
down	tow
row	row
owl	snow
bow	bow
town	window
brown	own
how	know
	bowl

Workbook answers

Focus

1 mouse	**2** house
3 scout	**4** clown
5 crown	**6** cow
7 cloud	**8** owl
9 crowd	**10** shout
11 growl	**12** mouth

Extra

1 brow	cow
2 scout	shout
3 clown	frown
4 loud	cloud
5 house	mouse
6 south	mouth

Resource sheet answers

Focus

Ⓐ cow   howl   loud   cloud   clown
   crown   mouse   house   mouth

Ⓑ cow   mouse   cloud   clown

Extension

Ⓐ

1 cloud	**2** crowd	**3** proud
4 owl	**5** house	**6** growl
7 loud	**8** mouse	**9** crown

Children should copy the words.

Ⓑ Dad <u>thought</u> Mum would have been
home an <u>hour</u> ago. We looked <u>through</u>
the windows but there is no one home.
Where is <u>our</u> Mum?

Supporting word lists

bow cow how now row sow brow
owl fowl howl growl prowl scowl
down gown town clown brown crown
drown frown
crowd

out bout lout pout rout tout
about clout trout scout spout stout
sprout shout
foul
loud cloud proud
noun
house louse mouse blouse
grouse spouse
bound found hound mound pound
round sound wound ground
count fount mount
ounce bounce pounce flounce trounce
couch pouch slouch crouch
mouth south

*could would should
*you your our hour
*thought through
*know

LEARNING TARGETS

Pupil Book: Focus

to match key words to pictures, and associated activity

Pupil Book: Extra

to complete a simple cloze activity focusing on target phonemes

Pupil Book: Extension

to complete a quiz using target words

Workbook: Focus

to match words to pictures

Workbook: Extra

to complete a simple cloze activity using **or**, **ore**, **aw** and **au** words

Resource sheet: Focus

to practise **ork**, **orn**, **ort**, **ore** and **aw** patterns and words

Resource sheet: Extension

to identify a selection of target words in puzzles and use them in sentences

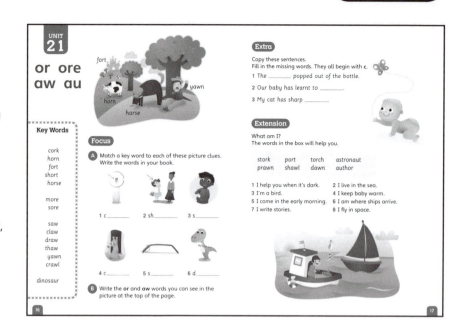

BACKGROUND NOTES AND SUGGESTIONS

These letter patterns make a nice complement to previous work on **ar** and **are** patterns, for even though they look similar (both being what are sometimes called **r** vowels) **or/ore**, unlike **ar/are**, have no discernible difference in sound.

Several **aw** words are similar in sound to other words, but not exactly the same, so cannot properly be described as homophones. Nevertheless, from the point of view of spelling they are sufficiently close to cause confusion and so warrant a group or class lesson. This might usefully lead on to consideration of other groups of similar sounding words that can cause occasional difficulty.

Nelson Grammar may be a helpful source of further reference, and contains several sets of exercises on homophones. Please note that homophones will vary depending on regional accents.

Pupil Book answers

Focus

A 1 cork   2 short   3 sore

     4 claw   5 saw   6 dinosaur

B yawn   horse   fort   horn

Extra

1 cork

2 crawl

3 claws

Extension

1 torch   2 prawn   3 stork   4 shawl

5 dawn   6 port   7 author   8 astronaut

Workbook answers

Focus

 1 horn   2 horse

 3 dinosaur   4 cork

 5 snore   6 shore

 7 saw   8 claw

 9 paw   10 crawl

11 sore   12 short

Extra

1 My <u>fork</u> fell on the floor.

2 I use my <u>torch</u> to read at night.

3 I <u>saw</u> my grandma.

4 My lamb sleeps on <u>straw</u>.

5 My dad has a loud <u>snore</u>.

6 I eat <u>more</u> chips than Mum!

7 The car beeped its <u>horn</u>.

8 I love <u>dinosaurs</u>.

Resource sheet answers

Focus

A fork   paw

B cork   horn   port   core

C port   fork   torn   sore

Extension

1 stork/torch

2 horse/sore

3 caught/paw

4 fort/port

5 law/floor

Teacher to check individual answers

Supporting word lists

or for

cord ford lord

cork fork stork

form storm

born corn horn morn torn worn

sworn shorn scorn

fort port sort snort sport short

gorge

force

gorse horse Morse

porch torch scorch

north

ore bore core more sore tore wore

store score snore swore shore

jaw law paw raw saw

claw thaw draw straw

dawn fawn lawn pawn yawn drawn

prawn spawn

bawl crawl trawl sprawl shawl

hawk

LEARNING TARGETS

Pupil Book: Focus
to match key words to pictures, and associated activity

Pupil Book: Extra
to sort words with the target phoneme into appropriate spelling patterns

Pupil Book: Extension
to build target words using component segments

Workbook: Focus
to match words to pictures

Workbook: Extra
to choose words to match to pictures

Resource sheet: Focus
to complete word sums using **air** and **ear**

Resource sheet: Extension
to consider other letter patterns that represent the target phoneme i.e. **ere** and **ear**

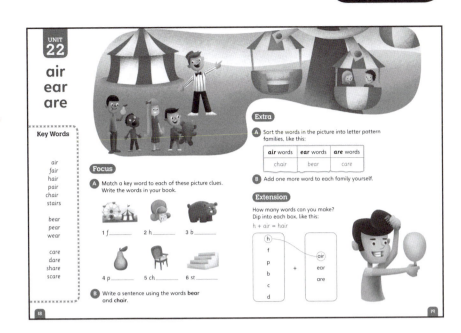

BACKGROUND NOTES AND SUGGESTIONS

The unit teaches the **are**, **air** and **ear** graphemes, when they represent the distinctive vowel phoneme heard in *bear, bare and hair*. It is helpful to refer the children to earlier work relating to the **ar** and **ai** vowel phonemes that can cause potential confusion.

More opportunities for work with homophones, which are quite frequent with **air/are** words, are offered in Pupil Book 2, Unit 27.

Pupil Book answers

Focus

A 1 fair   2 hair   3 bear
    4 pear   5 chair   6 stairs

B Teacher to check individual answers

Extra

A chair   bear   care
    fair   pear   dare
    hair   wear   scare

B Teacher to check individual answers

Extension

hair   hear   hare
fair   fear   fare
pair   pear   pare
bear   bare
care
dear   dare

Workbook answers

Focus

1 hair	2 stairs
3 fair	4 pear
5 tear	6 bear
7 care	8 scare
9 hare	10 wear
11 dare	12 chair

Extra

hare
hair
scare
chair
pear
care
funfair
airport

Resource sheet answers

Focus

A Children should copy the letter patterns and words.

B 1 fair   2 bear   3 share
    4 chair   5 pear   6 scare
    7 wear   8 hair

Extension

A 1 The <u>scared</u> <u>hare</u> jumped over the <u>chair</u>.
    2 "Take <u>care</u> not to lose your new <u>pair</u> of socks when you <u>wear</u> them," said Mum.
    3 "I haven't enough <u>spare</u> money for the bus <u>fare</u>," said my friend.
    4 Look! <u>There</u> is a <u>hare</u> with long ears.
    5 I've never been as <u>scared</u> as I was at the <u>fair</u> last night.

B 1 hair   2 spare   3 stairs
    4 mare   5 airport   6 bear
    7 stare

Supporting word lists

bare care dare fare hare mare rare
glare spare stare scare snare share

air fair hair pair
flair stair chair

ear dear fear gear hear near
rear tear year
clear smear spear beard

LEARNING TARGETS

Pupil Book: Focus
to match key words to pictures

Pupil Book: Extra
to organise key words according to spelling pattern

Pupil Book: Extension
to complete word sums incorporating the target spelling patterns

Workbook: Focus
to match key words to pictures

Workbook: Extra
to identify rhyming words

Resource sheet: Focus
to practise the **ook** and **oon** patterns and words; to practise writing other **oo** words

Resource sheet: Extension
to complete word sums using **oo** and **u** letter patterns; to sort **oo** words by their rhyme patterns

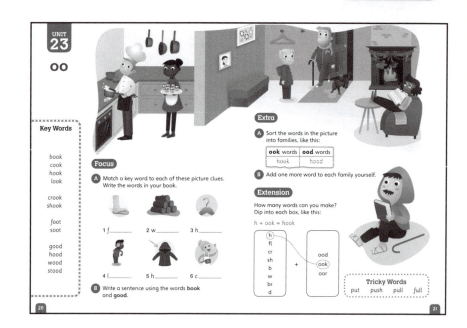

BACKGROUND NOTES AND SUGGESTIONS

There are two clearly recognised vowel phonemes represented by **oo**; as in *room* and as in *book*. There is also a third, **oor** as represented in *poor*, though few will spot it, and it is quite sufficient at this stage to recognise it as a spelling pattern sub-division of the other groups depending on regional pronunciation, especially as not all **oor** words have the same standard pronunciation.

The phoneme can also be represented in a few high frequency words as **u**. These are listed in the Tricky Words box, and should be practised as a group.

Pupil Book answers

Focus

Ⓐ 1 foot   2 wood   3 hook
   4 look   5 hood   6 cook

Ⓑ Teacher to check individual answers

Extra

hook   hood
book   wood
look   stood

Extension

hood hook
flood floor
crook
shook
book
wood
brood brook
door

Workbook answers

Focus

1 wood   2 cook
3 look   4 book
5 soot   6 shook
7 foot   8 good
9 hook   10 stood
11 hood   12 crook

Extra

1 book   cook   look
2 good   wood   hood
3 pool   tool   fool
4 boot   shoot   hoot
5 goose   moose   loose
6 hoop   loop   scoop
7 room   broom   groom
8 crook   shook   brook

Resource sheet answers

Focus

Ⓐ Children should copy the letter patterns and words.

Ⓑ moo   zoo   room   boot
   food hoof roof

Extension

Ⓐ 1 moon   2 noon   3 soon
    4 spoon   5 room   6 broom
    7 look   8 book   9 took
   10 brook   11 full   12 pull
   13 bush   14 push

Ⓑ root   book   soon
   hoot   brook   moon
   boot   look   noon
   shoot   crook   spoon
   scoot   shook

Supporting word lists

book cook hook look rook took
crook brook shook
foot soot
good hood wood stood
wool
put pull push full

LEARNING TARGETS

Pupil Book: Focus
to practise writing days of the week by completing picture captions;
to answer simple comprehension questions based on the *Solomon Grundy* nursery rhyme

Pupil Book: Extra
to complete a cloze activity concerning the name origins of days of the week

Pupil Book: Extension
to complete a quiz activity concerning the origins of names of months

Workbook: Focus
to write days of the week in order

Workbook: Extra
to write a simple diary entry for each day of the week

Resource sheet: Focus
to complete a quiz concerning the days of the week

Resource sheet: Extension
to complete a cloze activity and quiz activity concerning the names of months

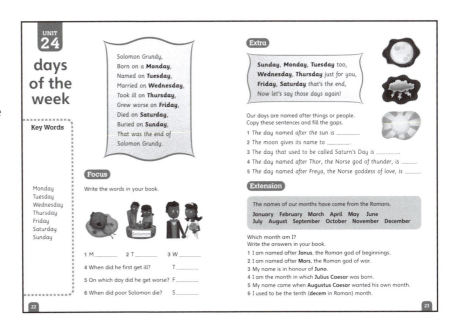

UNIT 24
days of the week

Key Words

Monday
Tuesday
Wednesday
Thursday
Friday
Saturday
Sunday

Solomon Grundy,
Born on a **Monday**,
Named on **Tuesday**,
Married on **Wednesday**,
Took ill on **Thursday**,
Grew worse on **Friday**,
Died on **Saturday**,
Buried on **Sunday**,
That was the end of Solomon Grundy.

Focus

Write the words in your book.

1 M _____ 2 T _____ 3 W _____
4 When did he first get ill?   T _____
5 On which day did he get worse? F _____
6 When did poor Solomon die?   S _____

22

Extra

Sunday, Monday, Tuesday too,
Wednesday, Thursday just for you,
Friday, Saturday that's the end,
Now let's say those days again!

Our days are named after things or people.
Copy these sentences and fill the gaps.
1 The day named after the sun is _____.
2 The moon gives its name to _____.
3 The day that used to be called Saturn's Day is _____.
4 The day named after Thor, the Norse god of thunder, is _____.
5 The day named after Freya, the Norse goddess of love, is _____.

Extension

The names of our months have come from the Romans.

January February March April May June
July August September October November December

Which month am I?
Write the answers in your book.
1 I am named after **Janus**, the Roman god of beginnings.
2 I am named after **Mars**, the Roman god of war.
3 My name is in honour of **Juno**.
4 I am the month in which **Julius Caesar** was born.
5 My name came when **Augustus Caesar** wanted his own month.
6 I used to be the tenth (**decem** in Roman) month.

23

BACKGROUND NOTES AND SUGGESTIONS

There are several traditional rhymes and songs that use the days of the week – this unit uses two of them.

It can be both a point of interest and a useful prompt for spelling to appreciate the origins of the names of the days of the week. These are summarised here but further research is highly recommended. The Greeks named them after the sun, the moon and the five known planets, which were themselves named after the gods. The Romans substituted their equivalent gods, as did the Germanic peoples. The history is similar when it comes to month names.

Finally, it is worth constantly reminding the children that both days of the week and months of the year begin with a capital letter.

Pupil Book answers

Focus

1 Monday   2 Tuesday
3 Wednesday   4 Thursday
5 Friday   6 Saturday

Extra

1 Sunday
2 Monday
3 Saturday
4 Thursday
5 Friday

Extension

1 January
2 March
3 June
4 July
5 August
6 December

Workbook answers

Focus

1 Saturday
2 Sunday
3 Wednesday
4 Friday
5 Monday
6 Thursday
7 Tuesday

Extra

Teacher to check individual answers

Resource sheet answers

Focus

1 Wednesday
2 Monday
3 Tuesday
4 Thursday
5 Sunday

Extension

Ⓐ

last month	this month	next month
February	*March*	*April*
August	*September*	October
April	May	*June*
October	November	December
July	August	September
September	October	*November*
December	*January*	February
October	November	*December*

Ⓑ 1 March
2 September
3 December
4 January
5 August
6 October
7 July
8 February

LEARNING TARGETS

Pupil Book: Focus
to use picture clues to complete compound words

Pupil Book: Extra
to use picture clues to create compound words

Pupil Book: Extension
to identify the syllables in two- and three-syllable words

Workbook: Focus
to match key words to pictures

Workbook: Extra
to use picture clues to create compound words

Resource sheet: Focus
to use picture clues to complete compound words

Resource sheet: Extension
to complete and use compound words; to identify the number of syllables in words

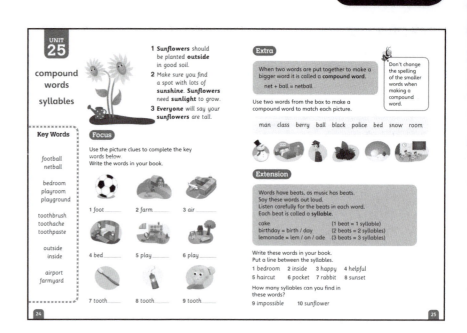

BACKGROUND NOTES AND SUGGESTIONS

Compound words are essentially two words joined together, although later pupils will become aware that compound words can be hyphenated. The important message at this stage is to understand that each part of the compound word is spelt as it would be if it were on its own.

This unit also gives a first introduction to syllables, as 'beats' in a word. Compound words are helpful in this regard as many are composed from two single syllable words and thus the beats are easy to appreciate, e.g. bed/room, out/side. But the notion of syllables needs to go beyond this.

For those that are ready, it can be pointed out that each syllable is built around a vowel phoneme, thus giving each syllable at least one vowel letter or **y**. Also, with double letters it is normal to split syllables between these i.e. *scruf/fy*.

Words of more than one syllable often have an unstressed syllable in which the vowel sound is unclear.

Pupil Book answers

Focus

1 football
2 farmyard
3 airport
4 bedroom
5 playroom
6 playground
7 toothbrush
8 toothpaste
9 toothache

Extra

snowman   bedroom   policeman
blackberry   snowball   classroom

Extension

1 bed/room
2 in/side
3 hap/py
4 help/ful
5 hair/cut
6 po/cket
7 rab/bit
8 sun/set
9 4
10 3

Workbook answers

Focus

1 toothache
2 toothbrush
3 playroom
4 playground
5 football
6 netball
7 inside
8 outside

Extra

1 blackbird
2 airport
3 daydream
4 tablespoon
5 grandmother
6 teacup
7 sunflower
8 rainbow

Resource sheet answers

Focus

bedroom   matchbox   farmhouse
football   toothbrush

Extension

A some + thing = something
some + where = somewhere
some + one = someone
every + thing = everything
every + where = everywhere
no + where = nowhere
no + thing = nothing

B Teacher to check individual answers

C bedroom = 2
moneybox = 3
policeman = 3
moonlight = 2

snowball = 2
fingerprint = 3

Supporting word lists

bedtime, blackbird, cowboy, cupcake, notepad, popcorn, rainbow, starfish, sunset

farmyard, butterfly, daylight, drumstick, flagpole, jellyfish, letterbox, notebook, raincoat, suntan, bathroom, catfish, sunglasses, footprint, lipstick, outside, pineapple, seashell, birthday, doorway, fireplace, homework, peanut, ponytail, snowflake

overcoat, railway, stepladder, teaspoon, waterfall, workbench, football, earring, necktie, playpen, seafood, skyscraper, sunrise, windmill, daydream, handshake, nightdress, racetrack, shoelace, spaceship, teardrop, textbook, toothbrush, windscreen

LEARNING TARGETS

Pupil Book: Focus
to match key words to pictures

Pupil Book: Extra
to answer clues with **wh** and **ph** words

Pupil Book: Extension
to practise creating compound words

Workbook: Focus
to match words to pictures

Workbook: Extra
To complete simple cloze activity using **wh** words

Resource sheet: Focus
to complete **wh** and **ph** word sums;
to match words to pictures

Resource sheet: Extension
to match pictures to words;
to recognise and use question words beginning with **wh**

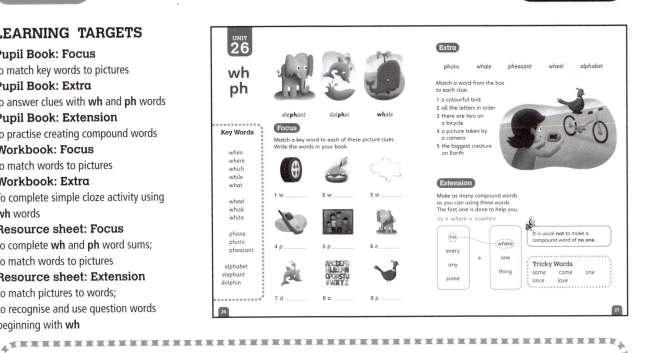

BACKGROUND NOTES AND SUGGESTIONS

Of the consonant digraphs **wh** and **ph**, **wh** is the far more significant at this stage. The question words are the most important **wh** words at the early stages, and can provide a useful focus for a lesson, as can *where* in compound words (*nowhere, anywhere, everywhere, somewhere*).

Unfortunately several **wh** words include irregular characteristics for the weaker spellers, so this is an opportunity for those children to practise the words using the 'Look, Say, Cover, Write, Check' technique.

Most words with the **ph** digraph are of Greek origin and are quite sophisticated. A selection of the rather more frequently used and accessible words is listed below. The /f/ sound is not usually spelt 'ph' in short, everyday English words.

Pupil Book answers

Focus

1 wheel	2 whisk	3 white
4 phone	5 photo	6 elephant
7 dolphin	8 alphabet	9 pheasant

Extra

1 pheasant	2 alphabet	3 wheel
4 photo	5 whale	

Extension

nowhere   nothing
everywhere   everyone   everything
anywhere   anyone   anything
somewhere   someone   something

Workbook answers

Focus

1 alphabet	2 pheasant	3 whisk
4 wheel	5 elephant	6 phone
7 dolphin	8 white	9 photo

Extra

1 My mum uses a <u>whisk</u> when she makes a cake.
2 I painted the swan in my picture <u>white</u>.
3 Tom and Isla always <u>whisper</u> to each other.
4 The <u>wheel</u> on my bike is broken.
5 The cat cleans her <u>whiskers</u>.
6 <u>Where</u> are my shoes?
7 My teacher blew her <u>whistle</u>.
8 <u>What</u> time is it?

Resource sheet answers

Focus

Ⓐ Children should copy the letter pattern.

Ⓑ whisk white wheel photo pheasant phone

Ⓒ photo whisk phone white

Extension

Ⓐ

1 dolphin		2 elephant
3 whisper		4 whisker
5 whistle		6 alphabet
7 whirlwind		8 pheasant

Ⓑ Teacher to check individual answers

Supporting word lists

whack
when
whip which whiz whisk
whisker whistle whisper
whale
wheel wheat
while whine white
why
whirl

Irregular wh words
as in hare:
where wherever
as in moo:
who whom whose whoever
as in rose:
whole wholly
as in dog:
what

pharaoh phone phonics
photo photograph phrase physical

apostrophe nephew orphan prophet
triumph trophy typhoon

LEARNING TARGETS

Pupil Book: Focus

to match key words to pictures, and an associated activity

Pupil Book: Extra

to understand the concept of prefixes by deconstructing words with the **un** prefix

Pupil Book: Extension

to create antonyms using the **un** prefix

Workbook: Focus

to match key words to pictures

Workbook: Extra

to label a picture with given **un** words

Resource sheet: Focus

to practise writing **un** words and match words to pictures

Resource sheet: Extension

to complete an **un** words word fan; to match the words to pictures

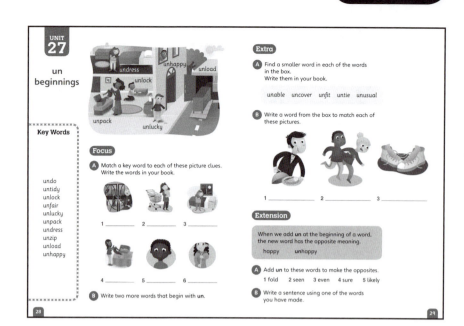

BACKGROUND NOTES AND SUGGESTIONS

The prefix **un** is added to the beginning of a word without the need for any adjustment to the spelling. This makes it a helpful way to introduce prefixes, which are developed further in Pupil Book 2, Unit 15.

Pupil Book answers

Focus

Ⓐ 1 unlock   2 unload   3 undress
4 unpack   5 unhappy   6 unzip

Ⓑ Teacher to check individual answers

Extra

Ⓐ unable: able
uncover: cover
unfit: fit   (it)
untie: tie
unusual: usual (us)

Ⓑ 1 uncover   2 unfit   3 untie

Extension

Ⓐ 1 unfold   2 unseen   3 uneven
4 unsure   5 unlikely

Ⓑ Teacher to check individual answers

Workbook answers

Focus

1 unhappy   2 unlock
3 undo   4 untidy
5 unpack   6 unload
7 undress   8 unzip
9 unfair

Extra

Teacher to check individual answers

Resource sheet answers

Focus

Ⓐ untidy undress unpack unhappy

Ⓑ unlock unhappy undo

Ⓒ untidy undress unpack

Extension

Ⓐ undo unfair unlock untidy
undress unzip unload unhappy

Ⓑ unlock undress unhappy
unzip untidy unload

Supporting word lists

unable unaided unarmed unaware
unbearable unclean uncover undo
undress uneven unfair unfit unfold
unlikely unload unlock unlucky
unpack untie

LEARNING TARGETS

Pupil Book: Focus
to identify missing letters in short sequences;
to answer questions on letter position

Pupil Book: Extra
to introduce the notion of
alphabetical ordering

Pupil Book: Extension
to sort words alphabetically by
first letter

Workbook: Focus
to write the alphabet in order using capital
letters

Workbook: Extra
to answer questions on letter position; to put
letters in alphabetical order

Resource sheet: Focus
to identify initial letters of words

Resource sheet: Extension
to order letters and words alphabetically

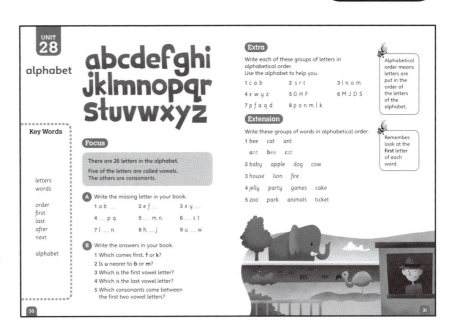

BACKGROUND NOTES AND SUGGESTIONS

The ability to sort alphabetically is required for much reference work through a child's school life, and beyond.
Unit 1 in Pupil Book 1A started to develop this skill; this is the next of several units in *Nelson Spelling* to take the
work forward.

Pupil Book answers

Focus

Ⓐ **1** a b c   **2** e f g   **3** x y z
   4 o p q   **5** l m n   **6** r s t
   7 l m n   **8** h i j   **9** u v w

Ⓑ **1** f   **2** m   **3** a
   4 u   **5** b c d

Extra

Ⓐ **1** a b c   **2** r s t
   3 l m n o   **4** w x y z
   5 F G H   **6** D J M S
   7 a d f p q   **8** k l m n o p

Extension

1 ant bee cat
2 apple baby cow dog
3 fire house lion
4 cake games jelly party
5 animals park ticket zoo

Workbook answers

Focus

ABCDE
FGHIJ
KLMNO
PQRST
UVWXY
Z

Extra

1 a
2 k
3 b
4 s
5 u o a
6 Teacher to check individual answers

Resource sheet answers

Focus

Ⓐ t = tap
   m = map
   d = door

Ⓑ **1** s   **2** d
   3 c   **4** p

Extension

Ⓐ **1** s t u
   2 b c d
   3 o p q
   4 g h i
   5 u v w
   6 f g h
   7 p q r
   8 q r s

Ⓑ / Ⓒ Teacher to check
individual answers

Check-Up 2

1 windy	**2** party	**3** dart
4 coin	**5** flower	**6** nurse
7 clown	**8** bear	**9** bedroom
10 boy	**11** beard	**12** bird
13 house	**14** horse	**15** elephant

Extension

1–3 Teacher to check individual answers

1 Monday	**2** Friday	**3** Wednesday

Book 2 Scope and Sequence

Unit	Pupil Book Focus	Pupil Book Extra	Pupil Book Extension	Workbook Focus	Workbook Extra & Extension	Resource Book Focus	Resource Book Extension
1	*a-e ai ay* key word matching	compound words	homophones	labelling a picture	word sums: adding *ing*; key word quiz	using *ai* and *ay* words	key exceptions: *said, says, again*; wordsearch
2	*ee ea e-e* key word matching	homophones; cloze activity	short *ea* cloze activity	labelling a picture	sorting words by *ee / ea*; writing rhyming words	*ee / ea* word sums; word matching	*ee / ea* puzzle; cloze activity with *please & heard*
3	*i-e igh y* key word matching	copying *ike y ice ight* rhyming words	target word quiz with poem	labelling a picture	completing words with *igh* and *y*; cloze activity	*y* word sums	rule for adding *ed / es* to words ending in *y*; *why*
4	*o-e oa ow* finding rhyming words	sorting words by long / short *ow*	vowel letters	labelling a picture	wordsearch; using given words in sentences	*oa / ow* word sums; word-matching	practising words with long 'o' phoneme
5	*u-e oo ew* key word matching	target word quiz	sorting words by long / short *oo*	labelling a picture with given words	word-matching; writing rhyming words	*ew / oo* word sums; word-matching	alphabetical ordering by 2nd letter
6	*ar* key word matching	identifying *ar* words in a picture; the *ar* grapheme as *or* phoneme	the *ar* phoneme when spelled *a*	labelling a picture with given words	building *art ar ark* words; writing sentences	*ar* letter patterns	word sums; letter pattern sorting
7	*oi oy* finding rhyming words	sorting words by *oil oin oy* patterns	completing words with *oi* or *oy*	labelling a picture	cloze activity; finding words in jumbled letters	*oil, oin, oint & oy* letter patterns	writing sentences
8	*ear ea* key word matching	sorting words by long / short *ea*	wordsearch	labelling a picture	writing rhyming words; word quiz	*ear & ead* letter patterns; word sums	sorting *ea* words
9	*er ir ur* key word matching	cloze activity with *ur* words	*ire* phoneme dictionary work	labelling a picture	completing words with *er, ir* and *ur*; sorting words	*er, ir* and *ur* word sums; word-matching	adding suffixes and doubling final consonant
10	*ou ow* key word matching	sorting words by different *ow / ou* sounds	cloze activity: irregular but high frequency *ou* words	labelling a picture	word quiz; wordsearch	*ou & ow* letter patterns	*could, should, would; ou* homophones
11	*or ore aw au* key word matching	suffix *ed / d*	homophones wordsearch	labelling a picture	word sums with *ing*; writing rhyming words	word fan; word-matching	homophones cloze activity
12	*air ear are* key word matching	homophone pairs wordsearch	compound words puzzle	labelling a picture	building *air ear are* words; alphabetical order	*ain & air* letter patterns; word sums	completing words; homophone practice
13	*all al* matching and using key words	*al* prefix	*al / ly* suffixes	labelling a picture	sorting words by *al / all*; cloze activity	target letter patterns; word sums	*al* prefix
14	unusual 'o' words key word matching	cloze activity using target words	word puzzle using target words	word-matching	identifying and writing rhyming words; completing words; sentence writing	word-matching; rhyming words	different phonemes using *o* in *o-e* words

The darker cells introduce statutory material for this year group in the National Curriculum for England.
The paler cells denote revision of a topic covered in previous years.

Unit	Pupil Book Focus	Pupil Book Extra	Pupil Book Extension	Workbook Focus	Workbook Extra & Extension	Resource Book Focus	Resource Book Extension
15	*un dis* key word matching, adding *un* & *dis*	cloze activity using target prefixes	writing sentences with target prefixes	labelling a picture	building words using the target prefixes; wordsearch	*dis* words fan; word-matching	target word puzzles; sentences
16	soft *c* matching and using key words	wordsearch with 'soft' and 'hard' c	word fan with *ace* pattern	labelling a picture	word-matching; writing sentences	word sums; word-matching	alphabetical ordering
17	soft *g ge dge* matching key words and building words	wordsearch	*ge dge* quiz	labelling a picture	cloze activity; finding words in jumbled letters	letter patterns; rhyming words	target word puzzle; sentences
18	*le el al il* endings key word matching; rhyming words	identifying letter patterns; answering clues	sorting letter patterns	labelling a picture	completing words with *le, el, al* & *il*; cloze activity	*le* letter patterns; rhyming clues	jumbled letters puzzle; wordsearch
19	adding *'s* or *s* adding missing apostrophes	adding missing apostrophes; shortening sentences using *'s*	plurals with *s* and *es*	labelling a picture	adding apostrophes; plurals with *s / es*	plural nouns with *s* & *es*	sentences with singular possessive
20	*y ey* endings matching and using key words	selecting and sorting *y* phonemes	vowel / *y* plurals	labelling a picture	completing words with *y* or *ey*; forming plurals in nouns ending in *y*	target letter patterns; rhyming words	adding *s* to words ending in *y*
21	adding *ing ed er* matching & using key words	double last letter before suffix	dropping *e* before suffix	labelling a picture	word sums with *ing* (magic) e; word sums	final consonant doubling	adding *ing* rules
						Extra practice 1 adjectives with *y*	**Extra practice 2** *er* and *est* with 'magic' *e*
22	silent letters matching and using key words	wordsearch; quiz	sorting words by silent letter	labelling a picture	identifying silent letters; silent *k, g, w* words	target letter patterns; word sums	identifying words with silent letters
23	*wa qua* key word matching	target word quiz	singular possessive	labelling a picture	cloze activity; finding words in jumbled letters	target letter patterns; word sums	cloze activity; wordsearch
24	adding *less ful ness ment ly* adding suffix to make target words	adding suffix to *y* endings	adding *ness, ment* to make new words	labelling a picture	building *full less* words; writing sentences	word fans with *less, full*	*less fully* suffixes
25	shortened words deconstructing contractions	forming contractions from two words	tricky contractions	matching contractions with their component words	using contractions in sentences	writing & 'exploding' contractions	writing contractions; using *its* & *it's*
26	*tion* matching & using key words	finding target words in wordsearch	the *zh* sound spelt 's'	labelling a picture	word-matching; using *tion* words in sentences	word sums; word-matching	completing words; wordsearch
27	homophones writing homophones	homophone cloze activity	homonyms	labelling a picture	differentiating between homophone pairs; homonym cloze activity	high frequency homophones	homophone practice
28	*y + er y + est y + ed* matching & writing key words	adding suffixes to words ending in *y*	comparative adjectives	labelling a picture	word sums; cloze activity	word-matching	rule for adding *er / est* to words ending in *y*

LEARNING TARGETS

Pupil Book: Focus
to match key words to pictures, and associated activity; to write **ay** rhyming words

Pupil Book: Extra
to practise compound words

Pupil Book: Extension
to introduce homophone use with the target digraphs

Workbook: Focus
to label a picture using given words

Workbook: Extra
to add **ing** to **a-e**, **ai** and **ay** words

Workbook: Extension
to answer clues using **a-e**, **ai** and **ay** words; to write rhyming words

Resource sheet: Focus
to use **ai** and **ay** words

Resource sheet: Extension
to practise the 'special' words *said, says, again*; to use clues to find key words in a wordsearch

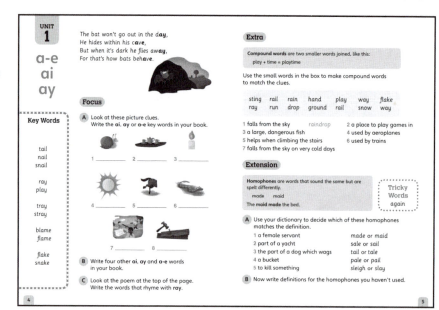

BACKGROUND NOTES AND SUGGESTIONS

The modifier ('magic') **e** work introduced earlier, in the context of the **a-e** digraph, and the other important vowel graphemes **ai** and **ay**, are revisited from Pupil Book 1, and the work extended.

Both **ai** and **ay** words often appear as components of compound words, and therefore this unit is a useful opportunity to work on compound words generally.

One of the more significant letter patterns associated with the vowel digraph **ai** is **air**. This is part of the focus of Pupil Book 2, Unit 12.

Pupil Book answers

Focus

A 1 snail 2 tray 3 flame
4 ray 5 tail 6 snake
7 play 8 nail

B Teacher to check individual answers

C away   day

Extra

1 raindrop 2 playground
3 stingray 4 runway
5 handrail 6 railway
7 snowflake

Extension

A 1 maid 2 sail 3 tail
4 pail 5 slay

B Teacher to check individual answers

Workbook answers

Focus

Teacher to check individual answers

Extra

1 playing 2 tracing 3 staging
4 paying 5 nailing 6 sailing
7 laying 8 saying 9 shaking
10 shaving

Extension

1 nail 2 play 3 tail
4 snake 5 flame 6 tray

Resource sheet answers

Focus

A sail nail rain tray

B tail snail pay play

C tray nail rails spray

Extension

A "Mum <u>says</u> we can use Dad's tools,"
<u>said</u> Ravi.
"But Dad <u>said</u> if he found us using
them <u>again</u> we'd be in big trouble!"
<u>said</u> Usha.

B 1 railway 2 play
3 aid 4 rain/spray
5 snail 6 stray
7 tray

C tray say lay ray way lay laid
rail spray rain

Supporting word lists

ace face lace race
place grace trace space

age cage page rage wage stage
blade spade
blame flame shame
brake flake stake shake snake
brave slave grave shave
crane plane
blaze graze
grape shape
crate grate plate slate
chase

bay day hay jay lay
may pay ray say way
lay clay play
ray bray pray tray stray spray
way sway
stay

aid aim
maid mail main
paid pail pain plain
raid rail rain
aid laid maid paid raid
bail fail hail jail mail nail pail rail sail tail
vail wail rail Braille frail trail sail snail

*said says again

LEARNING TARGETS

Pupil Book: Focus
to match key words to pictures, and associated activity

Pupil Book: Extra
to introduce and provide practice with homophones

Pupil Book: Extension
to introduce the grapheme **ea** representing the phoneme as a short /e/

Workbook: Focus
to label a picture using given words

Workbook: Extra
to sort words according to letter patterns

Workbook: Extension
to write rhyming words for given words

Resource sheet: Focus
to complete **ee** and **ea** word sums; to match words with pictures

Resource sheet: Extension
to use **ee** and **ea** words to answer a puzzle; to use the 'special' words *please* and *heard* in a cloze passage

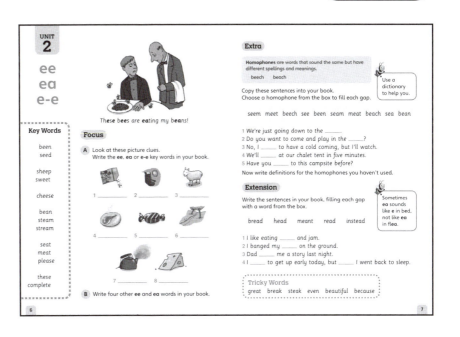

BACKGROUND NOTES AND SUGGESTIONS

These vowel digraphs are extremely common in the words young children read and write. They therefore warrant a little extra time and attention. They are also ideal digraphs to support revision of the consonant sequences and consonant digraphs from earlier units.

Whilst one of the main objectives of this unit is to revisit words with the simple **ea** sound, it should be noted that other **ea** sound/letter correspondences are covered in this unit and returned to in Pupil Book 2, Unit 8. Because of these sound variations many **ea** words are associated with homophones and homonyms. These are introduced here and this might be a good time to start a class collection of homophones and homonyms.

Relatively few significant words have the target phoneme represented by the modifier ('magic') **e**, e.g. *these, theme, complete*. These might usefully be introduced and practised at this time.

Pupil Book answers

Focus

A 1 seed   2 seat   3 sheep
4 meat   5 sweet   6 stream
7 steam   8 cheese

B Teacher to check individual answers

Extra

1 beach   2 sea   3 seem
4 meet   5 been

Extension

1 bread   2 head
3 read   4 meant instead

Workbook answers

Focus

Teacher to check individual answers

Extra

words with **ee**	words with **ea**
green	*clean*
reef	dream
sheep	meal
sweet	cream
speed	peach
weed	team

Extension

Teacher to check individual answers

Resource sheet answers

Focus

A Children should copy the patterns.
B *Upper activity*
bee tree sweet sea seat steam stream
Lower activity
tree bee sweet steam

Extension

A 1 feet   2 tree   3 beans
4 beach   5 weeds   6 bee
7 stream   8 seal   9 steel

B "Dad, <u>please</u> can Zak come to tea?" asked Will.
"I've <u>heard</u> he can be rude!" said his dad.
"I don't know where you <u>heard</u> that," replied Will.
"He always says <u>please</u> and thank you."

Supporting word lists

ee fee see free tree
eel feel heel peel reel steel
deed feed need seed weed
bleed breed greed speed tweed
been keen seen green
deep jeep keep peep seep weep
sleep creep steep sheep
feet meet fleet sleet tweet sweet sheet
leek week
see seed seek seen seem
bee beef been
fee feel feet

+ing
feeding needing seeding weeding
bleeding speeding
peeping weeping sleeping creeping
seeping feeling meeting

pea sea tea flea
eat beat heat meat neat peat teat
bleat treat cheat
bean jeans lean mean clean
beam seam team gleam cream dream
steam scream stream
deal heal meal peal seal veal steal
beak leak teak freak speak sneak tweak
streak
bead lead read plead
heap leap reap cheap
each beach peach reach teach
bleach preach
east beast feast least yeast
heave leave weave
sea seal seam seat
tea teak team teat
pea peal peat peak
leaf leak lean leap leach

*please heard

these theme complete

LEARNING TARGETS

Pupil Book: Focus
to match key words to the pictures, and associated activity

Pupil Book: Extra
to identify rhyming words related to significant spelling patterns for the target phoneme

Pupil Book: Extension
to find **igh** words in a poem to answer clues

Workbook: Focus
to label a picture using given words

Workbook: Extra
to complete words using **igh** or **y**

Workbook: Extension
to complete a simple cloze activity

Resource sheet: Focus
to complete word sums using **y**

Resource sheet: Extension
to introduce the rule for adding **ed** and **es** to short words ending in **y**

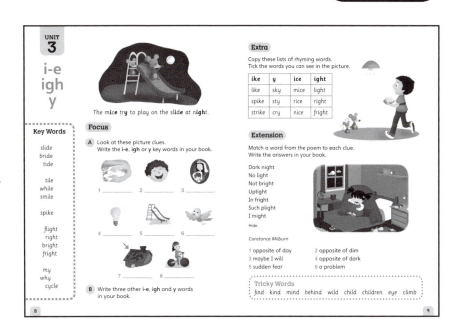

BACKGROUND NOTES AND SUGGESTIONS

igh is traditionally thought of as being one of the trickier vowel graphemes, but unlike many others it has no phonemic variations, and thus once mastered can be very satisfying for the children to use.

Pupils who did the earlier work on these vowels can be directed to the significance of this group of words in which one of the representations of the phoneme has no vowel letter other than the 'semi-vowel' **y**. The point can be made that whenever it stands as a vowel, it takes the place of an **i**, usually 'long' (*my*, *cry*) – though not always (*gym*).

The Resource sheet Extension activity demonstrates a simplified version of the spelling rule:
- to make the plural of a noun that ends in a consonant +**y**, change **y** to **i** and add **es** (*fly*, *flies*).

Pupil Book answers

Focus

A 1 tide   2 smile   3 bride
    4 light   5 slide   6 flight
    7 tile   8 cycle

B Teacher to check individual answers

Extra

mice, light, rice, fright

Extension

1 night   2 bright   3 might
4 light   5 fright   6 plight

Workbook answers

Focus

Teacher to check individual answers

Extra

1 fly   2 high
3 sly   4 light
5 sky   6 bright
7 sigh   8 my
9 dry   10 flight
11 sight   12 why

Extension

1 The ball was kicked <u>high</u> in the <u>sky</u>.
2 The <u>mice</u> come out at <u>night</u>.
3 The <u>light</u> is very <u>bright</u>.
4 The <u>fly</u> flew <u>right</u> into my eye!
5 The <u>bride</u> has a lovely <u>smile</u>.

Resource sheet answers

Focus

A Children should copy the words.
B *Upper activity*
cry try fry dry fly sky spy
Lower activity
cry fry fly sky

Extension

A cried cries
   fried fries
   dried dries
   spied spies

B Teacher to check individual answers

Supporting word lists

ice dice mice nice rice
slice price spice twice splice
spike strike
spite sprite
stile while smile
spine swine twine shine
glide slide bride pride
crime grime prime slime
tripe swipe
drive

by my
fly sly
cry dry fry try
sky spy sty shy
type style

high sigh thigh
fight light might night right sight tight
light blight flight slight
right bright fright
brighten frighten lighten tighten

LEARNING TARGETS

Pupil Book: Focus
to find and copy rhyming **o-e** and **oa** words

Pupil Book: Extra
to compare and practise words with the two main phonemes represented by **ow**

Pupil Book: Extension
to introduce the notion of vowel letters

Workbook: Focus
to label a picture using given words

Workbook: Extra
to find **o-e**, **oa**, **ow** words in a wordsearch

Workbook: Extension
to use **o-e**, **oa** and **ow** words in a sentence

Resource sheet: Focus
to complete word sums involving **oa** and **ow** digraphs; to match words to pictures

Resource sheet: Extension
to practise words with the 'long o' phoneme represented by **o**

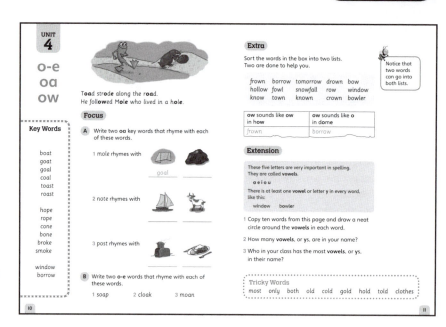

BACKGROUND NOTES AND SUGGESTIONS

This unit seeks to secure and develop the skills and knowledge previously introduced in Pupil Book 1A, Unit 13.

A noteworthy feature of most words that have the ending **ow** is that it represents the 'long' **o** phoneme (as in *rose*), rather than the regular **ow** sound (as in *cow*).

It is also worth focusing on the modifier ('magic') **e** situation where there is no intervening consonant, e.g. *doe*. Draw parallels with **ie** and **ue** endings.

The phoneme is often represented by a single **o**, notably in some frequently used 'special' words, e.g. *most almost cold*. The important **old** letter sequence is the subject of the Resource sheet Extension for this unit.

Some children will be able to appreciate that the bottom group of words in the Supporting words lists have the long **o** sound because they are all (except *own*) past tense and their root words have a final (long) **ow**.

Pupil Book answers

Focus

Ⓐ goal   coal
    boat   goat
    toast   roast

Ⓑ Teacher to check individual answers

Extra

frown	borrow
drown	tomorrow
bow	bow
fowl	hollow
row	snowfall
town	row
crown	window
	know
	known
	bowler

Extension
Teacher to check individual answers

Workbook answers

Focus
Teacher to check individual answers

Extra

k	c	b	s	n	o	w	f
h	w	e	f	l	p	t	l
o	g	r	o	a	n	h	o
p	a	o	a	u	o	r	a
e	j	p	m	r	t	o	t
h	k	e	d	s	e	w	i
t	o	m	o	r	r	o	w

snow, groan, rope, tomorrow, float, note, throw, foam, hope

Extension
Teacher to check individual answers

Resource sheet answers

Focus

Ⓐ Children should copy the patterns.

Ⓑ *Upper activity*
goat coat toad goal crow blow snow
Lower activity
goat crow toad goal

Extension
Upper activity
Children should copy the words.
Lower activity
Teacher to check individual answers

Supporting word lists

bone cone lone tone zone
stone scone throne
code rode strode
dope hope mope rope slope grope
dole hole mole pole role vole stole
home
coke joke poke woke yoke
broke bloke spoke smoke choke
hose nose pose rose
close prose chose those
note tote vote
drove
robe globe probe
froze
doe foe hoe toe
*one gone come some

oats boat coat goat moat
float throat stoat bloat
coal foal goal shoal
foam roam
coax hoax
load road toad
loan moan groan

bow low mow row sow tow know
blow flow glow slow crow grow stow
snow show throw
arrow barrow harrow marrow narrow
bellow fellow yellow elbow
billow pillow willow widow window
minnow
follow hollow
burrow furrow tomorrow sorrow sparrow
shadow shallow swallow
rainbow crossbow hedgerow

owned sown blown flown grown shown
thrown known

LEARNING TARGETS

Pupil Book: Focus
to match key words to pictures, and associated activity

Pupil Book: Extra
to match key words to clues in a puzzle

Pupil Book: Extension
to distinguish the two phonemes represented by **oo**

Workbook: Focus
to label a picture using given words

Workbook: Extra
to choose words to match pictures

Workbook: Extension
to write rhyming words for given words

Resource sheet: Focus
to complete word sums involving **ew** and **oo** digraphs; to match words to pictures

Resource sheet: Extension
to practise alphabetical ordering by second letter

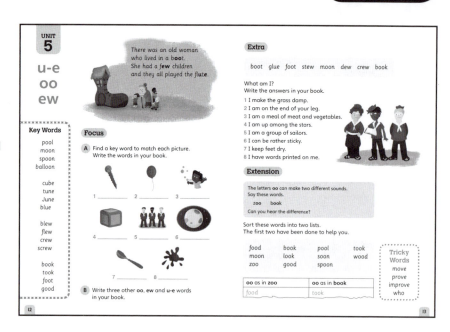

BACKGROUND NOTES AND SUGGESTIONS

In Received Pronunciation, **oo** represents three different vowel sounds (as in *moon book door*). This unit focuses on the first two of these, which are the most common.

A frieze of a herd of cows, each with a long **oo** word, can be effective, as can pictures in a frieze of eyes or glasses representing 'look', each with a short **oo** word.

The **ew** vowel digraph is often found associated with the letter **r**, as can be noted in the Supporting word lists below.

Pupil Book answers

Focus

A
1 screw	2 balloon	3 blew
4 cube	5 crew	6 moon
7 spoon	8 blue	

B Teacher to check individual answers

Extra

1 dew	2 foot	3 stew
4 moon	5 crew	6 glue
7 boot	8 book	

Extension

oo as in zoo: food pool moon soon
             spoon

oo as in book: took look wood good

Workbook answers

Focus
Teacher to check individual answers

Extra

1 spoon	2 chew	3 cube
4 boot	5 crew	6 flute
7 book	8 shrew	9 June

Extension

A e.g. moon, balloon, soon

B e.g. chew, flew, screw, blew

C e.g. tune, June

D e.g. took, look, cook

Resource sheet answers

Focus

A Children should copy the pattern.

B *Upper activity*
new chew crew shrew zoo food boot
Lower activity
chew shrew food boot

Extension

A blew flew stew
chew dew threw

B saw sow stew
screw shawl spawn
claw cow crew
new nil now

Supporting word lists

boo moo too zoo shoo
boom doom room zoom bloom gloom
broom groom
boot coot loot hoot root toot
shoot scoot
food mood brood
fool pool tool spool stool

hoof roof proof
hoop loop scoop snoop swoop stoop droop
moon noon soon spoon
boo boom boot
hoof hoop hoot
roof room root

June dune tune prune
lute cute flute brute
duke fluke
rule
use fuse
rude nude
cube tube
blue clue glue true

yew dew few mew new stew chew
blew flew
brew crew drew grew
screw threw shrew

LEARNING TARGETS

Pupil Book: Focus
to match key words to pictures, and associated activity

Pupil Book: Extra
to identify and write target words from a picture; to select words where the **ar** grapheme represents the **or** phoneme

Pupil Book: Extension
to introduce the target phoneme **ar** when represented by the single letter **a**

Workbook: Focus
to label a picture using given words

Workbook: Extra
to build words by joining letters

Workbook: Extension
to choose words and use them in a sentence

Resource sheet: Focus
to practise **ar** letter patterns and related words

Resource sheet: Extension
to complete word sums and sort words by letter patterns

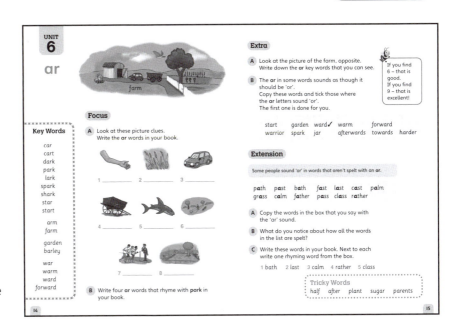

BACKGROUND NOTES AND SUGGESTIONS

The unit revises and revisits work from Pupil Book 1B, Unit 16, but progresses to encompass the spelling patterns in which the phoneme normally associated with the grapheme **ar** is represented by the single letter **a** and where it represents the **or** phoneme. As there are many high and medium frequency words in this group it is important to ensure as many children as possible are taught to understand and spell these words.

The related **are** phonemes are introduced and taught in Pupil Book 2, Unit 12. However, some children might be ready to be made aware of the potential confusion with words such as *care* and *fare*.

Pupil Book answers

Focus
A 1 arm   2 barley   3 car
   4 cart   5 shark   6 park
   7 start   8 garden

B Teacher to check individual answers

Extra
A barn, garden, bark, lark, car, cart, bar, dark (inside barn), barley, spark (from fire)

B *Words to tick:* ward warm forward warrior afterwards towards

Extension
A This answer is very much regional dependent.

B The 'ar' sound is spelt 'a'.

C Teacher to check individual answers

Workbook answers

Focus
Teacher to check individual answers

Extra
e.g. wart, war, bar, bark, dart, dark, shark, part, par, park, spar, spark, start, star, stark, lark, cart, car, jar

Extension
Teacher to check individual answers

Resource sheet answers

Focus
A Children should copy the patterns.

B dark arm star shark

C farm shark car cart

Extension
A 1 car   2 dart   3 dark
   4 lark   5 spark   6 shark
   7 garden   8 starling   9 bath
   10 fast   11 grass   12 class
The 'a' sounds 'ar' in the last four words.

B lark   smart   alarm
   park   start   farm
   spark   cart   arm
   bark   part   harm
   shark   dart

C Teacher to check individual answers

Supporting word lists
bar car far jar tar star scar
ark bark dark lark mark park
shark spark
arm farm harm
art cart dart part tart start smart
barn darn yarn
card hard lard yard
harp scarp sharp
scarf
harsh marsh
ark arm art
bar bark barn
car card cart
dark darn dart
hard harm harp

bath path
cast past fast last mast
pass class grass
palm calm half
father rather
after
plant

*are care fare

LEARNING TARGETS

Pupil Book: Focus
to select rhyming key words to match pictures, and associated activities

Pupil Book: Extra
to sort target words according to their spelling patterns

Pupil Book: Extension
to complete words using the correct vowel digraph

Workbook: Focus
to label a picture using given words

Workbook: Extra
to complete a simple cloze activity

Workbook: Extension
to find **oi** and **oy** words in mixed-up letters

Resource sheet: Focus
to practise **oil**, **oin**, **oint** and **oy** letter patterns and related words

Resource sheet: Extension
to use a selection of target words in sentences

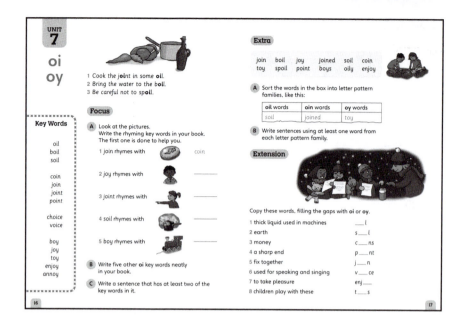

BACKGROUND NOTES AND SUGGESTIONS

The vowel sound represented by **oi/oy** never appears as the letter pattern **oi** at the end of a word. **oy** appears frequently in a medial position if preceding a suffix (e.g. *joyful*) or exceptionally in *groyne, royal*.

Pupil Book answers

Focus

A
1 coin	2 boy
3 point	4 boil
5 toy	

B Teacher to check individual answers
C Teacher to check individual answers

Extra

A
soil	joined	toy
boil	join	joy
spoil	coin	boys
oily	point	enjoy

B Teacher to check individual answers

Extension

1 oil	2 soil
3 coins	4 point
5 join	6 voice
7 enjoy	8 toys

Workbook answers

Focus

Teacher to check individual answers

Extra

1 The children planted a small tree in the <u>soil</u>.
2 My puppy chewed my best <u>toy</u>.
3 I want to <u>join</u> a football club.
4 The class made a lot of <u>noise</u> so the teacher told them off.
5 Ben hid his last <u>coin</u> so his sister would not spend it.
6 I like to annoy my <u>brother</u>!

Extension

1 point	2 boy
3 coin	4 voice

Resource answers

Focus

A Children should copy the patterns.

B point toy join soil

C voice boil boy joint

Extension

Upper activity
Children should copy the words.

Lower activity
Teacher to check individual answers

Supporting word lists

join joint joist
soil spoil spoilt
oil boil coil soil toil spoil
coin join
joint point
hoist joist moist
voice choice
noise poise

boy joy toy ploy
groyne

LEARNING TARGETS

Pupil Book: Focus
to match key words to pictures, and associated activities

Pupil Book: Extra
to compare examples of words with different **ea** phonemes

Pupil Book: Extension
to find short **e** phoneme **ea** words in a wordsearch puzzle

Workbook: Focus
to label a picture using given words

Workbook: Extra
to write rhyming words for given words

Workbook: Extension
to answer clues with **ear** and **ea** words

Resource sheet: Focus
to practise the **ear** and **ead** letter patterns; to complete word sums using the patterns

Resource sheet: Extension
to sort words according to the phonemes represented by the **ea** grapheme

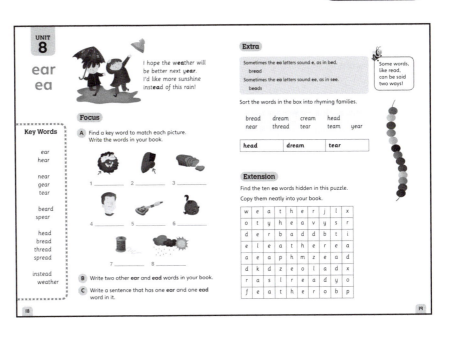

BACKGROUND NOTES AND SUGGESTIONS

Before commencing this unit, remind the children that the 'regular' and most frequent phoneme for the **ea** grapheme is represented in words such as *tea* and *heat*. Some children will find the auditory distinction between **ea** in these words and **ea** in *year* difficult at this stage.

There are a significant number of irregular **ea** words, falling into two groups, as shown. This unit practises the important 'irregular' short **ea** (*head*) words. Some teachers may choose to use the device of describing the **a** in this group as 'silent'.

More work on these sound/letter pattern correspondences follows later in the course in Book 4, Unit 1.

Pupil Book answers

Focus

A 1 beard   2 ear
    3 bread   4 head
    5 spread   6 tear
    7 thread   8 weather

B Teacher to check individual answers

C Teacher to check individual answers

Extra

head	dream	tear
bread	cream	near
thread	team	year

Extension
weather, heavy, leather, ready, feather, dead, read(s), heather, bread, steady

Workbook answers

Focus
Teacher to check individual answers

Extra

1	ear	
2	fear	
3	bread	
4	tear	
5	head	
6	feather	

Extension
1 spread
2 head
3 weather
4 sea
5 near

Resource sheet answers

Focus

A Children should copy the patterns and words.

B hear year tear head bread tread spread

Extension

beach	pear	head
steamer	wear	weather
tear	tear	dread
nearly		tread
spear		feather
team		spread
treated		leather
teacher		dead
year		

Supporting word lists
dead head lead read
bread dread tread stead
thread spread
breadth instead bedspread

ear dear fear gear hear
near rear tear year
clear smear spear
beard

LEARNING TARGETS

Pupil Book: Focus

to match key words to pictures, and associated activities

Pupil Book: Extra

to choose **ur** words to complete a cloze exercise

Pupil Book: Extension

to use a simple dictionary to find definitions of some target words

Workbook: Focus

to label a picture using given words

Workbook: Extra

to complete words using **er**, **ir** or **ur**

Workbook: Extension

to sort words into **er**, **ir** and **ur** groups

Resource sheet: Focus

to complete word sums using **er**, **ir** and **ur** words; to match words to pictures

Resource sheet: Extension

to add **er**, **ed** or **ing** to words, noting when the final consonant must be doubled

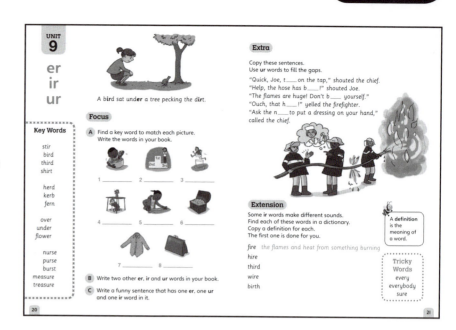

BACKGROUND NOTES AND SUGGESTIONS

This unit practises a group of frequently occurring **r** vowel sounds. Phonemically the medial **er** in the words listed below and the final **er** are different vowel sounds, the latter being a schwa vowel, and sounding more as a grunt (similar to the word *a*). Nevertheless, most teachers find the grouping of the medial and final **er** letter pattern rarely causes problems and is usually helpful.

A useful spin-off with work on the final **er** pattern is that children can work on double letter patterns that might be causing problems, similar to those listed in the Supporting word lists.

Whilst it is not a vowel digraph which appears very frequently, several of the words in which **ir** does occur are used quite often by children. Also, the **ire** letter pattern, whilst containing **ir**, has a separate and distinct phoneme. This is demonstrated in the Extension section of this unit.

Some children might find using a dictionary a novel experience and appropriate support will need to be given.

The **ur** vowel digraph occurs quite often (see also Book 4, Unit 3), but in spelling acquisition its most significant context is in the suffixes **sure** and **ture** (see Book 3, Unit 23).

Pupil Book answers

Focus

A 1 stir 2 third 3 over
4 under 5 measure 6 treasure
7 shirt 8 purse

B Teacher to check individual answers

C Teacher to check individual answers

Extra

turn burst burn hurt nurse

Extension

Teacher to check individual answers

Workbook answers

Focus

Teacher to check individual answers

Extra

1 ve**r**b 2 bu**r**n 3 cu**r**l
4 sti**r** 5 thi**r**d 6 he**r**d
7 pe**r**ch 8 nu**r**se 9 flowe**r**

10 shi**r**t 11 treas**u**re 12 fe**r**n
13 bi**r**d 14 p**u**rse 15 di**r**t

Extension

er words	ir words	ur words
verb	stir	curl
perch	shirt	burn
herd	bird	purse
flower	third	treasure
fern	dirt	nurse

Resource sheet answers

Focus

A Children should copy the pattern.

B *Upper activity*
herb perch letter bird stir skirt
nurse burst
Lower activity
nurse perch burst skirt

Extension

shopper	shopped	shopping
swimmer		swimming
slipper	slipped	slipping
spinner		spinning
flipper	flipped	flipping
digger		digging
mixer	mixed	mixing
zipper	zipped	zipping
printer	printed	printing
sitter		sitting
hopper	hopped	hopping
dropper	dropped	dropping
tripper	tripped	tripping
twister	twisted	twisting

Supporting word lists
her herd
herb kerb verb
fern stern
jerk perk
perm term germ
nerve serve swerve
perch

There are numerous examples of words
with final er. Here are a few which also
have either tt or pp patterns.
letter litter better trotter potter spotter
gutter butter sitter fitter hitter
slipper hopper zipper shopper chopper
supper clipper trapper stopper

fir sir stir
bird third
dirt flirt skirt shirt
firm
swirl twirl
first thirst
chirp
birth mirth

fire hire wire shire tired

urn burn turn churn
fur
curl hurl
hurt
surf turf
urge surge
curse nurse purse
curve
burnt
burst
nature future
picture puncture
texture mixture
sculpture scripture
structure fracture
denture adventure
furniture
measure treasure pleasure

LEARNING TARGETS

Pupil Book: Focus
to match key words and pictures, and associated activities

Pupil Book: Extra
to differentiate between the different phonemes represented by the graphemes **ou** and **ow**

Pupil Book: Extension
to focus on the irregular but high frequency **ou** words

Workbook: Focus
to label a picture using given words

Workbook: Extra
to answer clues using **ou** and **ow** words

Workbook: Extension
to find **ou** and **ow** words in a wordsearch

Resource sheet: Focus
to practise **ou** and **ow** patterns and words

Resource sheet: Extension
to secure the spelling of key **ould** words;
to practise significant **ou** homophones

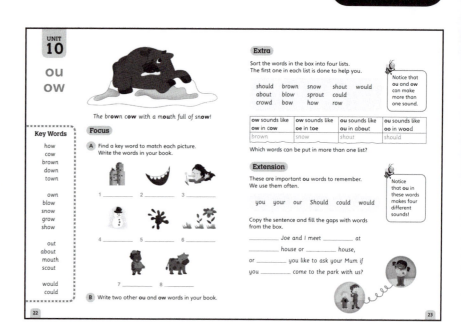

BACKGROUND NOTES AND SUGGESTIONS

This unit revisits the simple **ow** sound (as in *cow*) and **ou** sound (as in *out*). However, the work develops to introduce the irregular phonemes represented by both **ou** and **ow**.

ou is an important letter pattern, though perversely the most frequent significant words using **ou** are phonemically 'irregular' and so this is the focus of the Extra and Extension work.

Pupil Book answers

Focus

A 1 town   2 mouth   3 blow
    4 snow   5 brown   6 grow
    7 scout   8 cow

B Teacher to check individual answers

Extra

brown	snow	shout	should
crowd	blow	about	would
how	row	sprout	could
bow	bow		
row			

Extension

Should	you	our/your	your/our
would	could		

Workbook answers

Focus

Teacher to check individual answers

Extra

1 snow
2 town
3 mouth
4 mouse
5 cow
6 shout

Extension

A

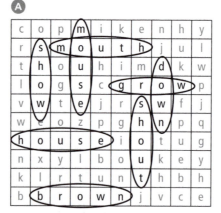

B mouth, house, shout, mouse, grow, show, down, brown

Resource sheet answers

Focus

A Children should copy the patterns.

B town cow snow blow
    cloud mouth scout mouse

C house town loud show

Extension

A Sam said I <u>could</u> go to her farm tonight if I'd like to.
I said I <u>would / could</u>, but I <u>should</u> ask Mum first.
I said I <u>would</u> ask her later.

I asked Sam if she <u>would</u> make sure her parents didn't mind.
She said she <u>would</u>.
They said I <u>could</u> come.

B 1 your you're   2 Our hour
    3 you ewe

Supporting word lists

bow cow how now row sow brow
owl fowl howl growl prowl scowl
down gown town clown brown crown
drown frown crowd

out bout lout pout rout tout about
clout trout scout spout stout
sprout shout
foul
loud cloud proud
noun
house louse mouse
blouse grouse spouse
bound found hound
mound pound round
sound wound ground
count fount mount
ounce bounce pounce flounce trounce
couch pouch slouch crouch
mouth south
*could would should
*you your our hour
*thought through
*know

LEARNING TARGETS

Pupil Book: Focus
to match key words to pictures, and associated activity

Pupil Book: Extra
to introduce rules relating to the use of the inflectional ending **ed**

Pupil Book: Extension
to find and write homophones with the target phoneme hidden in a wordsearch

Workbook: Focus
to label a picture using given words

Workbook: Extra
to build words by adding **ing**

Workbook: Extension
to write rhyming words

Resource sheet: Focus
to complete a word fan and match target words to pictures

Resource sheet: Extension
to select target word homophones in a cloze activity

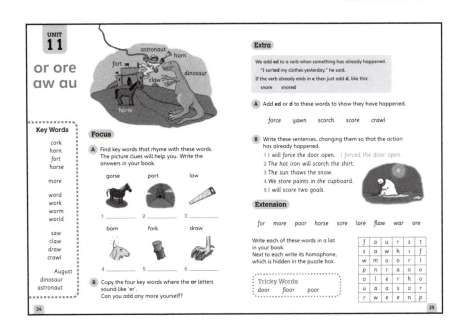

BACKGROUND NOTES AND SUGGESTIONS

These letter patterns complement work on **ar** and **are** patterns, for even though they look similar, both being what are sometimes called **r** vowels, **or / ore**, unlike **ar / are**, has no discernible difference in sound.

Several **aw** words are similar in sound to other words, but not exactly the same, so are better described as 'near homophones'. Nevertheless, from the point of view of spelling they are sufficiently close to cause confusion and so warrant a group or class lesson. This might usefully lead on to consideration of other groups of similar sounding words that can cause occasional difficulty. (*Nelson English* may be a helpful source of further reference and contains several sets of exercises on homophones. Note that homophones will vary depending on regional accents.)

au is a relatively infrequent grapheme though it appears in a few important words (see Supporting words list below).

Pupil Book answers

Focus

A 1 horse   2 fort   3 saw
   4 horn   5 cork   6 claw

B Teacher to check individual answers

Extra

A forced   yawned   scorched   scored   crawled

B 1 I forced the door open.
   2 The hot iron scorched the shirt.
   3 The sun thawed the snow.
   4 We stored paints in the cupboard.
   5 I scored two goals.

Extension

for	four	more	moor
poor	pour	horse	hoarse
sore	saw	lore	law
flaw	floor	war	wore
ore	oar	(inside 'hoarse')

Workbook answers

Focus
Teacher to check individual answers

Extra

1 storing   2 forming   3 thawing
4 yawning   5 scoring   6 crawling
7 forcing   8 scorching   9 pawing
10 drawing

Extension

A e.g. horn, corn, torn,

B e.g. shore, wore, tore

C e.g. saw, claw, draw

Resource sheet answers

Focus

A Children should copy the pattern.

B saw   paw   law   jaw   claw   straw
   draw   thaw

C saw   claw   draw   thaw

Extension

1 roar raw   2 saw sore
3 floor flaw   4 poor pour paw
5 sure shore   6 court caught

Supporting word lists

or for
cord ford lord
cork fork stork
form storm
born corn horn morn torn worn sworn
shorn scorn
fort port sort snort sport short
gorge
force
gorse horse Morse
porch torch scorch
north

ore bore core more sore tore wore store
score snore swore shore
jaw law paw raw saw
claw thaw draw straw
dawn fawn lawn pawn yawn drawn
prawn spawn
bawl crawl trawl sprawl shawl
hawk
awkward awful
author August astronaut dinosaur

LEARNING TARGETS

Pupil Book: Focus
to match key words to pictures and associated activity

Pupil Book: Extra
to find and write pairs of homophones from a wordsearch

Pupil Book: Extension
to identify and write compound words of the target phonemes from a word puzzle

Workbook: Focus
to label a picture using given words

Workbook: Extra
to build words by joining letters and patterns

Workbook: Extension
to put words in alphabetical order by their first letters

Resource sheet: Focus
to practise the **ain** and **air** letter sequences; to complete word sums using the sequences

Resource sheet: Extension
to complete words using clues; to practise homophones that incorporate the **air** phoneme

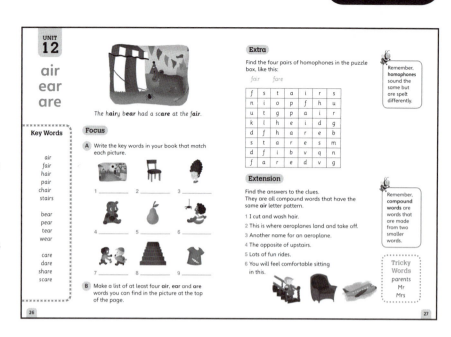

BACKGROUND NOTES AND SUGGESTIONS

The unit teaches the **are**, **air** and **ear** graphemes when they represent the distinctive vowel phoneme heard in *bear, bare* and *hair*. It is helpful to refer the children to earlier work relating to the **ar** and **ai** vowel phonemes that can cause potential confusion.

The unit gives an opportunity to practise homophones and compound words, which are quite frequent with **air/are** words, and can be extended to words with other spelling patterns.

Pupil Book answers

Focus

A
1 fair	2 chair	3 hair
4 bear	5 pear	6 scare
7 share	8 stairs	9 tear

B fair
bear
scare
(hair)
(air)
(dare)

Extra
stairs	stares
pair	pear
hair	hare
fair	fare

Extension
1 hairdresser	2 airport (airfield)
3 aircraft	4 downstairs
5 funfair (fairground)	6 armchair

Workbook answers

Focus
Teacher to check individual answers

Extra
fair, fare, fear, chair, hair, hare, hear, pair, pear, scare, stair, stare, tear, wear, ware

Extension
1 bear pear tear wear
2 air chair hair pair
3 care dare hare scare

Resource sheet answers

Focus
A Children should copy the patterns and words.

B chain stain pain chair stair pair

Extension
A
1 chain
2 chair
3 stare
4 complain
5 chase
6 there

B Teacher to check individual answers.

Supporting word lists

bare care dare fare hare mare rare
glare spare stare scare snare share

air fair hair pair
flair stair chair

bear pear tear wear

LEARNING TARGETS

Pupil Book: Focus
to match key words to pictures, and associated activity

Pupil Book: Extra
to introduce the prefix **al**

Pupil Book: Extension
to introduce the suffixes **al** and **ly** and demonstrate how sometimes they are used together

Workbook: Focus
to label a picture using given words

Workbook: Extra
to sort words according to whether they end in **al** or **all**

Workbook: Extension
to complete a cloze exercise

Resource sheet: Focus
to practise target letter patterns and complete word sums

Resource sheet: Extension
to secure the **al** prefix

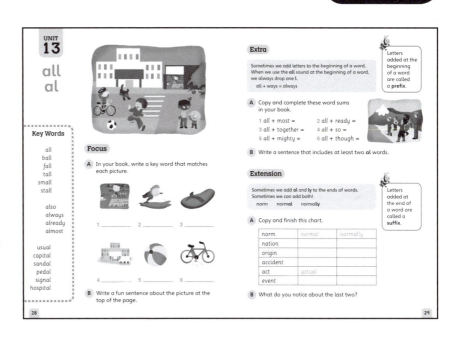

BACKGROUND NOTES AND SUGGESTIONS

The vowel sound in *ball* is represented by the vowel digraph **al**, not, as is often assumed, **all**. This is important in helping to clarify the letters representing the vowel in words such as *talk* and *walk*. It also helps to explain why, when **al** forms a prefix (e.g. *always*), it has a single **l**.

There are no rules to determine whether a word should end in **al** rather than **le** or **el**. The only limited support available is to remember that when added as a suffix to a word ending in **ic** or **on** it will be **al** (e.g. *musical, national*).

Pupil Book answers

Focus
A 1 stall   2 fall   3 sandal
    4 hospital   5 ball   6 pedal

B Teacher to check individual answers

Extra
A 1 almost   2 already   3 altogether
    4 also   5 almighty   6 although

B Teacher to check individual answers

Extension
A
norm	normal	normally
nation	national	nationally
origin	original	originally
accident	accidental	accidentally
act	actual	actually
event	eventual	eventually

B Child to indicate the addition of **u** to suffix

Workbook answers

Focus
Teacher to check individual answers

Extra

words ending in *al*	words ending in *all*
usual	all
sandal	ball
capital	fall
signal	small
hospital	stall
pedal	tall

Extension
1   The winning runner was given a <u>medal</u>.
2   Arun's <u>ball</u> smashed a window when he kicked it.
3   I must remember to write a <u>capital</u> letter at the beginning of my name.
4   My brother was rushed to <u>hospital</u> when he hurt his arm.
5   Please can I have a <u>small</u> cake?
6   We <u>all</u> had a great time at the party.

Resource sheet answers

Focus
A Children should copy the pattern and words.

B vandal
    dental
    bridal
    hospital
    pedal
    petal

Extension
A Teacher to check individual answers.

B Teacher to check individual answers.

Supporting word lists
initial vowel a
actual sandal vandal capital natural national factual radical casual

initial vowel e
medal metal pedal petal dental medical central mechanical special general equal

initial vowel i
signal clinical historical accidental bridal final spiral

initial vowel o
coral comical topical tropical hospital horizontal moral original occasional total postal local

initial vowel u
usual musical

other
normal royal loyal crystal

prefix al
already always altogether also although almighty almost

LEARNING TARGETS

Pupil Book: Focus
to match key words to pictures, with an associated activity

Pupil Book: Extra
to complete a cloze exercise with selected target words

Pupil Book: Extension
to select answers to a word puzzle from target words

Workbook: Focus
to match words to pictures

Workbook: Extra
to identify and write rhyming words

Workbook: Extension
to complete words using **ove**, **ome** and **one**, and use them in sentences

Resource sheet: Focus
to match words to pictures and find rhyming words

Resource sheet: Extension
to identify the different phonemes represented by **o** in **o-e** words

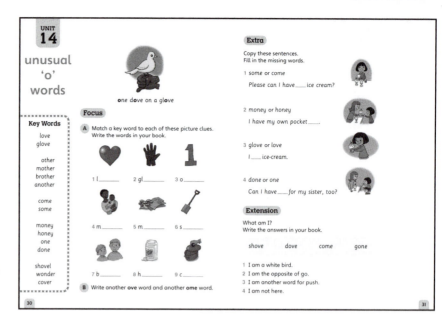

BACKGROUND NOTES AND SUGGESTIONS

Opinions differ as to how best to describe this 'family' of words; teachers will reach their own conclusion as to whether they prefer 'irregular 'magic' e words' or 'silent e words' or indeed neither of these. Note that they do not have a common grapheme/phoneme relationship.

But the group is an important one, and is worth some emphasis, as it contains so many high frequency words (*one, once, gone, done, none, come, some, something, love, above*).

Many of these words have evolved from Old English, resulting in this characteristic pronunciation.

English words hardly ever end with the letter **v**. The letter **e** usually needs to be added after the **v** (e.g. *love, dove, have, give, live*).

Pupil Book answers

Focus

A 1 love   2 glove   3 one
   4 mother   5 money   6 shovel
   7 brother   8 honey   9 cover

B Teacher to check individual answers

Extra
1 some   2 money   3 love   4 one

Extension
1 dove   2 come   3 shove   4 gone

Workbook answers

Focus
 1 glove   2 mother   3 love
 4 come   5 some   6 one
 7 done   8 honey   9 cover
10 shovel   11 brother   12 above

Extra
1 love   glove   (dove)
2 come   some
3 none   one
4 above   dove   (glove)
5 stone   throne

6 brother   mother
7 money   honey

Extension
1 g<u>love</u>   2 <u>move</u>   3 <u>honey</u>
4 thr<u>one</u>   5 <u>some</u>   6 ab<u>ove</u>

Teacher to check individual answers

Resource sheet answers

Focus

A one love come honey
   glove cover above some

B glove move one love

Extension

A The bricks should be coloured as follows:
   Red: shone gone
   Blue: one above done come dove love glove shove none some
   Green: move prove
   Not coloured: hope chose rope throne vote slope stone toe

B 1 glove   2 hope
   3 stone   4 gone

C Teacher to check individual answers

Supporting word lists
gone scone shone
one done none

come some

dove love glove shove above
move prove

lose

Check-Up 1

Focus

1 snake	**2** tail	**3** sheep	**4** night
5 bride	**6** rope	**7** balloon	**8** shark
9 bath/bathroom	**10** boy	**11** spread	**12** bread
13 nurse	**14** treasure	**15** snow/snowman	**16** scout
17 saw	**18** dinosaur	**19** chair	**20** pear
21 bear	**22** pedal	**23** honey	**24** glove

Extension

A Teacher to check individual answers

B Teacher to check individual answers

C **1** tale **2** sail **3** bean **4** meet **5** would **6** four

D **1** moon **2** glue **3** point **4** bread **5** hear **6** third

LEARNING TARGETS

Pupil Book: Focus

to match key words to pictures, and an associated activity

Pupil Book: Extra

to complete a cloze activity with the target prefixes

Pupil Book: Extension

to write sentences incorporating the target prefixes

Workbook: Focus

to label a picture using given words

Workbook: Extra

to build words using the target prefixes

Workbook: Extension

to find and write words in a wordsearch

Resource sheet: Focus

to complete a **dis** words word fan; to match words to pictures

Resource sheet: Extension

to identify in puzzles and use in sentences a selection of target words

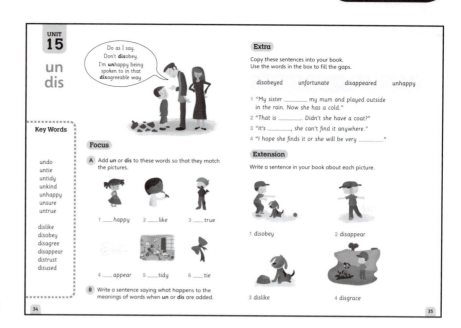

BACKGROUND NOTES AND SUGGESTIONS

This unit revisits the prefix **un** and introduces **dis**. Both are added to the beginning of a word without the need for any adjustment to the spelling. This makes it a helpful way to introduce prefixes, developed further in several later units of the course.

Pupil Book answers

Focus

A 1 unhappy   2 dislike   3 untrue
    4 disappear   5 untidy   6 untie

B Teacher to check individual answers

Extra

1 disobeyed   2 unfortunate
3 disappeared   4 unhappy

Extension

Teacher to check individual answers

Workbook answers

Focus

Teacher to check individual answers

Extra

1 unkind   2 disagree
3 unhappy   4 untidy
5 untrue   6 unused / disused
7 undo   8 dislike
9 disappear   10 distrust
11 unsure   12 untie
13 uncover/discover
14 disobey   15 unload

Extension

A undo, disobey, dislike, untidy, untrue, uncover, disappear, disagree

B

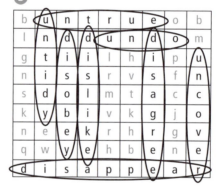

Resource sheet answers

Focus

A Children should copy the pattern.

B dislike disused disagree distrust
     disobey disappear disconnect disarm

C disagree dislike disobey

Extension

1 incorrect / inaccurate
2 unhappy / untidy
3 dislike / disobey
4 improve / important
5 demand / decided
6 mistake / mislead

Teacher to check individual answers

Supporting word lists

unable unaided unarmed unaware unbearable unclean uncover undo undress uneven unfair unfit unfold unlikely unload unlock unlucky unpack untie

negative prefix forms

disable disagree disappear discharge discolour disconnect dishonest dislike disloyal disobey displease disprove disqualify disregard distrust

negative 'sense'

disaster disease distress disturb dismal disgust dismiss

LEARNING TARGETS

Pupil Book: Focus
to match target words to pictures, and associated activity

Pupil Book: Extra
to find and list 'soft' and 'hard' **c** words in a wordsearch

Pupil Book: Extension
to complete a word fan with the spelling pattern **ace**; to make a word fan using the spelling pattern **ice**

Workbook: Focus
to label a picture using given words

Workbook: Extra
to choose words to match pictures

Workbook: Extension
to write sentences using given 'soft' **c** words

Resource sheet: Focus
to copy letter patterns; complete word sums; match words to pictures

Resource sheet: Extension
to secure alphabetical ordering

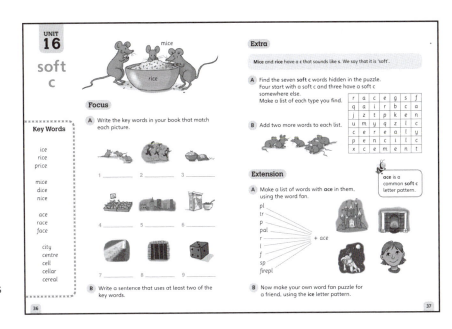

BACKGROUND NOTES AND SUGGESTIONS

A useful way to introduce this unit is to arrange for the class or group to collect words which include the **ca, ce, ci, cy, co** and **cu** letter patterns, and from these to draw out that **ce, ci** and **cy** usually have the effect of 'softening' the **c**. *Celt* and *Celtic* are sometimes exceptions to this.

Notice also what happens to words with the **cc** pattern, e.g. *succeed*.

Pupil Book answers

Focus

A 1 mice 2 race 3 rice
    4 price 5 city 6 cereal
    7 cellar 8 cell 9 dice

B Teacher to check individual answers

Extra

A city   pencil
    cereal   race
    cell   fancy
    cement

B Teacher to check individual answers

Extension

A place trace pace palace race lace face space fireplace

B Teacher to check individual answers

Workbook answers

Focus
Teacher to check individual answers

Extra
1 cereal 2 face 3 mice
4 race   5 circle 6 juicy
7 fence   8 dance 9 police

Extension
Teacher to check individual answers

Resource sheet answers

Focus

A Children should copy the pattern.

B *Upper activity*
    rice mice dice price face lace race
    Lower activity
    face race price mice

Extension

A 1 Jacob's <u>face</u> looked red after he ran in the <u>race</u>.
    2 Mum thought the <u>nice</u> skirt I liked was a good <u>price</u>.
    3 I eat <u>cereal</u> for breakfast.
    4 I added <u>ice</u> to my drink to make it taste <u>nice</u>.
    5 Dad and I went to the <u>city</u> <u>centre</u> to meet Nan.

B 1 face lace race
    2 dice mice nice
    3 ice price rice
    4 fancy juicy spicy

Supporting word lists

initial ce
cell cent cease cedar cellar cement
centre central ceiling certain centaur
celery cereal century certify celebrate
centipede cemetery centurion
ceremony certificate

medial ce
recent accept excel except cancel
excess exceed process proceed
success succeed grocer concert
December excellent innocent

final ce
ace face lace pace race
ice dice mice nice rice slice price spice
twice splice notice office police service
truce spruce peace

initial ci
city civic civil
cinder circus circuit circle citrus
cinema circular citizen

medial ci
acid pencil icing decide
accident ferocity electricity simplicity

initial cy
cycle cyclone Cyclops cymbal cygnet
cynic cylinder

final cy
icy lacy fancy juicy spicy agency
currency frequency conspiracy

final nce
dance lance glance prance trance chance
advance distance entrance
fence offence pence sentence defence
absence commence
mince since wince prince convince ounce
announce bounce pounce

LEARNING TARGETS

Pupil Book: Focus
to match key words to pictures and
associated activities

Pupil Book: Extra
to find target **age** words in a wordsearch and
use one in a sentence

Pupil Book: Extension
to complete **ge** and **dge** words

Workbook: Focus
to label a picture using given words

Workbook: Extra
to complete a cloze exercise with selected
target words

Workbook: Extension
to identify the letters that make given words,
in jumbled letters

Resource sheet: Focus
to copy letter patterns; to select target words
and rhyming words

Resource sheet: Extension
to use target words in a puzzle and sentences

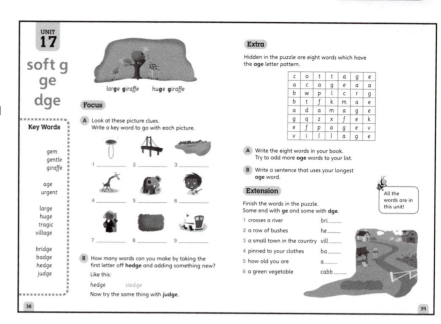

BACKGROUND NOTES AND SUGGESTIONS

The letter **j** is never used at the end of English words – the sound is represented by **dge** or **ge**.

Although not usually classed as such, it can be helpful for children to think of the **d** in **dge** pattern words as 'silent'.
Thus, revision of other silent-letter words can usefully be carried out as an extension of this unit (see Book 2,
Unit 22).

Elsewhere in words the 'j' sound is usually spelt as **g** when it comes before **e, i** or **y**, e.g. *gem, giant, energy.*

Pupil Book answers

Focus

A 1 gem   2 bridge   3 village
   4 giraffe   5 huge   6 badge
   7 judge   8 hedge   9 urgent

B hedge ledge sledge wedge
   judge fudge nudge grudge trudge

Extra

A cottage, cabbage, garage, damage,
   village, cage, page, age

B Teacher to check individual answers

Extension

1 bridge   2 hedge   3 village
4 badge   5 age   6 cabbage

Workbook answers

Focus

Teacher to check individual answers

Extra

1 A dog jumped off a <u>bridge</u> into the
   water!
2 I want a <u>large</u> slice of cake.
3 I watched a baby <u>giraffe</u> with its mother.
4 Ellie hid behind the <u>hedge</u>.

5 The child was <u>gentle</u> when she stroked
   the cat.
6 My grandmother lives in a <u>village.</u>

Extension

1 badge
2 gem
3 large
4 hedge

Resource sheet answers

Focus

A Children should copy the patterns.

B bridge hedge badge fridge

C bridge judge hedge cage

Extension

A 1 fudge
   2 judge
   3 sledge
   4 hedge
   5 bridge
   6 fridge
   7 edge
   8 ledge

B sludge   edge   ridge
   fudge   sledge   bridge
   nudge   hedge   midge
   judge   ledge   fridge

C Teacher to check individual answers

Supporting word lists

badge badger cadge cadger gadget
edge edger hedge ledge ledger wedge
midge midget bridge porridge
dodge lodge lodger
fudge judge nudge grudge trudge
budget

final ge (without silent d)
age cage page rage sage wage
cabbage damage garage garbage
package advantage
huge bulge

LEARNING TARGETS

Pupil Book: Focus
to match key words to pictures, and associated activity

Pupil Book: Extra
to recognise a range of spelling patterns associated with the **le** ending

Pupil Book: Extension
to sort words by their endings

Workbook: Focus
to label a picture using given words

Workbook: Extra
to complete words using **le, el, al** and **il**

Workbook: Extension
to choose words to complete a cloze exercise

Resource sheet: Focus
to complete words using **le** letter patterns and rhyming picture clues

Resource sheet: Extension
to complete a jumbled letters puzzle and find key words in a wordsearch

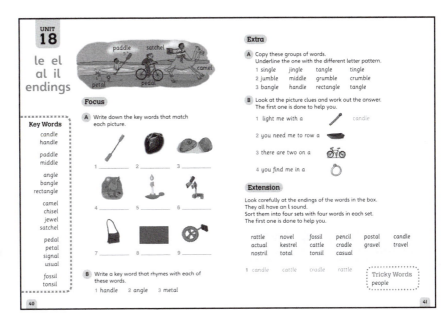

BACKGROUND NOTES AND SUGGESTIONS

There are very many words ending in **le**; indeed it is the most common spelling for this sound at the end of words. The sets of words listed below are 'regular', thus enabling the child to focus without confusion on the final **le**. It is usually advantageous to work on groups of words with similar spelling patterns before mixing them.

There are no rules to determine whether a word should end in **al** rather than **le** or **el**. The only limited support available is to remember that when added as a suffix to a word ending in **ic** or **on** it will be **al** (e.g. *musical, national*).

Also, **el** is used after **m, n, r, v, w** and, more often than not, after **s**.

There are very few words ending in **il**.

From the Supporting word lists it can be seen that many of the **el** words have medial double letters, and others have rhyming patterns. Select groups for individuals to learn as appropriate.

Pupil Book answers

Focus
A 1 paddle   2 jewel   3 fossil
    4 camel   5 candle   6 chisel
    7 satchel   8 rectangle   9 pedal

B 1 candle   2 bangle   3 petal

Extra
A *(Underline)*
    1 tangle   2 middle   3 handle

B 1 candle   2 paddle
    3 pedal   4 jewel

Extension
1 candle cattle cradle rattle
2 novel kestrel gravel travel
3 fossil pencil nostril tonsil
4 postal actual total casual

Workbook answers

Focus
Teacher to check individual answers

Extra
1 camel   2 signal   3 fossil
4 candle   5 handle   6 jewel
7 pedal   8 petal   9 tonsil
10 label   11 medal   12 jungle
13 model   14 hospital   15 rectangle

Extension
1 The candle holder has a handle.
2 I dropped the paddle in the middle of the river.
3 The camel carried the jewel across the desert.
4 A chisel was used to free the fossil.
5 My bike pedal fell off, as usual!

Resource sheet answers

Focus
A *Upper activity*
    puddle   bangle   jumble
    paddle   tangle   grumble
    saddle   rectangle   crumble

    Lower activity
    rectangle   tangle
    saddle   puddle

B crumble middle bangle saddle

Extension
A 1 handle   2 paddle
    3 single   4 couple
    5 rectangle   6 bangle

B jumble angle handle camel
    jewel signal petal tonsil fossil

Supporting word lists

gamble ramble bramble scramble
bumble fumble humble jumble mumble
rumble crumble grumble stumble
dimple pimple simple
rumple crumple
candle handle
kindle spindle dwindle swindle
bundle trundle
angle bangle dangle jangle tangle
spangle strangle rectangle
jingle mingle single tingle
bungle jungle
tinkle winkle crinkle twinkle sprinkle
nestle trestle
bristle gristle thistle
bustle hustle rustle
jostle

initial vowel a
actual sandal vandal capital natural
national factual radical casual
initial vowel e
medal metal pedal petal dental medical
central mechanical special general equal
initial vowel i
signal clinical historical accidental bridal
final spiral
initial vowel o
coral comical topical tropical hospital
horizontal moral original occasional total
postal local
initial vowel u
usual musical
other
normal royal loyal crystal
initial vowel a
camel panel barrel pastel channel flannel
gravel travel cancel label
parallel
channel satchel
caramel mackerel
initial vowel e
kennel vessel kestrel level
initial vowel i
tinsel swivel minstrel shrivel chisel
initial vowel o
hovel novel grovel shovel model mongrel
hostel cockerel
initial vowel u
duffel funnel tunnel mussel fuel cruel
other
parcel vowel towel scoundrel
pencil fossil nostril

LEARNING TARGETS

Pupil Book: Focus
to introduce the singular possessive (**'s**)

Pupil Book: Extra
to practise using **'s** in the context
of sentences

Pupil Book: Extension
to revise adding **s** or **es** to form plural nouns

Workbook: Focus
to label a picture using given words

Workbook: Extra
to add apostrophes and use given phrases
in sentences

Workbook: Extension
to revise adding **s** or **es** to form plural nouns

Resource sheet: Focus
to revise adding **s** or **es** to form plural nouns

Resource sheet: Extension
to rewrite sentences using the singular
possessive (**'s**)

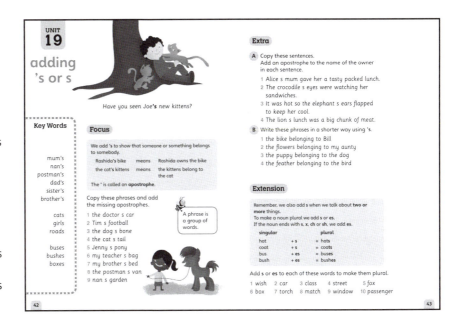

BACKGROUND NOTES AND SUGGESTIONS

This is the first introduction in this series to the use of an apostrophe to indicate the possessive form. Here we restrict consideration to the singular.

Many children (and many adults, too!) get highly confused about the use of apostrophes in association with **s**. Plenty of reinforcement might be needed in oral sessions to establish the notion of ownership. Only when this has been embedded can the child begin to realise when and how to use **'s** to denote the possessive.

The correct formulation of plurals is an important skill for spelling. Fortunately the vast majority of words conform to a few basic rules and 'sub-rules'. These are introduced here and in later units and then revised throughout the rest of the course as opportunities lend themselves.

In this unit, the rules addressed are:
- most nouns, including those that end in **e**, simply add **s**
- for words that end with **s**, **x**, **ch** or **sh** we add **es**.

Pupil Book answers

Focus

1 the doctor's car   2 Tim's football
3 the dog's bone   4 the cat's tail
5 Jenny's pony   6 my teacher's bag
7 my brother's bed   8 the postman's van
9 nan's garden

Extra

A 1 Alice's mum gave her a tasty
     packed lunch.
   2 The crocodile's eyes were watching
     her sandwiches.
   3 It was hot so the elephant's ears
     flapped to keep her cool.
   4 The lion's lunch was a big chunk
     of meat.

B 1 Bill's bike
   2 my aunty's flowers
   3 the dog's puppy
   4 the bird's feather

Extension

1 wishes   2 cars   3 classes
4 streets   5 foxes   6 boxes
7 torches   8 matches   9 windows
10 passengers

Workbook answers

Focus

Teacher to check individual answers

Extra

Teacher to check individual answers

Extension

1 girls   2 boxes
3 brushes   4 toys
5 carrots   6 babies

Resource sheet answers

Focus

1 drums   2 branches   3 clocks
4 gases   5 books   6 dresses
7 bikes   8 crashes   9 elephants
10 guesses   11 circles   12 peaches
13 letters   14 postboxes 15 cups
16 brushes   17 hands   18 rashes
19 lambs   20 indexes

Extension

1 Jake's dog has run away.
2 Mrs Scott's coat is all muddy.
3 Harry lost Ben's book.
4 Farmer Hill found the sheep's lamb.
5 Leah ate Isla's sweets.
6 Kamil kicked Dan's football.
7 Matthew's cat is not very well.
8 The policeman's car broke down.

Supporting word lists

Words that take s
There are a great number, including:
game table pen cup pond book school
teacher

Some words that take es
ash bush glass inch watch brush dish
kiss tax box grass pass bus gas
sandwich fox class

LEARNING TARGETS

Pupil Book: Focus
to match key words to pictures, and associated activity

Pupil Book: Extra
to differentiate between the phonemes made by a final **y**

Pupil Book: Extension
to introduce plural nouns formed from words with a final **y**

Workbook: Focus
to label a picture using given words

Workbook: Extra
to complete words by adding **y** or **ey**

Workbook: Extension
to write plural nouns formed from words with a final **y**

Resource sheet: Focus
to select target words and rhyming words

Resource sheet: Extension
to add **s** to words ending in **y**

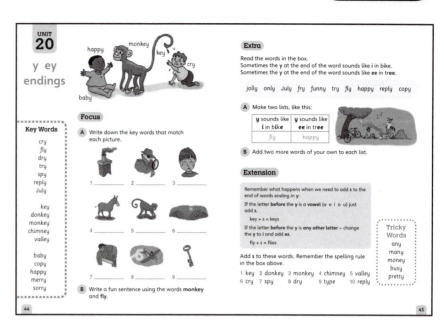

BACKGROUND NOTES AND SUGGESTIONS

This unit highlights the two phonemes (long /e/ and /i/) represented by the letter **y** in a final position. Remind the children about vowel letters and about the anomaly of **y** being able to take the role of a vowel, as in *fly*.

The Extension gives a first introduction to the rule for making plurals of words ending with **y**:
- if the letter before the **y** is a vowel, just add **s** e.g. keys
- if the letter before the **y** is any other letter, change the **y** to **i** and add **es** e.g. flies

Although the following rules will be returned to later, this unit is a good opportunity to begin to discuss them:
- nouns can be made into adjectives by adding **y**
- if the letter before the last is a single vowel then double the last letter (*mud, mu**dd**y*)
- if the word ends in **e**, drop the **e** before adding the **y** (*slim**e**, slimy*)

The **y** (sounding ee) nouns (and adjectives) offer an opportunity to practise some of the other letter patterns learnt earlier in the course. The Supporting word lists are arranged in groups to help facilitate this.

By selecting words from the Key Words list, the effect of double consonants 'shortening' the preceding vowel can be demonstrated (e.g. *baby, happy*).

Pupil Book answers

Focus

A
1 chimney	2 spy	3 cry
4 donkey	5 monkey	6 valley
7 dry	8 fly	9 key

B Teacher to check individual answers

Extra

A
fly	happy
fry	only
try	funny
july	jolly
reply	copy

B Teacher to check individual answers

Extension

1 keys	2 donkeys
3 monkeys	4 chimneys
5 valleys	6 cries
7 spies	8 dries
9 types	10 replies

Workbook answers

Focus

Teacher to check individual answers

Extra

1 cry	2 valley	3 key
4 July	5 donkey	6 sorry
7 try	8 chimney	9 baby
10 reply	11 happy	12 monkey
13 dry	14 merry	15 spy

Extension

1 monkeys	2 spies
3 babies	4 valleys
5 trolleys	6 butterflies

Resource sheet answers

Focus

A cry baby happy monkey chimney

B fly key donkey rainy

C cry monkey lorry dry

Extension

1 keys	2 dries	3 replies
4 babies	5 monkeys	6 chimneys
7 tries	8 cries	9 valleys
10 spies	11 donkeys	12 alleys
13 copies	14 dragonflies	15 berries
16 hurries	17 ladies	18 trolleys
19 jockeys	20 fries	

Supporting word lists
cranky flashy scratchy messy smelly
rocky frosty lucky dusty rusty rainy
brainy milky risky frilly windy chilly fussy
sleepy cheeky leafy creaky creamy
mighty croaky moody sooty salty stormy
hardy marshy dirty cloudy
dotty bossy foggy spotty chatty muddy
tubby runny funny sunny nutty furry
lazy hazy crazy wavy easy icy slimy
bony rosy smoky stony noisy greasy
nouns
daddy nanny nappy tabby granny
jelly jetty penny teddy berry cherry
dolly holly hobby lorry poppy
buggy dummy gully mummy
puppy tummy
baby lady gravy
story
other word classes
flashy scratchy lazy crazy
messy smelly pretty
silly chilly
dotty bossy foggy rocky spotty
fussy muddy funny sunny
lucky mucky dusty rusty
rainy brainy
easy leafy creaky creamy
sleepy cheeky

LEARNING TARGETS

Pupil Book: Focus
to match key words with the **ing** suffix to pictures, and associated activity

Pupil Book: Extra
to master the rule for adding the suffix **ing**

Pupil Book: Extension
to master the rule for adding the suffixes **ing**, **ed** and **er** after ('magic') **e**

Workbook: Focus
to label a picture using given words

Workbook: Extra
to complete word sums using **ing**

Workbook: Extension
to complete word sums with ('magic') **e** using **ing**

Resource sheet: Focus
to double the final consonant of short words before adding **ed**

Resource sheet: Extension
to secure adding **ing** rules, particularly dropping the final ('magic') **e**

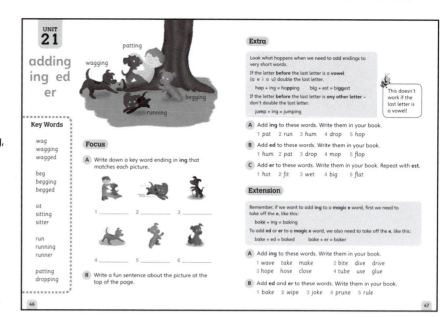

BACKGROUND NOTES AND SUGGESTIONS

In this unit the focus is on the letter pattern **ing** when it forms an inflectional ending (as opposed to the consonant digraph **ng** as in words like *bang*). Also, similar rules apply to the suffixes **ed** and **er**.

For most short words containing a single short vowel before the final consonant, we double the final consonant (e.g. *big/bigger/biggest*). But, remember, the **x** is never doubled!

For most words ending in **e** we drop the **e** before adding the suffix (e.g. *bake/baking, late/later*).

Pupil Book answers

Focus

A 1 patting 2 running 3 dropping
4 wagging 5 begging 6 sitting

B Teacher to check individual answers

Extra

A 1 patting 2 running 3 humming
4 dropping 5 hopping

B 1 hummed 2 patted 3 dropped
4 mopped 5 flopped

C 1 hotter hottest
2 fitter fittest
3 wetter wettest
4 bigger biggest
5 flatter flattest

Extension

A 1 waving taking making
2 biting diving driving
3 hoping hosing closing
4 tubing using gluing

B 1 baked baker
2 wiped wiper
3 joked joker
4 pruned pruner
5 ruled ruler

Workbook answers

Focus

Teacher to check individual answers

Extra

1 dropping 2 crying
3 wetting 4 skipping
5 running 6 begging
7 smashing 8 calling
9 copying 10 kicking

Extension

1 racing 2 shaded
3 glider 4 pacer
5 glued 6 roping
7 voted 8 tuning
9 arriving 10 wiper

Resource sheet answers

Focus

A 1 jumped 2 helped
3 splashed 4 licked

Teacher to check individual answers.

B 1 chopped 2 mopped
3 dripped 4 dropped
5 planned 6 hopped
7 clapped 8 skipped
9 slipped 10 shopped

Extension

A 1 sitting 2 bathing
3 sleeping 4 boxing
5 selling 6 jumping
7 cutting 8 shopping
9 blowing 10 shooting
11 banging 12 singing
13 replying 14 pressing
15 trying

B 1 waved 2 raking
3 bouncing 4 sliding
5 saver 6 driver
7 sloping 8 grazed

Supporting word lists

Some words to which ing/ed can be added without modification:
act pant camp land stand help melt bend mend send milk film lift limp list sulk hunt bump dump jump dust rust grunt

Words with short single vowels
thin fat big hot glum flat sad red

LEARNING TARGETS

Resource sheet: Focus 1
extra practice: est and y endings
to make adjectives by adding **y**
Resource sheet: Focus 2
extra practice: est and y endings
to practise adding **er** and **est** to
'magic' **e** words

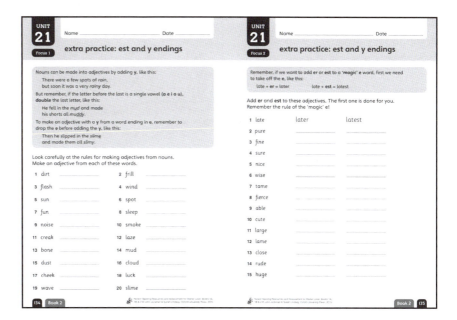

BACKGROUND NOTES AND SUGGESTIONS

In these pages, we look at two spelling rules in detail.

Focus 1 explores the rules for making nouns into adjectives:

- nouns can be made into adjectives by adding **y**
- if the letter before the last is a single vowel then double the last letter (*mud, mudd*y)
- if the word ends in **e**, drop the **e** before adding the y (*slime, slimy*)

Focus 2 is concerned with adding the **er** and **est** suffixes to adjectives ending in **e**, building on the work completed in the Extension activity of Pupil Book 2, Unit 21.

Resource sheet answers
Extra practice: est and y endings

Focus 1

1 dirty	2 frilly	3 flashy
4 windy	5 sunny	6 spotty
7 funny	8 sleepy	9 noisy
10 smoky	11 creaky	12 lazy
13 bony	14 muddy	15 dusty
16 cloudy	17 cheeky	18 lucky
19 wavy	20 slimy	

Focus 2

1 later	latest
2 purer	purest
3 finer	finest
4 surer	surest
5 nicer	nicest
6 wiser	wisest
7 tamer	tamest
8 fiercer	fiercest
9 abler	ablest
10 cuter	cutest
11 larger	largest
12 lamer	lamest
13 closer	closest
14 ruder	rudest
15 huger	hugest

Supporting word lists

cranky flashy scratchy messy smelly
rocky frosty lucky dusty rusty rainy
brainy milky risky frilly windy chilly fussy
sleepy cheeky leafy creaky creamy
mighty croaky moody sooty salty stormy
hardy marshy dirty cloudy
dotty bossy foggy spotty chatty muddy
tubby runny funny sunny nutty furry
lazy hazy crazy wavy easy icy slimy
bony rosy smoky stony noisy greasy

Words with a final e
nice fine wise safe late tame brave rude
ripe close

LEARNING TARGETS

Pupil Book: Focus
to match key words to pictures, and associated activities

Pupil Book: Extra
to identify silent **w** letters from a wordsearch puzzle; to answer clues

Pupil Book: Extension
to introduce and teach a range of other silent-letter words

Workbook: Focus
to label a picture using given words

Workbook: Extra
to identify the silent letter in given words

Workbook: Extension
to write words with the silent letters **k**, **g** and **w**

Resource sheet: Focus
to practise target letter patterns and complete word sums

Resource sheet: Extension
to identify words with silent letters

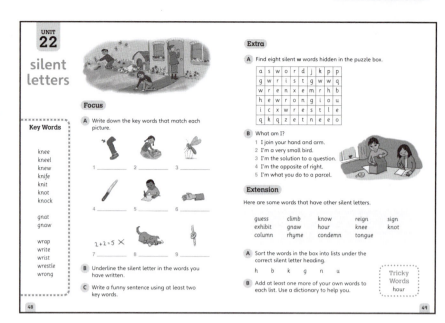

BACKGROUND NOTES AND SUGGESTIONS

The children will be intrigued to realise that in days gone by many silent letters were pronounced, but due to the general evolution of language they have become silent.

This is the first unit to focus on silent letters. Other silent letters feature in Book 3, Units 4, 17 and 26 and Book 4, Unit 5. Any silent letters can be introduced at any stage, so activities developed from this unit might usefully also introduce other silent letters.

As was mentioned previously, many vowel letters are not sounded individually and teachers may choose to teach them as silent (e.g. **a** in *head;* **e** in *gone*), though the term is conventionally reserved for consonant letters. However, if identified in the Extension resource, these should be allowed as correct.

Related to silent letters are the unstressed letters, especially vowels, and these are covered in depth as the course progresses. There are some specific patterns to explore with the children in this unit, including:
- silent **k** at the beginning of a word is always followed by **n**
- silent **w** is normally associated with an **r**, though there are exceptions to this

It is interesting to ask the children to spot other silent letter associations (e.g. **wh, mb, gn, mn, st**).

Pupil Book answers

Focus

A **B**

1 <u>k</u>nee	2 <u>w</u>rap	3 <u>g</u>nat
4 <u>k</u>nife	5 <u>w</u>rite	6 <u>w</u>rist
7 <u>w</u>rong	8 <u>g</u>naw	9 <u>k</u>not

C Teacher to check individual answers

Extra

A
sword	wrist	wren
wrong	wrestle	wreck
write	whole	

B 1 wrist 2 wren 3 answer
   4 wrong 5 wrap

Extension

A h exhibit hour rhyme
   b climb

k	know	knee	knot
g	reign	sign	gnaw
n	column	condemn	
u	guess	tongue	

B Teacher to check individual answers

Workbook answers

Focus
Teacher to check individual answers

Extra
1 w	2 g	3 k
4 k	5 w	6 w
7 k	8 w	9 g
10 w	11 w	12 k

Extension
Teacher to check individual answers

Resource sheet answers

Focus

A Children should copy the patterns.

B knot knee knock lamb crumb climb

Extension

Thomas and <u>Ch</u>loe had gone to help their dad for a <u>c</u>ouple of <u>h</u>ours. Their dad was a plum<u>b</u>er.

He had to <u>w</u>riggle into small spaces and <u>w</u>restle with heavy pipes. <u>Th</u>omas and <u>Ch</u>loe especially liked to watch him get covered in water if a pipe burst.

One day, he <u>k</u>nelt on the floor and cut his <u>k</u>nee. This made him drop his hammer on his thum<u>b</u> and he leapt up and <u>k</u>nocked his head on a beam.

Luckily he was all right. They all laughed and the t<u>w</u>o children still remember the event!

94

Supporting word lists

knit knob knot

knelt knack knock

knee kneel knife knight knew known

knuckle

wrap wrapper wrapped wrapping

wriggle wriggled wriggler wriggling

wrinkle wrinkled wrinkly

write written wrote

wreck wrecker wrecked wreckage

wringer wretched wrangle wrist

whole wholemeal wholesome wholly

sword swordfish

answer answered answering

gnat gnaw reign resign design sign

Some other silent letter words:

h

wheel whether which whisker whisper

white

hour honest honour

rhyme rhythm rhubarb rheumatism

b

climb tomb plumber comb thumb

n

hymn autumn column condemn

t

thistle whistle castle listen Christmas

LEARNING TARGETS

Pupil Book: Focus
to match key words to pictures

Pupil Book: Extra
to secure key words by practising in a puzzle activity

Pupil Book: Extension
to revise the singular possessive apostrophe

Workbook: Focus
to label a picture using given words

Workbook: Extra
to complete a cloze activity using target words

Workbook: Extension
to identify words in jumbled letters

Resource sheet: Focus
to copy target patterns and words and complete word sums

Resource sheet: Extension
to complete a cloze activity using high frequency **wa** words; to identify **wa** and **qua** words in a wordsearch

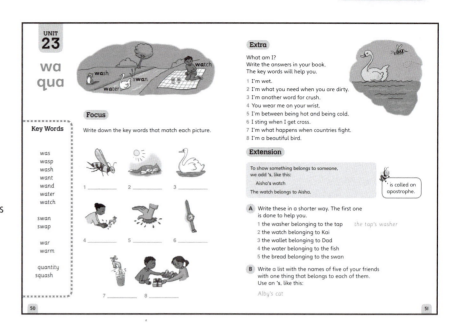

BACKGROUND NOTES AND SUGGESTIONS

Four very high frequency words (*was, wasn't, want, water*) make this one of the more significant 'irregular' letter patterns.

qua is far less significant in children's language usage, and is liable to 'exceptions' e.g. *quay*.

The singular possessive apostrophe is revisited from Book 2, Unit 19 in the Extension section.

Pupil Book answers

Focus

1 wasp	2 warm	3 swan
4 wash	5 squash	6 watch
7 water	8 swap	

Extra

1 water	2 wash	3 squash
4 watch	5 warm	6 wasp
7 war	8 swan	

Extension

Ⓐ 1 the tap's washer 2 Kai's watch
   3 Dad's wallet 4 the fish's water
   5 the swan's bread

Ⓑ Teacher to check individual answers

Workbook answers

Focus

Teacher to check individual answers

Extra

1 I must <u>wash</u> my hands before tea.
2 Can I <u>swap</u> my drink for yours?
3 The <u>swan</u> glided up the river.
4 Alex was very hot so had to drink lots of <u>water</u>.
5 We had to <u>squash</u> into a small tent when it rained.
6 We collected a large <u>quantity</u> of litter.

Extension

Ⓐ 1 water   2 swan
   3 watch   4 wasp

Resource answers

Focus

Ⓐ Children should copy the patterns and words.

Ⓑ was   want   wash
   water   swan   swat

Extension

Ⓐ Wanda didn't <u>want</u> to wash. She just <u>wanted</u> to watch her favourite television programme. Mum <u>was</u> cross because she <u>wanted</u> Wanda to have her dinner. So Mum got the <u>water</u> ready and told Wanda she <u>wanted</u> her to wash "NOW!"

Ⓑ watch water wasp want wash was squash quantity

Supporting word lists

was wasn't wasp wallet wand want wash watch water

war ward warden warm warn

swan swap swamp swab swat

quantity quality qualify squash

quad (bike) quarrel quarry quarter quartet

LEARNING TARGETS

Pupil Book: Focus
to select the appropriate suffix to complete a key word to match a picture

Pupil Book: Extra
to add suffixes to words ending with **y**

Pupil Book: Extension
to select the appropriate suffix to make a new word

Workbook: Focus
to label a picture with given words

Workbook: Extra
to build words using word sums

Workbook: Extension
to use the words built in Extra in a sentence

Resource sheet: Focus
to complete word fans adding the suffixes **less** and **ful**

Resource sheet: Extension
to secure the spelling of target words with the **less** and **fully** suffixes

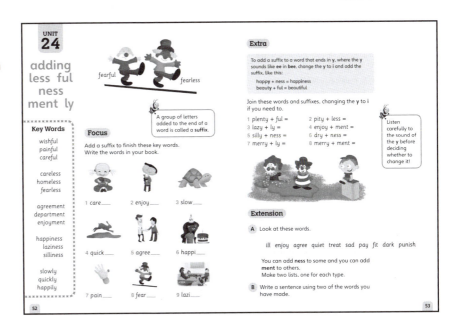

BACKGROUND NOTES AND SUGGESTIONS

Developing an awareness and understanding of the meaning and function of suffixes can be a significant aid to good spelling, e.g.

ful means 'full of';
less means 'without';
ment means 'condition of';
ness means 'state of'.

Although these might sound sophisticated, children can enjoy getting to grips with these ideas when comparing the root word with the word after the suffix is added.

All five suffixes that are the focus of this unit are common and frequently used in the writing of children of this age.

The work might be introduced by writing on the board words from the same family, each containing one of the suffixes, e.g. *careless, careful, carefully*. It is important to teach that these particular suffixes are 'consonant' suffixes (i.e. the first letter of each is a consonant) and thus follow the rule that whilst they can be added to most words without adaptation, if the root word ends in **y** (and sounds like **ee**), it must be changed to **i**.

Note that **ly** is often, though by no means always, used in conjunction with **ful**.

Pupil Book answers

Focus

1 careless	2 enjoyment	3 slowly
4 quickly	5 agreement	6 happiness
7 painful	8 fearless	9 laziness

Extra

1 plentiful	2 pitiless	3 lazily
4 enjoyment	5 silliness	6 dryness
7 merrily	8 merriment	

Extension

A

quietness	agreement
sadness	treatment
fitness	payment
darkness	punishment
illness	enjoyment

B Teacher to check individual answers

Workbook answers

Focus
Teacher to check individual answers

Extra
careful, colourful, fearful, hopeful, painful, useful, wishful, careless, colourless, fearless, homeless, hopeless, painless, useless

Extension
Teacher to check individual answers

Resource sheet answers

Focus

A Children should copy the pattern.

careless	helpless
hopeless	painless
thoughtless	

B Children should copy the pattern.

careful	helpful
hopeful	painful
thoughtful	

Extension

A

1 thoughtless	2 careless
3 mindless	

Teacher to check individual answers

B Teacher to check individual answers

C

1 thoughtfully	2 carefully
3 cheerfully	4 purposefully
5 hopefully	

Teacher to check individual answers

Supporting word lists

careful dreadful faithful grateful helpful
thoughtful sorrowful wonderful
plentiful beautiful dutiful fanciful
merciful

helpless hopeless pointless senseless
useless careless thoughtless homeless
lifeless fearless jobless thankless
headless speechless endless
merciless

darkness illness weakness greyness
greenness meanness likeness soreness
laziness ugliness nastiness happiness
emptiness heaviness business dryness

attachment agreement payment enjoyment
entertainment treatment
improvement statement basement
pavement involvement excitement
encouragement advertisement judgement
arrangement replacement argument

Some other ment words:
fragment cement implement monument
department ornament parliament

LEARNING TARGETS

Pupil Book: Focus
to 'explode' simple contractions

Pupil Book: Extra
to form contractions from two words

Pupil Book: Extension
to consider some exceptions

Workbook: Focus
to match up contractions with the words that make them

Workbook: Extra
to use target contractions in sentences

Workbook: Extension
to write contractions and use them in sentences

Resource sheet: Focus
to write and 'explode' simple contractions

Resource sheet: Extension
to write contractions; to understand when to use *it's* and *its*

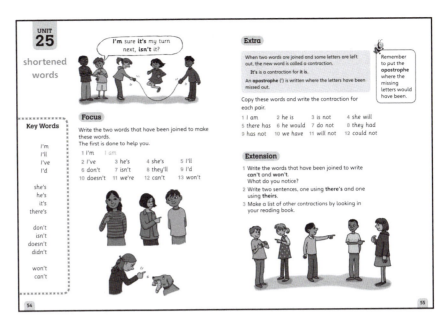

BACKGROUND NOTES AND SUGGESTIONS

The most important point for children to appreciate is that when writing abbreviations, the apostrophe should be placed exactly where the letter or letters have been omitted. There are a few circumstances where this is not quite straightforward (e.g. *shan't*, where letters have been omitted in more than one position i.e. *shall not*).

Another point to teach is that our language has evolved to create a few contraction spellings that are at variance with the words apparently contracted (e.g. *won't*, the contraction of *will not*).

When appropriate, draw to the children's attention the homophone issue (*its/it's* and *theirs/there's*).

Pupil Book answers

Focus

1 I am	**2** I have	**3** he is
4 she is	**5** I will	**6** do not
7 is not	**8** they will	**9** I would
10 does not	**11** we are	**12** cannot
13 will not		

Extra

1 I'm	**2** he's	**3** isn't
4 she'll	**5** there's	**6** he'd
7 don't	**8** they'd	**9** hasn't
10 we've	**11** won't	**12** couldn't

Extension

1 Child to indicate *can't* is abbreviation of a single word, or two words, without changing letters, and *won't* has letters changed (*will not*).

2 Teacher to check individual answers

3 Teacher to check individual answers

Workbook answers

Focus

I'm	I am
don't	do not
there's	there is
I've	I have
isn't	is not
he's	he is
I'd	I would
doesn't	does not

Extra
Teacher to check individual answers

Extension
Teacher to check individual answers

Resource sheet answers

Focus

A

1 don't	**2** doesn't
3 isn't	**4** it's
5 she'll	**6** didn't
7 I'll	**8** here's

B

1 <u>I'll</u> see you later.	I will
2 I <u>don't</u> know when.	do not
3 <u>Where's</u> your house?	where is
4 We <u>won't</u> see it from here.	will not

Extension

A

1 who's	**2** when's	**3** couldn't
4 what's	**5** what'll	**6** that'll
7 they're	**8** they'll	**9** we're
10 haven't	**11** where's	**12** hasn't
13 shouldn't	**14** who'll	**15** weren't
16 wouldn't		

B

1 its
2 It's
3 its
4 It's

Supporting word lists

I'm I'll I've I'd (I had / I would)
he's she's it's there's that's
you're we're they're
you've we've they've
you'd he'd she'd we'd they'd
don't can't isn't doesn't won't aren't
shan't
haven't couldn't wouldn't shouldn't
wasn't weren't
o'clock pick 'n' mix ma'am

LEARNING TARGETS

Pupil Book: Focus

to match key words to pictures, and associated activity

Pupil Book: Extra

to identify and copy target words from a wordsearch

Pupil Book: Extension

to consider some phonemic exceptions

Workbook: Focus

to label a picture using given words

Workbook: Extra

to match words with pictures

Workbook: Extension

to use **tion** words in sentences

Resource sheet: Focus

to complete word sums and write words to match pictures

Resource sheet: Extension

to use target word endings to complete words; to identify **tion** words in a wordsearch

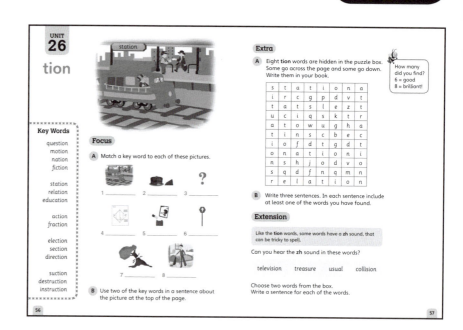

BACKGROUND NOTES AND SUGGESTIONS

This is an important suffix. Note that **tion** words tend to be more common than the related **sion** words (see Book 3, Unit 13). The prefix **tion** is commonly preceded by an **a**.

The Extension activity explores the 'zh' sound, which can cause confusion with some children.

Pupil Book answers

Focus

A
1 station	2 fraction
3 question	4 instruction
5 election	6 direction
7 destruction	8 suction

B Teacher to check individual answers

Extra

A
station	traction	action
suction	attraction	nation
situation	relation	

B Teacher to check individual answers

Extension

Teacher to check individual answers

Workbook answers

Focus

Teacher to check individual answers

Extra
1 motion	2 relation	3 section
4 fraction	5 fiction	6 instruction
7 station	8 attraction /action	
9 infection		

Extension

Teacher to check individual answers

Resource sheet answers

Focus

A Children should copy the pattern.

B *Upper activity*

question fiction station relation

direction fraction instruction

Lower activity

direction fraction station question

Extension

A fraction section suction

traction election instruction

attraction direction destruction

B destruction election fraction

C station question education action

fraction election section direction

suction instruction

Supporting word lists

ation

nation station ration

location relation vacation

celebration conservation

conversation education explanation

occupation operation population

situation vaccination examination

investigation multiplication

ition

ambition condition edition ignition

position addition tuition

ammunition competition recognition

repetition expedition

otion

lotion potion devotion

motion emotion promotion

commotion

etion

completion deletion discretion

ption

eruption disruption deception

reception caption option

description

ction

action faction fraction traction

attraction extraction subtraction

section connection direction

election infection objection

selection fiction friction distinction

suction instruction

function junction

ntion

mention attention detention

intention invention

LEARNING TARGETS

Pupil Book: Focus
to write homophones for given words

Pupil Book: Extra
to complete a cloze activity which requires differentiation of homophones

Pupil Book: Extension
to introduce the concept of homonyms

Workbook: Focus
to label a picture using given words

Workbook: Extra
to differentiate the meanings of pairs of homophones

Workbook: Extension
to choose the correct homophone to complete a cloze activity

Resource sheet: Focus
to secure some high frequency homophones

Resource sheet: Extension
to secure further homophones that sometimes cause confusion

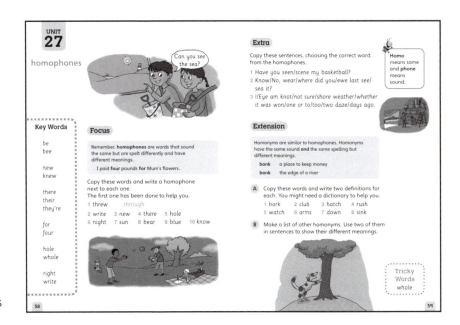

BACKGROUND NOTES AND SUGGESTIONS

Homophones are words with the same (*homo*) sound (*phone*) but a different spelling and meaning, whereas **homonyms** have the same spelling and sound but different meanings.

In this unit we focus on the homophones of, or related to, words which are high-frequency in children's writing. Elsewhere in the course (e.g. Book 5, Unit 19) less common homophones are introduced.

Please note that homophones will vary depending on regional accents and dialects. Some near homophones, e.g. quite and quiet might cause confusion too.

Pupil Book answers

Focus

1 threw through	2 write, right
3 new, knew	4 there, their
5 hole, whole	6 night, knight
7 sun, son	8 bear, bare
9 blue, blew	10 know, no

Extra

1 seen   2 No, where, you, see
3 I, not, sure, whether, one, two, days

Extension

Ⓐ Teacher to check individual answers

Ⓑ Teacher to check individual answers

Workbook answers

Focus

Teacher to check individual answers

Extra

1 write right	2 knew new
3 blew blue	4 ewe you

Extension

1 I <u>knew</u> the <u>new</u> dress would look lovely.
2 Jacob was <u>right</u>, he could also <u>write</u> with his left hand.
3 Did <u>you</u> see the <u>ewe</u> giving birth to the lamb?
4 The <u>blue</u> sailing boat <u>blew</u> close to the rocks.

5 Look over <u>there</u>, <u>their</u> dog has run into a shop!

Resource sheet answers

Focus

Ⓐ
1 ark	2 blue	3 break
4 buy	5 sent	6 cheap
7 creak	8 dear	9 you
10 eye	11 fair	12 fur
13 four	14 hare	15 hear
16 our	17 one	18 pore

Ⓑ Teacher to check individual answers.

Extension

Ⓐ "I left my boots just <u>there</u>, under the bench," I said.
Jess said, "<u>They're</u> the same colour as my boots."
Arun and Callum said <u>their</u> boots were left <u>there</u> as well.

Ⓑ Mrs Lindsay said, "I could <u>hear</u> you <u>two</u> arguing from <u>here</u>."
"Bring all the boots <u>here</u> <u>to</u> me," she said.
"Shall we get ours, <u>too</u>?" asked Arun and Callum.
"Yes bring them all <u>here</u>. I'm sure there are enough for you all to have <u>two</u> boots each!"

Supporting word lists

Some of these are not strictly homophones, but are 'near homophones' and are being included because in some regions they can sound very similar and cause confusion.

were we're
where wear
there their they're
you yew ewe
to two too
be bee
new knew
right write
through threw
hole whole
are our
see sea
no know
morning mourning
great grate
I eye
in inn
heard herd
might mite
place plaice
eyes ice
for four
of off

LEARNING TARGETS

Pupil Book: Focus
to match key words to pictures; to select and copy double-letter words

Pupil Book: Extra
to secure the rule for adding suffixes to words ending in **y**

Pupil Book: Extension
to introduce comparative form of adjectives

Workbook: Focus
to label a picture using given words

Workbook: Extra
to complete word sums using **er**, **est**, and **ed**

Workbook: Extension
to add **er** and **est** to words to complete a cloze activity

Resource sheet: Focus
to match key words to pictures

Resource sheet: Extension
to secure the rule for adding **er** and **est** to words ending in **y**

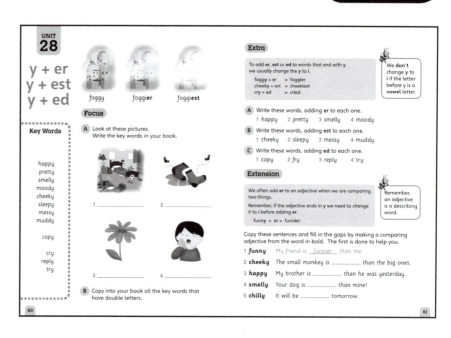

BACKGROUND NOTES AND SUGGESTIONS

It might be useful to remind the children that a final **y** can sound as a 'long i' or as 'ee'. Adding suffixes to a final **y** often causes confusion so this concluding unit is hoped to secure some of the learning previously touched on in this book.

For most words, when forming the comparative (**er**) or superlative form (**est**) we just add the suffix (*quicker, quickest*). For words ending in **y** we change **y** to **i** before adding the suffix (e.g. *chillier, chilliest*).

(However, for most words ending in **e** we drop the **e** before adding the suffix, e.g. *later, latest*. For most short words containing a single short vowel before the final consonant, we double the final consonant, e.g. *bigger, biggest*.)

It will be possible to extend this work with some children by considering that there are many important exceptions when forming these comparing adjectives e.g. *good, better, best; far, farther, farthest*. Also, consider what happens to such base words as *curious, sensible, intelligent*, i.e. we use *more* and *most*.

Pupil Book answers

Focus

A 1 messy   2 smelly
    3 pretty   4 sleepy

B happy pretty smelly moody
    cheeky sleepy messy muddy

Extra

A 1 happier   2 prettier
    3 smellier   4 moodier

B 1 cheekiest   2 sleepiest
    3 messiest   4 muddiest

C 1 copied   2 fried
    3 replied   4 tried

Extension

1 My friend is funnier than me.
2 The small monkey is cheekier than the big ones.
3 My brother is happier than he was yesterday.
4 Your dog is smellier than mine!
5 It will be chillier tomorrow.

Workbook answers

Focus

Teacher to check individual answers

Extra

1 cheekier   2 smelliest
3 cried   4 dustiest
5 cloudier   6 replied
7 copied   8 noisier

Extension

1 Today is the <u>windiest</u> day since the storm.
2 My boots are <u>muddier</u> than my brother's.
3 My sister's room is the <u>messiest</u> room in the house!
4 Mr Kaur told a <u>funnier</u> joke than Mr Golding.
5 Li felt she was the <u>luckiest</u> girl ever when she got a puppy.

Resource sheet answers

Focus

A Children should copy the letter patterns.

B 1 happy   2 messy   3 cry
    4 muddy   5 reply   6 smelly
    7 pretty   8 copy   9 sleepy

Extension

	+er	+est
milky	milkier	milkiest
cloudy	cloudier	cloudiest
crazy	crazier	craziest
creaky	creakier	creakiest
smoky	smokier	smokiest
slimy	slimier	slimiest
frosty	frostier	frostiest
smelly	smellier	smelliest
spotty	spottier	spottiest
rocky	rockier	rockiest
chatty	chattier	chattiest

Supporting word lists

happy cranky hilly milky frilly chilly floppy
spotty fussy dusty lazy crazy rainy
sleepy easy greasy icy mighty bony
smoky stormy noisy

Check-Up 2

Focus

1 mice	**2** face	**3** badge	**4** giraffe
5 candle	**6** camel	**7** pedal	**8** fly
9 monkey	**10** baby	**11** knife	**12** station
13 ball	**14** wasp	**15** swan	**16** television

Extension

A **1** untie **2** unkind **3** dislike **4** disagree

B Teacher to check individual answers

C **1** sadness **2** hopeful **3** plentiful **4** happiness **5** beautiful

D **1** Sam's coat **2** Jayden's bike **3** Amber's dog **4** Arjun's football **5** Aimee's friend

E **1** knee **2** gnat **3** knife **4** knot **5** wrong

F **1** birds **2** sheds **3** cats **4** buses **5** brushes **6** foxes **7** stories **8** days **9** babies

G **1** I'm **2** he'd **3** isn't **4** they'd **5** won't **6** couldn't

H **1** ant cat dog elephant

2 water when window wing

3 boy brother day night

I **1** jumping **2** running **3** hopping **4** flying

J **1** quickly **2** merrily **3** lazily **4** happily

K **1** copier **2** muddier **3** smellier **4** cheekier

Glossary

affixes
prefixes and suffixes which are added to word roots, such as **un**cover**ed**

auditory memory
short-term memory of sound-letter relationships

blending
smooth running together of individual sounds, usually referring to consonant blends, such as **bl**ot, **cl**ap, sa**nd**, **str**ap

consonants
the letters and letter sounds that are not vowels

cvc
abbreviation for *consonant/vowel/consonant* as in h-a-t

cue
the clues used to help identify a word. These can be 'phonic' (predictable from sound), 'grammatical' (predictable from word ordering) or 'semantic' (predictable from meaning).

decoding
translating print into spoken words

digraph
a pair of letters that operate together to represent a single sound, such as c**low**n, **ch**in

> **consonant digraph**
> pair of consonant letters that operate together to represent a single consonant sound, such as **ch th sh**
> **vowel digraph**
> pair of vowel letters that operate together to represent a single vowel sound, such as **ow ee oo**

etymology
word origins and roots

grapheme
the written form of the smallest sound segment of a word, such as individual letters or digraphs

homographs
words that are spelt the same but sound different and have different meanings, such as *row* (argument) and *row* (with an oar)

homonyms
words that sound the same, are spelt the same but have different meanings, such as *saw* (cutting tool) and *saw* (past tense of 'see')

homophones
words that sound the same but have different spellings and meanings, such as *there, their*

inflections
the endings of verbs to indicate tense or singular/plural, such as

> jump**ed** jump**ing**; jump jump**s**

or the endings of nouns to indicate plurals, such as
> dog**s**, box**es**

kinaesthetic
physical sense of awareness

mnemonics
memory joggers, such as, 'When you are emba**rrass**ed, you turn **r**eally **r**ed and **s**tart to **s**tutter.'

morphology
the study of the elements of words that carry the meaning

orthographic
concerned with spelling

phoneme
the spoken form of the smallest sound unit of a word, such as individual letter sounds or digraph sounds

phonemic
the approach to spelling based on sound-symbol relationships

phonics
the relationship between the spoken and written forms of words; often used to mean the method of teaching reading using the phonetic values of letters or groups of letters

position
in a word, position is often defined as
> initial (**sh**eep)
> medial (sh**ee**p)
> final (shee**p**)

prefix
element added to the beginning of a word to change or modify meaning, such as **un**necessary

rhyme
identity of sound, though not necessarily of letter pattern, between words or the endings of words

segmentation
process of identifying constituent parts of words

stem
core part of a verb, to which inflections may be added as required

suffix
element added to the end of a word to change or modify meaning, such as care**ful**

syllable
a part of a word including a vowel and its attached consonant sounds

tactile
concerning the sense of touch

vowels
the sounds at the heart of every syllable, that are represented by **a e i o u** and sometimes **y**

whole-word approaches
memorising of individual words by rote